MASTER OF CEREMONIES

3⁵⁰
PRN

Also by David Henry Sterry

Chicken
Satchel Sez (with Arielle Eckstut)
Putting Your Passion Into Print (with Arielle Eckstut)
Travis & Freddy's Adventures in Vegas (as Henry Johnson)

MASTER OF CEREMONIES

A True Story of Love, Murder, Roller Skates & Chippendales

David Henry Sterry

CANONGATE
Edinburgh · New York · Melbourne

First published in Great Britain in 2007 by
Canongate Books Ltd., Edinburgh, Scotland

Published simultaneously in Canada
Printed in the United States of America

FIRST AMERICAN EDITION

ISBN-10: 1-84195-876-x
ISBN-13: 978-1-84195-876-7

Canongate
841 Broadway
New York, NY 10003
Distributed by Publishers Group West
www.groveatlantic.com

08 09 10 11 12   10 9 8 7 6 5 4 3 2 1

To Michael Amy Lynne Rodriguez Sterry Cira Scippo,
for getting me through all this shit, and always always
being there.

ACKNOWLEDGMENTS

Jamie Byng cannot be thanked enough. But here's a start: *Molto grazie!* David Graham is a true force of nature, and I thank him for that. Morgan Entrekin, for putting his muscle behind me. Tad Floridis, my hard rocking editor, has been an island of calm smarts in the sea of G-strings and sweaty balls. *Gracias, señor.* Colin McClear must get mad props for massive help re. ms, but also for greasing the wheels from the git-go. Many readers helped immensely: the lovely and talented Veronica Monet, Grandmaster Sheffie Sheff, Seth Jacobs, darling Ariel Levine, dear Emily Ogden and Sue Hecht for typing. Thanks to Frannie, Jenny, Sheila, Polly, Jo, Francis, and all the fabulous staff at Grove and Canongate. My copy editor, Heather Angell, was great. Made the book lots better. The sweet sassy saucy sexy Elise Cannon and the PGW crew are here kindly appreciated. Tamim Anssary, the Plot Doctor, is a marvel, and was a wonderful sounding board, and the SF Writers Group was, and continues to be, extremely good. Scott James is a fucking genius, and his notes kept me on track when the wheels were falling off. Arnolpho d'Alencar Araripe Pimenta de Mello makes me happy to be alive: Thanks, baby! Many thanks to everyone at Chippendales. Frank Hoolihan, how we miss ye! To all the women who made Chippendales what it was. And Nick de Noia, for teaching me so much. Thanks to Milo for keeping it real. Thanks to Sweet Lou, for keeping it surreal. Thanx Katie for helping me get organized, and for looking so fab! Michael Amy Cira, my oldest and dearest friend, must be thanked for the past, the present, and the future. Here's a big smackeroo for you: Mwwwa! And of course the source from which it all flows: the Snow Leopard, the inimitable, indomitable lion, Arielle Eckstut, sock mogul extraordinaire. She read the book about a billion times and I couldn't honestly have done it without you. All love.

GROUND RULES

I was the Master of Ceremonies at Chippendales Male Strip Club from 1985 to 1987. This is what I remember, hopefully with all the boring bits sucked out. Occasionally the time has been condensed to make for more pleasurable reading. Lotsa people in this book are still alive, and I didn't think it was fair to out them, so I changed the names and blended the bodies and actions and characters of the Men of Chippendales. The only names I didn't change are Brooke Shields, her mom, Jason Alexander, Billy Idol, Dorothy Dalmatian, Chippendales director Nick de Noia, his business partner Steve Banerjee, and Arnolpho d'Alencar Araripe Pimenta de Mello.

Plus, of course, my own.

READ THIS FIRST

Chippendales is tight, quiet, frantic. Something's off, I can feel it the second I roll in. Something bad. Something worse than usual. Wait a second, is that a cop?

Arnolpho whips past in a fast version of his dancer's walk, flying by like some fabulous flaming South American comet. Seeing me he screeches to a halt, leans in close, touches me on the chest with intimate familiarity, and purrs in a sex-drenched Brazilian whisper:

'Oh, hhhoney, have you heard?'

His face is so brown and beautiful and smooth. I forget sometimes how gorgeous he is. Arnolpho is delighted, rapturous almost. That's because he's in possession of some delicious dishy dirt.

I wait for him to tell me. Of course he won't. He wants to

milk me first for all I'm worth. He wants me to ask. No, he wants me to beg.

'OK,' I say, 'I'll play. Have I heard what?'

'Nick de Noia . . .'

Arnolpho nods his stunning head with wicked insinuation: Something evil this way comes.

I'm hooked, he's got me, and he knows it. Now he's gonna play with me like a fat cat that's batting around a blind church mouse.

'What happened to Nick?' I'm uncomfortable with how much need-to-know quivers in my voice.

'Bay-bee, your mind isss gonna get blown into tiny li'l pieces.' Arnolpho's smile reminds you of a samba at the beach on a hot day when everybody's randy and sticky. He's having such fun.

'Arnolpho, for God's sake, what happened to Nick?'

An incredibly average man in an incredibly average suit approaches and addresses me without a trace of an accent:

'What do you do here?'

'I'm . . . uh . . . ,' I stutter, 'the emcee, the Master of Cere-monies – why, what—'

'Could you come with me?'

The man walks. I heel. I look over my shoulder at Arnolpho and toss him a *holy shit!* look. He nods his perfectly coiffed yet casually styled head very slowly, like:

Tha's what I'm talkin' 'bout, bay-bee!

I'm hardly ever inside the tiny, mirrored dressing room when it's not full of beautiful, shaved-smooth Men either putting on or taking off clothes. Now that it's just me and the incredibly average man, I'm struck by the bad-cologne, musky-funk, semen'n'sweat smell, all soured from not having had a proper scrub for a very long time.

'So,' says the incredibly average man, 'what can you tell me about your relationship with Nick de Noia?'

So this is an interrogation. Frankly, I'm a little disappointed. I always thought when I got grilled, it'd be at the hands of some tough-guy hard man who could make me his bitch in a New York minute. This guy looks like a seventh-grade geography teacher. I can't imagine him playing Ricki-Tikki-Tavi on some evil bastard's skull.

Luckily, I have training in How to Be Interrogated. Rule number five: Say as little as possible. Rule number six: When in doubt, say even less. So I say:

'Well, you know . . . he's my boss.'

The incredibly average man leans in steely and spits:

'Where were you yesterday afternoon?'

Suddenly I've got a bad case of the deep willies, and I feel incredibly guilty, even though I didn't do anything. Suddenly I have no idea where I was yesterday afternoon. Now I see his game. He comes across like he's a wouldn't-hurt-a-fly guy, so you let down your defense, then he springs at you like a fully-loaded Doberman.

'Uh . . .' I start the sentence without knowing where I'm going. Always a bad move.

Stop. Think. Ah, yes:

'I had an audition. Then I went and harangued my agent about getting me more auditions. Then I had some sushi. I gotta receipt.'

The incredibly average man goes back to being incredibly average. It's an astonishing transformation. Scary detective to geography teacher in half a heartbeat. He writes down something in a notebook, then, without even looking at me, asks:

'Do you know anybody who might want to kill Nick de Noia?'

Air leaves my lungs like a bullet.

Nick de Noia is dead.

Nick de Noia, the man who basically invented Chippendales, the most famous male strip show in the history of Western civilization, is dead.

Do I know anybody who might want to kill Nick de Noia? Hhmmmmmm.

I look into the detective's incredibly average eyes and say: 'Do you want the short list or the long list?'

MASTER OF CEREMONIES

PART I

WELCOME TO CHIPPENDALES, MUTHERFUCKER

CHAPTER 1

BARBRA STREISAND AND THE HOIPEE

1984. I've been alive a quarter of a century. Seems so much longer. Five years out of college, ten years out of Dumpster-diving, I cram as many of my prized possessions as I can into my tiny baby-shit green Toyota Corolla and give away everything else I own in a ridiculously misguided attempt to get all Zen. Worst decision in a life crammed full of bad decisions.

In the last three years I've done approximately five thousand sets of stand-up comedy, opening for everyone from Robin Williams to Milton Berle to a guy dressed like a big yellow banana, performing everywhere from the mecca of Bay Area comedy – the Holy City Zoo – to the shittiest dive at the end of the universe – the Sutro Bath House – where I did comedy in front of fifty nude swingers in metal folding chairs that squeaked every time their flabby flesh fidgeted. Mostly I sucked, but eventually I made a living. If you can call below-poverty-level, starving-but-for-food-stamps life a living.

I've decided I'm ready to take my shot at the big time, so like a turtle on speed I flee San Francisco with two thousand dollars in my pocket, a thousand head shots and résumés in my trunk, and a big fat dream in my heart. I'm bound for New York City, gonna take a bite of the Big Apple, maggots and all. I figure the two Gs'll last me a year easy, and by that time I'll be a star, baby!

I whip through the heartland of America, blasting tunes on my boom box, smack-dab in the middle of the cash-happy coke-crazy 80s when money-moving stockbroking masters of the universe rule the roost from Wall Street, and girls just wanna have fun, and it's raining men, and we all sit around watching *Lifestyles of the Rich and Famous*, and *Dallas*, and *Dynasty*, hey, great is good, man, haven't you heard? Let's go watch Rambo kill some gooks at the movies, while we drink 'new' Coke and Michael Jackson's hair catches on fire. Reagan, flush with the rush of re-election, funds drug thugs while his designer-clad Stepford-Wife First Lady gives grateful drug addicts everywhere the key to sobriety: Just Say No! In the midst of this flood of money, a bankrupt Iowa farmer kills his wife, his neighbor, and his banker. His wife and his neighbor I can understand. But his banker? In San Diego a guy walks into a McDonald's and blows away twenty citizens sucking down Happy Meals. 'Born in the USA' tops the charts for eighty-four weeks, a mirror reflecting the Vietnam hangover hanging over America.

Ten days after I leave my heart in San Francisco, Manhattan's monumental twin towers appear on the horizon, and my jaw drops:

'New York City, just like I pichered it, skyscrapers an' eve'ythang!'

I rent a small room in a big apartment on Seventeenth Street. With a kiss and a prayer I launch a hundred head shots and carefully crafted hand-calligraphed letters of introduction into the world. I'm convinced I'll be deluged by NY, NY's finest agents furiously fighting to handle me.

Three agents call.

Ninety-seven rejections.

Looking back, 3 percent was a pretty decent return, but at the time all I can hear is the universe telling me that the only possible outcome is failure.

Agent 1 sets up a meeting for Monday afternoon. That morning his secretary calls to tell me the man died over the weekend. My first thought: How rude! But as it sinks in I take his death as further evidence that the universe has it in for me.

Agent 2 is just under five feet tall and just over 120 years old. She smokes an unbroken chain of unfiltered cigarettes. Her office is swathed in a smog overcoat as she peers at me through the haze and in the voice of a two-pack-a-day troll growls:

'Y'll nevva woik in dis bizness widdout extensive plastic soigery.'

My heart stops for a second as she confirms my worst suspicions. I was right; I am hideously ugly.

'Foist of all ya nose's too big. Y'll nevva make it in dis bizness wid a honkah like dat, trust me. An dose ears, my Gawd, ya look like a cab wid de daws open. And ya've gotta hoipee on ya lip.'

'A what?'

'A hoipee.'

'A what?'

'A hoipee.'

'A herpe?'

'Dat's what I said.'

'No, no,' I protest, 'that's not a herpe, it's a mole.'

'Well,' she croaks, 'it looks like a hoipee ta me. Trust me, y'll never work in dis bizness wid a big hoipee on ya lip.'

Flattened and shattered, I see now that I should move to South Africa or South Alabama and help the needy.

'Dis is my nephew's cahd. He's a wonduful plastic soijun.' The Troll leans in for effect, and a wrinkly mottled spotty hand gives me a business card as her moldy odor wafts over me. 'Mention my name y'll getta fawty p'cent awff.' She winks at me, but her eye gets stuck shut so she lights another cigarette. 'Cawll me when yer awll healed up.'

I slouch out of her den of nicotine, trying to imagine what my new hoipee-free, tiny-eared, normal-nosed, symmetrical, surgically straightened face will look like. What if they make my ears too small and I end up some mutilated lobeless freak? And how am I gonna pay for it? I've only been here a few months, and my two grand is practically gone. I suppose it'll be worth a few years of eating pizza and salad if I get to be a star. As I trudge into the bustling hustle of Midtown Manhattan, my hideousness settles like a pox upon my kingdom. I am, as I suspected, damaged goods, and I now know there's only one way to fix me: extensive cosmetic surgery.

As if in a movie, the sun bursts through the clouds and jolts me out of my mind, BAM! onto Fifty-seventh Street, where a sunbeam throws a spotlight on a face gracing the cover of a leading national magazine: Barbra Streisand. That supernova goddess diva, with her huge honker and her too-close-together eyes in her crooked face, looks as gorgeous as ever. I don't have to get my nose cut or my ears lopped or have the mole that looks like a hoipee chopped off. I dump the Troll's card in the trash, sad for all the other suckers butchered by her nephew.

Thanks, Babs.

Agent 3 interviews me and agrees to represent me. She only does commercials but promises to send me out soon and often.

No cosmetic surgery required.

I'm living on five dollars a day now, hungry all the time. I cull *Backstage*, the weekly showbiz rag full of mostly barrel-bottom gigs. *Annie Get Your Gun* at the Moosejaw Rep. Downtown avant-garde wank-o-ramas: *Spanking the President's Monkey* at the Vomiting Iguana. Corporate Industrials films: *Drunk Driving: Don't Do It.*

An ad captures my eye. Wanted: Master of Ceremonies at upscale exotic male revue. Quirky, high energy, improv skills, must be a great roller-skater. That's me to a T. Except the roller-skating. But I can learn to roller-skate. How hard could it be?

I have no idea that this innocuous-looking ad will bring me face-to-face with true love, fake sex, and real life Death.

That night my baby-shit green Toyota Corolla, with three windows already broken in, all mirrors ripped off, and side door smashed, is stolen.

CHAPTER 2
MY TESTICLES SHRINK

'Chippendales,' screams the marquee over the door I enter on Sixty-first and First, just up the block from the Fifty-ninth Street Bridge, where countless homeless citizens are just saying, 'No.' Across the street is a most excellent pizzeria, a mom'n'pop news shop, a homely bodega, and some old-school apartment buildings. Just up First Ave. is Dangerfield's Comedy Club, where nobody gets any respect.

I've heard of Chippendales Male Strip Club, of course. Everyone has. They're in the gossip column on Page 6 of the *New York Post*. Johnny Carson jokes about them on the *Tonight Show*. Sally Jessy Rafaël, a leading afternoon talk show host, has the Men on her show all the time, half-nude in their trademark skin-thin black spandex pants, bow tie, collar, and cuffs. But I'm not really aware that this is one of the hottest shows in New York City, or that the calendar sells millions of copies every year, or that Chippendales is, in fact, the most successful male strip show in history.

In the lobby, life-size glossy photos of the Men of Chippendales smolder at me: bulging bulges, mountain peak pecs, 6-pack man-rack abs, and cheekbones for miles. Too-too-blue eyes follow me wherever I go, and as I stare at these magnificent specimens I can actually feel my testicles shrink.

Five or six other googly-faced fools mutter underbreath, preparing to audition to be the next Master of Ceremonies at Chippendales. I don't know it at the time, but hundreds and hundreds of guys will audition for this plum of a job. Four days a week, two hours a day, two thousand bucks a month, six hundred screaming women a night.

This must be clear. Apart from the crooked face, the huge honker, the elephantine ears, and hoipee, I'm a reasonably pleasant-looking fellow. I have brown tousled hair, dimple-filled cheeks, and I'm easy with a laugh. But standing next to an Adonis I'm a frog.

A squashed woman with black plastered lacquered hair and a stylish plus-size blouse ushers me through red velvet curtains into the guts of the ratty, tacky club. Smells like bad booze and soiled cigarettes, with a musty undertow of coke, as she leads me to a man who stands in the shadows.

'This is . . . ,' purrs the round compacted woman with the pearly voice that sounds like she's selling perfume or doing phone sex. 'This is David . . . uh, Scary.'

I don't correct her. One time a casting director called me David Sterny, and I made the mistake of setting her straight. I never got called back. If this one wants me to be David Scary, I'll be David Scary. 'Cuz the two grand I brought to New York, New York, is now officially gone, and I really need this job.

A man spins out of the shadows with the muscular grace of Gene Kelly, eyes sparkling, salted, peppery, perfectly coiffed hair, lovely little leather jacket, and peach silk shirt open at the neck with a gold chain peeking its cocky head out. Tailored, freshly pressed blue jeans, tassel-happy Italian shoes, and a 20-gigawatt mile-wide smile beaming in the middle of it all.

I really want him to like me. That's the kind of guy he is. But I get the feeling he already hates me. That's the kind of guy I am.

'I'm looking for a cross between a baggy pants comic,' he says, smooth as the silk in his peach shirt, 'and a Joel Grey, *Cabaret*-type Master of Ceremonies.' He spears me with a svelte index finger. '*You* are the most important person in this show, because *you* speak for the Ladies. *You* say what they *wish* they could say.' He squints, leans in to me, and points to his palm. 'And you have to have them right here! It's your job to tell the Ladies of America that it's OK to grab a handful of hot young ass and give it a good squeeze!' His face is electric. 'I'm looking for someone who can go out there and really sparkle, who can be naughty and nice, who can ride these Ladies hard and put them up wet, as they say!' This guy's like a pimp you want to love you. 'Any questions?'

'No, I think I got it.' I try a smile, but there's way too much need-to-please in it, and a panicky clammy dread fills me. I'm certain once again that the only possible outcome is failure.

I walk to the center of the red sunken dance floor. It's unnaturally quiet in this dark cave of a club, lotsa little empty tables and chairs on two sides, a long liquor-filled bar at one end, and a raised stage at the other.

I turn my back to the man and his sex-voiced assistant, and marshal my forces. An adrenaline flash jacks right through me, as I spin around and throw an arm up while booming:

'The Men! Of! Chippendales!'

The Muse sinks her spike into my arm and pumps me full of juice as I ride the melody of the words, busting off the ends of the punch lines like I'm cracking a whip.

This is it, this is what I live for, center stage, completely engaged, not having to think about my shitty little life.

It's one of those auditions you dream about, where everything just flows and you go with it, and you somehow manage to tap into the life force that connects all living things, at which point you can do no wrong. When I'm done, bathed in sweaty happy afterglow, all I can think is, Why couldn't I have been auditioning for Steven Goddamn Spielberg instead of at Chippendales Male Strip Club? Story of my life. I note that even in triumph I manage to find a way to make myself miserable.

'That. Was. Faaaaaaabulous. Fab. U. Lous. Are you . . . available?' asks the charismatic man.

Available. The golden word. They can tell you you're faaaaaaabulous till you're blue in the balls, but they don't ask you if you're *available* unless they're actually interested.

Oh, God, I need this job!

'Well . . . yeah, I could be available . . .' I sound like the most available man in the world trying to pretend he's not available.

'And you do . . .'

The suave man pauses dramatically. All that smooth and charm's got me hypnotized.

'Roller-skate, of course, don't you?'

Roller-skate? Shit. Forgot about the roller-skating. I have no idea how to roller-skate. But again, I think: How hard could it be?

I call on all my actor training to stop the panic from invading my face as I lay out my bald-faced lie:

'Sure, I roller-skate.'

The debonair man whispers to his velvet-voiced assistant. She whispers back. He does a picture-perfect pirouette and sticks out his hand like we're in a Fred Astaire movie and I'm Ginger Rogers. He cocks his dashingly handsome head to one side, familial yet slightly sexy, and says:

'This isn't official, but barring any unforeseen circumstances, welcome to the Chippendales family.'

I smile, take his hand, and shake it. His hand is soft but his grip is hard. He's intimate yet impersonal. Relaxed yet professional. Friendly yet chilly. Welcoming yet intimidating. Reassuring yet terrifying.

And thus I'm introduced to Nick de Noia.

I'm ecstatic as he welcomes me into my second family of freaks.

CHAPTER 3

THUMP! THUMP! THUMP! THUMP! THUMP!

The Chippendales script is a sick thick three-hundred-page behemoth. Turns out the show's a ninety-minute monologue delivered by the Master of Ceremonies. Me. I'm responsible for triggering EVERY light cue, EVERY sound cue, EVERY video cue, and the removal of EVERY cuff, collar, and G-string. Every day my debut draws nearer, that script weighs a little bit more, until by my opening night it's a two-ton yoke of a lodestone.

As I memorize and memorize and memorize and memorize and memorize, I see endless variations of two scenarios:

(1) Finishing my first show, I pump my fists in triumph as the Ladies go crazy, and almost-nude, buff-bronze Chippendales Men congratulate me like I'm a conquering hero. Women can't wait to suck face with me and have my babies. Nick de Noia rushes backstage to tell me he's gonna personally see to it that I become a big shining star!

(2) I'm in the middle of the pit, all eyes are upon me: ladies, men, DJ, Nick de Noia, New York City, America, God. Klieg lights trap me like a bug in amber, and I freeze up solid, gears locking, brain crashing, as I draw a blank and stand there mute, six hundred furious flesh-craving $-waving Ladies staring me down. It's all MY FAULT they don't get to ogle twenty-five of the most beautiful dudes on the planet. The Men are furious. It's all MY FAULT they don't get to strut their stuff, make bank, get laid. And I'll never work in this town or this business ever again.

Sheer desperate terror, if used properly, is a marvelous motivational tool. I memorize when I wake up. I memorize when I eat lunch. I memorize when I go to bed. I memorize in my sleep – that is, when I'm not having nightmares of falling flat on my fat face. I write out the entire show in longhand, then break it down using my own cryptic short-hand code so it fits on fifty index cards I carry with me like a cheatsheet binky.

But no matter how much I study, my brain keeps sending up smoke signals:

DISASTER AHEAD! QUIT NOW BEFORE IT'S TOO LATE!

Then there's the roller-skating. They're old-school roller skates: black boots with four red wheels on each, fronted by red plastic knobby toe stops. I start out practicing in my radically tilted hardwood-floored East Village hovel. I stand at the high end of the living room and let gravity have its way with me, slowly rolling to the low end. I stop by slamming into the wall. Effective, if painful.

As I progress to the wide-open spaces of Union Square, I introduce my ass to asphalt so often they're on a first-name basis, slowly transforming my coccyx into one huge bruise.

Soon I'm moving a little smoother, so I decide to brave the mean streets of the city that never sleeps. Ten P.M. Pretty quiet for a Wednesday night. One week till my date with destiny at Chippendales. I'm skating rhythmically, flashing up First Avenue: left right left right left right, building up a good head of steam while slamming down a small hill. The little-kid wind-in-my-hair happiness is intoxicating, I'm zooming, cruising superfast.

Out of nowhere a solid block of headlights flashes up over the hill in front of me and fills First Avenue, all lanes jam-packed with taxicabs, vans, and other deadly heavy-metal high-beamed vehicles speeding straight at me.

Hyperventilating, wide-eyed, and terrified, I frantically search for an avenue of escape. Luckily, I have lots of practice keeping my head in the face of extreme danger. One hundred feet ahead a slender opening between two parked cars presents itself. Seems my best shot at yet again escaping death. I map out the necessary angles, make the appropriate adjustments, and when I reach the hole I swerve to my right, barely miss what looks like a Buick, flashing past its rear bumper. But now I'm gonna plow head-on into what's definitely a Mercedes. I see my leg breaking, shin shattering, kneecap splattering. So I go airborne and violently twist my body to the right, pulling my left leg away from the Mercedes. It brushes the bumper as I desperately spin, miraculously managing not to smash into the hard car metal.

I jerk my left skate toward the earth, trying manically to right my ship and restore balance, thisclose to calamity. But when I bend my knees a little, I manage to recapture balance and commence speeding breakneck up the Upper East Side sidewalk. Attempting a toe stop is an invitation to a tumble that at this speed would probably result in bone breakage and blood loss. I'm closing fast on a restaurant awning anchored by two brass poles. If I grab a pole maybe I can stop my progress and avoid breaking my entire body.

Crouching, I spring and grab the brass pole, which stops the top half of my body. But my bottom half continues to speed forward, roller-skated feet flying up off the sidewalk like they're the tip of a whip. I try with all my might to hold on to the pole, but centrifugal force commands my hands to follow my feet, and I release my arms before they're ripped from their sockets.

I'm now completely disconnected from the earth, flying through the air, trying to figure out how I can land without shattering my ass. Out of my eye corner I see a couple coming out of the restaurant ahead, as I descend like a jet whose landing gear has malfunctioned.

MAYDAY! MAYDAY! MAYDAY!

I do an emergency ass crash landing.

THUMP! THUMP! THUMP! THUMP! THUMP!

As I regain my senses I shake my head: stupid! I decide I'm gonna go home, call the club, and leave a message for Nick de Noia at Chippendales:

'Hi, this is David Scary. I know I haven't actually started yet, but I'm gonna have to quit. I apologize, but I can't be your Master of Ceremonies.'

As I slowly roll home, a New York tabloid with a grisly picture of a murdered gangster glares at me:

'MAFIA BOSS GUNNED DOWN! DID GOTTI DO IT?'

Seeing that bullet-ridden corpse bleeding from the front page infuses me with confidence. All of a sudden I don't feel so bad anymore. Yes, I can be the Master of Ceremonies. And what's the worst that'll happen if I fuck it all up?

I almost certainly won't get shot in the head.

CHAPTER 4

BOOMBOOMBOOM

My opening night is finally here. To the naked eye, it looks like just another naked Wednesday at Chippendales. But for me, it's the beginning of the rest of my life, where I metamorphose from a cockroach into a star.

Seven P.M., still an hour till showtime and already Sixty-first and First is live-wired, as a humming circle of lady bees buzzes around the Chippendales hive. Even the homely bodega and the mom'n'pop news shop seem more glamorous tonight. I half expect John Travolta to strut out of the most excellent pizzeria and bust some *Saturday Night Fever* moves right here on First Avenue.

The Ladies arrive: bimbos in limos and bevies of bachelorettes, coeds gone wild and booming grannies, supermodels, and supermoms. Huge poufy puffy fluffy hair. Creased blue denim and shock-me-pink tight-as-skin Norma Kamali: jumpsuits with shoulder pads so huge you could use them in the National Football League and never miss a beat. Vagina-clinging camouflage-chic fatigues. Oversized sweatshirt miniskirts clinging high on the thigh. And yes, Virginia, the miniskirt is back with a vengeance. Shiny plastic miniskirts, blue-jean miniskirts, and tutu miniskirts. Bustiers worn on the outside courtesy of Madonna, desperately seeking stardom. Jennifer Beals dirty flash-dancing leg warmers. Lime green high-tops, combat boots, and stiletto heels.

A Chippendales studmuffin stands next to the ticket booth with a tux collar around his naked beef-laden neck. Fluffed-up hair floats over acres of bronze, bare, hairless chest.

A brassy broad brays at him. She's fiftyish, with a tower of hair, tropical-fish eye makeup, and rouge raging on her face like scarlet fever:

'Hey asshole, I ordered these tickets three weeks ago, all my girlfriends are here!'

Studmuffin could not look more bored as he totally and completely ignores her.

Walking into the club, I'm trying to remember to breathe, but my nerves are stretched so tight all I can see is me tripping on my toe stop and taking a header into some stripper's ass.

In the lobby's low light the larger-than-life pics of the Chippendales Men and their larger-than-life pecs are so bright they suck my eyes right to them, and I'm overwhelmed by how much I need extensive cosmetic surgery.

And MY GOD! the Ladies are EVERYWHERE. It's so packed and saturated with excited expectation, it's electric to be a man in the middle of all this raging estrogen.

The disco inferno heat seeps through the red velvet curtain

as the beat goes boomboomboom, and I can feel the massive raw energy of Chippendales sucking everything toward it. The natives are clearly restless.

Sometimes you don't know your whole life's about to change. But as I stand before the dressing room door of Chippendales Male Strip Club, I heave a deep sigh, knowing that once I walk through that door, I will never be the same.

And, of course, I'm right.

CHAPTER 5
THE DICK PULL

When I was a kid in Minnesota, we'd sit in the sauna and get all sweaty, and then we'd run out and roll around in the snow. That's the shock to the system I feel, going from such high volumes of estrogen to that testosterone overload in the Chippendales dressing room. I wonder, if you exposed lab rats to this over and over, would they, too, crave sex and coke?

Fluorescent lights make the teeny tiny dressing room harsh, mirrored walls cramjampacked with the man skin of a dozen primping, preening, iron-pumping, oiled-up, slicked-down, tanning-bed-browned, blow-dried, hair-product-stiffened Men of Chippendales. It's like being inside a thermonuclear Man device ready to blow.

In the corner stands a lanky Man with outstanding hair wearing nothing but tux cuffs'n'collar and black spandex pants, unzipped. He pulls on his unsheathed penis like it's modeling clay and makes it longer, one stroke at a time, until it's at full extension. Then he meticulously lays his most prized possession on the inside of his thigh and snaps the spandex over it fast, yanking his pants shut, then quickly slithering his zipper over his Velcro-covered hip. In a mirror he admires his throbbing johnson knob, nodding his cocky head, like: Wow! I *do* look hot.

He's just done the Dick Pull. The principle is simple: If you snap the spandex over your penis fast enough, the blood remains trapped, creating a permanently erect hammerheaded trousersnake.

The Man catches me checking him out. So he cocks his fud and busts a gust of loud foul gas that explodes out of him like a sick goose honking on a foggy morn. Then he scrunches up his face and squawks in a cartoon voice:

'Hey Ma, I fahted!'

Everybody cracks up. Well, not everybody. Only those not lost in the Mirrors of Narcissus.

I laugh long after everyone else has stopped. I'm slightly embarrassed, but that vanishes when I realize no one is paying the slightest attention to me. It's a feeling I will become increasingly familiar with.

The dressing room is steamy, body-heat hot. I just stepped in and I'm already shvitzing. A nervous queeze freezes me. There's no air in here. Feels like if my head weren't tethered to my neck it would float away. Suddenly I'm acutely aware of being surrounded by some of the most breathtaking nude Men in the world. All making mad $ cuz of how hot they are. Why didn't I just get the plastic surgery? Stupid!

A half-naked, spandex-clad man with a bitchin' hot bod, big blond streaked hair, and 70s pornstar mustache cockwalks into the dressing room. He is the Snowman, the Man among the Men of Chippendales.

'Blond twins, corner of the Pit, they got my name on 'em, so hands off, assmunchers!' The Snowman mimes receiving fellatio from blond twins by flapping his arms on either side of his body, palms moving imaginary heads toward his very real penis. 'Doubleheader, baby!'

Hoots and hollers. Guttural grunts and guffaws.

The Snowman grabs a couple of hulking dumbbells, pumps them hard for thirty seconds, and spins into the mirror. When he flexes, his knotted muscles pulse, veins twitching like rivers on a moving relief map.

'Cut like a Ginsu knife!' crows the Snowman. Then he slips a very small white folded envelope to an impossibly gorgeous, absurdly sculpted guy. Hhmmmm. What's all this, then? I've heard there's lots of cocaine at Chippendales. Hell, coke is to the eighties what a dry martini was to the fifties. Me wonders, is that how the Snowman got his moniker?

Tall, thin, faceless lockers stand opposite the wall of mirrors. Crudely written over one of them is 'David Skerry.' I think for a minute that I should cross out the *k* and replace it with a *t*. But in the end, I don't wanna piss anybody off, so I don't.

I open my locker. Inside reside:

1 pair black tux pants with shiny pipes
1 black tux jacket with protruding tail
1 white button-up tux shirt
1 red cummerbund
1 red bow tie
1 black top hat
2 black roller skates with 8 red wheels

Seeing my costume eases me. Suddenly I'm Sir Galahad staring at his armor before going out to slay the exotic dancing man dragon.

I hang up my green Cossack jacket and my black drawstring pants. Put my red high-tops on the locker floor. Now I'm naked but for one red sock and one blue sock.

I turn around. Caught in the mirror with all those beautiful nubile nudes is a puffy white Marshmallow Man.

I chuckle.

Marshmallow Man chuckles. I'm embarrassed for the guy. If only he could see how grotesque his pallid fatness is next to the love gods of Chippendales.

I stop smiling and shake my head.

He stops smiling and shakes his head.

Wait a minute—

OHHHHHH NOOOOOOO!

I AM THE MARSHMALLOW MAN!

Mortified, I grab my tux and hightail my fat ass into the costume room, disappearing like a chubby cottontail into the bush.

CHAPTER 6
CAN YOU FEEL THE LOVE?

Johnny has a needle and thread in one hand, the Barbarian's fur loincloth in the other, and a strip of Velcro in her mouth. She looks about twenty, Latina with a swirly sea of curly brown hair, styly ripped jeans and white sailor-suit shirt with sweet coffee flesh floating underneath, two pouts for lips, and hips that make my knees weak. She seems to barely notice that a puffy white Marshmallow Man has just sprinted into her costume-strewn lair in a state of naked panic. This is part of her charm.

'Uh, do you mind if I . . . uh, you know, change . . . uh, back . . . here?' I stammer, plummeting: How in God's name am I gonna go out there in front of all those people and say all those words when I can barely ask the Costume Mistress if I can change in her room?

'Whatever.' Johnny lobs back half a smile, like we're both

in on the same joke, me naked and clutching my tux, her fastening Velcro to the Barbarian's fur loincloth.

Immediately I like her. Immediately I want her. Immediately I know she will never want me. I vow then and there I'm gonna bust my ass till I, too, am cut, buff, and muscular.

'God*damn* it, Johnny—'

A blast of mean ugliness blows in from the dressing room like the frigid wind of a nor'easter. That voice can only belong to one man:

Nick de Noia.

Our boss arrives a skosh later in a tailored charcoal suit that perfectly complements the salt and pepper of his hair.

'Why do the monkeys look like they have goddamn mange?! Helloooooooooo—?'

Nick notices me and does a double take. An old-fashioned, theatrical, look-away, look-back-at-me double take.

I watch him process the information.

The new Master of Ceremonies is in the costume room.

The new Master of Ceremonies has just caught him tongue-lashing Johnny at his whipping post.

Nick de Noia breathes with the ease of a trained dancer, pivots ever so slightly toward me, and says:

'Oh, hello, David, I was looking for you. Did you see the roses? They're on the counter.' Nick pours charm all over me like it's hot fudge and I'm his banana split.

Ladies and gentleman, step right up and watch Nick the Magnificent pull a Rico Suave gentleman out of his own belligerent ass.

'Thanks, that's . . . nice,' I say, smiling back like a goofy inmate in a loony bin. How did I miss the roses? That was so sweet of Nick.

'David, you're going to be faaaaaabulous tonight. Do you know how I know? Because I picked you, and I have incredible taste!' Nick de Noia's big easy laugh is contagious, and I catch it. But the laugh barks out of me too loud, like I'm in pain.

Johnny lets out a barely audible minichortle that drips cynicism. Makes me like and want her even more.

Nick's too busy being Nick to notice.

'The most important thing tonight is to go out there and have fun. This is your party, David. Go out there and sparkle for me!'

A flow of calm confidence oxygenates my blood, and suddenly my life makes sense. Yes, it's all been leading me here, so I can be Nick de Noia's Master of Ceremonies. So he can fix me.

Nick de Noia doesn't think of Chippendales as some cheap stupid male stripper show. And that's why it's not. Nick wants to change the world, give women the opportunity to ogle, fondle, and sexualize hot men, with upscale, old-fashioned, postmodern Folies Bergère style: classy not crude, fun not lewd, artistic not rude. And, of course, he wants to get rich doing it. Nick sees himself as equal parts Julius Caesar, P. T. Barnum, the Marquis de Sade, and Bob Fosse. And this show is his legacy to the world.

When Nick de Noia, the king of Chippendales, pirouettes on his heel and glides gracefully from the room, a cold snap and a heat wave swoosh out with him.

'Can you feel the love?' Johnny eye-rolls like an old soul trapped in a twenty-year-old hotty body. Then she viciously bites off a thread coming out of the Barbarian's fur loincloth, where in an hour his barbaric balls will be.

'Oh, is that what that is?' I crack back.

Johnny laughs, and I relax a little.

I fumble with my bow tie, can't get the little thingamajig into the doohickey.

Johnny steps in: hooks it, adjusts it, centers it, and stepping back, gives me the full once-over. She nods her approval, then goes back to attacking the mangy monkey masks.

A slight, lithe, finger-popping, wiggle-hipped, brown-sugar-skinned Brazilian slides into the room like K-Y Jelly. He's oh-so-fashionable in soft ecru slacks, funky short white tux jacket, and buttery five-hundred-dollar shoes wrapped around his twinkling toes. *Dios mio*, he's beautiful. I don't know him yet, but it's clear he's an Ensemble Dancer, one of the chorus that backs up the stars. Like me, he's here to make the Men of Chippendales look good.

'Girlfrien', Buddy is makin' me cray-sssee. An' I don't jus' mean cray-sssee, I mean CRAY-SSSEE!'

He suddenly sees me, the virgin MC. He stops what he's doing, studies me a moment, then meows in his Eurotrash accent:

'Ohhhhhh bay-bee, the spider has caught a fly!'

He and Johnny lock eyes, while he says:

'The black widow loves her man . . .'

They wag heads, snap fingers, and they say with saucy synchronicity:

'Then she bites his head off!'

He turns to me like the old-pro queen chorine he is. 'Hhhhoney, don' worry 'bout nothin'. Believe me, bay-bee, nobody gives a shit about you or me anyway. The mos' impor-tant thing is: Get my name right. Ahhhhhnolfo Djallenca Arraripe Pimenta Djimello.'

'Ahhhhhnolfo Djallenca Arraripe Pimenta Djimello,' I parrot exactly.

Like a mix of Mae West and Oscar Wilde, he nods at me sideways while wisecracking to Johnny:

'Where they find her?'

Johnny rolls out a silly Southern drawl.

'In the funny pay-puhs.'

After I laugh I can breathe better.

'Break a leg, bay-bee.' Arnolpho smiles at me, 'Jus' don' break mine!' He and Johnny double-airkiss, then Arnolpho flits away like a Brazilian Tinkerbell.

I strap on my cummerbund and stride into my jacket.

Johnny tugs at my tie, pulls at my pants, and shifts my shirt. Feels so nice having her fuss over me. I know she's just being a professional, but I can't help fantasizing about us hooking up. Suddenly I see Johnny with my baby in her belly, and blackness swallows my brain, as I stumble into the terrible reality that someone like her could never fall in love with someone like me.

As I reenter my body, I observe that Johnny, the I-don't-give-a-shit chick, is also mother hen to these Men, who, let's face it, are mostly big little boys.

'Not bad for a geek in a tux,' she chuckles. It's fun having my chops busted by Miss Johnny. Would my chances of making her love me improve if there weren't so many jaw-dropping, mouth-watering Men at Chippendales everywhere? Doubtful.

'Break a leg,' Johnny says as she smiles nice.

I see myself slipping on a piece of ice and fracturing my tibia, shattered bone puncturing skin—

Johnny feels me freak the fuck out, and stepping out from

behind her cool-chick facade, she shows me some genuine
concern:

'You all right?'

I step out from behind my desperate need and say:

'Yeah, thanks.'

And so Johnny, diva costume mistress, master disher, whipping post, fag hag, flirt, kid sister, and den mother, becomes
my friend.

CHAPTER 7

SEVENTY, GOING ON DEAD

I claw my way through the dressing room: duck a dumbbell, dodge a cock, and slither through all that oily tanned skin to my locker. As I pull on my roller skates, I'm interrupted by furious voices pounding out of the upstairs office, where all the $ lives. Can't make out the words, but I can sure feel the rancorous anger.

Mister Nick de Noia busts outta the upstairs office like a salt-and-pepper tsunami and slams the door so hard the wall shakes. He jams down the shitty, rickety spiral staircase and we hold our collective breath like a cranky psycho killer's got a loaded Uzi in the room.

Nick de Noia shoots through the dressing room and when he yanks open the door to the club, music floods in. With another slam he's gone, and the music mutes.

The Edwards brothers, Nick's NY $ partners, appear on

the landing of the upstairs office, in their dark hair and suits. There's a heaviness that hangs around the Edwards brothers. They whisper to each other, intense and compressed. They're the guys who sign the checks. I met them after I got hired, and nicknamed them the Tweedle brothers. They were wearing different dark suits then. I sat across from Dum, the older thinner one. Or was it Dee, the younger fatter one? I can't keep them straight. But even as they welcomed me to the Chippendales family, I felt some ugly unspoken undertow flow out of them. Or maybe it was seeping out of me.

An old gray man joins them on the landing, looking like a vulture that hasn't eaten in a while. He looks seventy, going on dead, with sickly thin translucent skin, a wicked comb-over covering his bald skull, a wobbling waddle, and a little piggy nose. A coke-laced teen queen in a little bitty miniskirt hangs from his withered arm in an I'm-hot-and-blowing-a-guy-old-enough-to-be-my-grandfather-for-coke kinda way.

Suddenly I notice the red roses Nick de Noia bought me. As soon as I see them, panic stabs me in the chest, wraps its hands around my throat, grabs my balls, and won't let go.

CHAPTER 8

GIRLS JUST WANNA HAVE FUN ON LADIES NIGHT WHEN IT'S RAINING MEN

When I open the dressing room door, the Wall of Sound pounds me, and the pressure of 600 palpitating ladies and 25 of the most beautiful Men on the planet waiting for me freezes my legs, and my skates won't roll. The Snowman is here to escort me to the Pit. He eyeballs me hard with ridiculously blue eyes. I didn't notice before how Paul Newman-blue his eyes are. I've never seen eyes that blue. Maybe he's wearing colored contact lenses.

'Are you wearing colored contact lenses?' The words are out of my mouth before I can stop them.

'What the fuck are you talkin' about?' The Snowman stares at me like I have an alien coming out of my forehead.

But that's all it takes to bring my legs to life. I'm on carpet, so there's no roll, but at least I'm lurching forward, albeit lock-kneed and tongue-tied, toward the stage, where destiny calls.

When the Snowman opens the red velvet curtain a blast of sex-factory air whacks me upside my top hat, while shapes and colors swirl in shooting pools and points of light around the club, like a Monet painting of panting women during a lightning storm.

Slowly focus comes. Ladies, ladies everywhere: Shoehorned into chairs, sardine-packed around tiny tables, hustling to get seated, restless in anticipation. They're power-drinking, primping, whispering, giggling, pecking and necking, flirting and being flirted with.

There are four classes of men at Chippendales:

The Stars: They have a featured number in the show. During the Kiss & Tip that follows their act, they exchange $ for kisses. There are only five of them.

The Waiters: They hustle drinks, drugs, snuggles, kisses, fondles, and whatever else they can. There are about ten of them.

The Hosts: They hustle seats, drugs, snuggles, kisses, fondles, and whatever else they can. There are about fifteen of them.

The Ensemble Dancers: Arnolpho and his ilk, professional chorus dancers, all under six feet tall. They don't get any $ except for their salary. There are five of them.

The Snowman leads me down a discreet path that's maintained with gestapoish zeal by the topless spandexed hunk Hosts, as the preshow starts, and 'Girls Just Wanna Have Fun' booms too loud, while a twenty-feet-tall crazy kooky-color-haired Cyndi Lauper flounces around on the giant video screen.

Where's the Snowman? He and his fabulous 70s porn-star mustache have vanished into the Amazon jungle. Shit. My toe stop catches in the carpet and I pitch forward. I grab at a Lady in front of me, but she feels me coming and jerks away. I know now I'm gonna faceplant, and there's not a single thing I can do about it. I land splat in the pungent rug, eye-level with high heels, high-tops, an occasional spike, and a black male-shoe or two.

The Snowman reappears, shakes his extremely annoyed and massively coiffed head, yanks me up, then drags me through the parting sea of Ladies like a half-naked Moses in black spandex.

The preshow continues, as 'Let's Get Physical' blasts, and a huge Olivia Newton-John grins in her sexy aerobic togs: tights, sweatpants, and leg warmers. She wants to hear my body talk.

The Pit, which serves as the main staging area for the show, is guarded by huge nude male backs. When the Snowman taps one, it opens like a flesh door, and I step through the looking glass, into the Land of Chippendales.

A long bench runs around the Pit's perimeter on three sides. Those are the cherry seats. And right now they're swollen with juice, jammed so full of Lady asses that at first glance you can't tell where one bum ends and the next begins.

Another blast of rampant estrogen slams into my solar plexus, rumbles in my guts, and bounces around my balls. The thumping music pounds my pulse, and my heart throbs with the bass as raw fear invades my face.

The Men of Chi-ppen-daaaaaales.

That's my first line.

The Men of Chi-ppen-daaaaaales.

Sloppy Sam, stage manager and head honcho on the floor, screams over the din:

'Hey man, you ready?'

He's in collar'n'cuffs, but he's the least handsome and muscle-cut of the studs. And he's the one in charge.

Sloppy Sam is keeper of the cordless microphone. It looks like a gray metal baton you might see used in a 400-meter relay race. It's very expensive. This fact has been mentioned to me by everyone even remotely connected to it.

'I said, "You ready!?"' Sloppy Sam repeats his scream.

'Yeah!' I yell back, all shaky and sketchy. I hope that if I sound like I mean it, I'll believe it myself.

I don't.

'What the fuck is wrong with you?!' Sloppy screams.

What the fuck *is* wrong with me? I wish I could answer that question.

I curse how little rehearsal I've had with the Men – just one afternoon that flew past so fast it was over before I even knew it started. I can barely tell one Man from another: All the tans and asses and fluffy puffy hair blend into one another.

Six hundred screaming alcohol-filled male-craving Ladies scream, and the music is soooooooo LOUD it rattles my marrow and scrambles my brain. The lights are too bright, synapses fire too fast: DANGER, DAVID SCARY: SENSORY OVERLOAD! I wanna throw up, go to sleep, sneeze, pee, and shit, all at the same time.

'Hey!' screams Sloppy Sam. 'Are you all right?'

I focus in on Sloppy Sam's sadsack face. He's so homely it makes me feel better.

'Yeah!' I scream my lie.

'Don't fuck around with this mic,' Sloppy yells, 'it's worth ten grand!'

'Right!' I yell back.

'What?!' screams Sloppy.

'Got it!' I give him the thumbs-up.

Then something odd happens. When Sloppy Sam gingerly hands me that outrageously expensive mic, it feels like a sacred scepter, and I see myself as a Messiah, ready to lead my people to the Promised Land: Let my Ladies come!

The Men of Chi-ppen-daaaaaales.

As the lights dim, a new roar rises up from twelve hundred ovaries, and I am filled with a deep transcendent love for mankind in general and women in particular.

The Weather Girls bust outta the speaker, wailing about how it's raining men.

Hallelujah!

The vast video screens flash an ancient phallic god with a rod of stone extending from chiseled groins, then Michelangelo's *David*, Casanova, Don Juan, Rudolph Valentino, James Dean, Marlon Brando, Paul Newman, Robert Redford, John Travolta, and Tom Cruise. The sequence climaxes with a series of quick pix of the Men of Chippendales, and a tornado of Lady yells blows through the room.

Any moment now there's going to be a pause in the music. This will be my cue to say:

'The Men of Chi-ppen-daaaaaales.'

There it is now.

The pause.

My cue.

Everyone's waiting.

My head is an empty blank.

Shit.

God help me.

SHIT!

Sloppy Sam nudges me with a shrug that says:

Hey asshole, start the show!

And that makes my engine turn over: I suck in a big breath as natural as a fish in water, put the priceless mic to my lips, and out of them soars with muscular intensity:

'The Men of Chi-ppen-daaaaales.'

A primal lioness roar lights up my insides like it's Chinese New Year, and I'm hot-wired right into all that grrrrl power, hot damn, shazam, ohhhhh man, that feels good! To this day, it's still the most carnage-charged powderkegged sound I've ever heard.

Cue lights: A blast of white hits the Pit like a meteor shower.

Cue music: A nut-thumping beat busts, as a butch bass rumbles under a heavy disco baritone about how it's Ladies Night, and the feeling is right.

Cue Men: Two lines of bare-chested, open-vested, top-hatted Chippendales Waiters and Hosts strut into the Pit, Dick Pulls bulging, clapping twice every fourth beat, waving, winking, blowing kisses.

The music changes, and the Men lip-synch a song specifically written for the show, a sort of musical mission statement of Chippendales in which it's postulated that the Ladies are foxes and the men are lambs. The Ladies get to wham bam while the Men say 'Thank you ma'am.'

I have no choice but to marvel at the majestic sight of all those monumental Men of Chippendales, as I slowly roll on shaking skates into the center of the Pit and they form a line on either side of me.

Scanning the six hundred Ladies I see I'm the only man here who's not ridiculously pretty and half-naked. With that comes a sickening realization.

I'm never gonna get laid at Chippendales.

The Ladies are almost all in packs. Each pack wears variations of the same hair and outfit, and each has an instigator, who's on her feet now, already half-plowed, awhoopin' and ahollerin', fueling her friends into having sex sex sexy fun.

Random pictures pop out of the crowd:

A wrinkled, pearled, high-collared grandma with blue hair sits with her granddaughter, who's got a mohawk that's a remarkably similar shade of blue.

A plus-size lady is on the Pit's fifty-yard line in a Scarlet-Letter-red low-cut dress that's overflowing with mounds of breast flesh. Turns out she's Big Alice, the regular's regular, front row and center more nights than not. She's screaming, 'Snowman! Ripped like a Ginsu knife, honey!' If you look close you can see a dollar bill peeking out from the bounty of her cleavage. Yes, Big Alice is open for business.

A modelly black babe in a high-fashion white dress and a modelly white babe in a high-fashion black dress sit in the corner of the Pit deepthroating each other's tongues. Ebony and Ivory run hands under dresses and up thighs. A hundred-dollar-a-pop bottle of Dom Pérignon luxuriates on the rail above, and several Men of Chippendales skulk around them, excited and confused.

I open my mouth, not sure if anything will come out. To my grateful amazement the sappy patter flows nice and easy. Seems my frantic, fanatic rehearsing is paying off after all.

I now teach the Ladies the most crucial thing in the entire Chippendales show:

'When I say, "Whattayaaa-wann'emmmmm-to-do?" you say, "Take it off." Ready?'

'Yeeeeeeseeeees!' the Ladies yell back.

'Whattttayaaa-wann'emmmmm-to-do?' I singsong, exactly like Nick de Noia taught me, long in the middle to build suspense, then snapped up hard and sharp at the end. Everything he told me works. Exactly like he said it would.

The Ladies roar gloriously:

'TAKE IT AWWWWWFF!'

Now I'm whipping through the introduce-the-Hosts-and-Waiters segment. This is the most important moment in the show for them. If they get a big roar here, they can be Superstarstud-for-a-Night, rake in many dead presidents, and get sexed with great vigor.

'In his spare time our next guy's a bowler, and Ladies, believe you me . . .' Pause pause pause, then I shout into the priceless mic:

'He's got a pair of sixteen pound balls . . . Tooooom Cat!!!'

A vulvic volcano flows molten from the Ladies as Tom Cat, long, lean, and lithe, smoldering coal eyes, sexwalks down the center of the elevated stage. Cat is gonna do very well tonight.

After I introduce fifteen or so Men, we're ready to begin the main body of the show, and it's all moving so fast now I don't have time to think about it.

Better that way, seeing's how my brain, at this point, is my worst enemy.

CHAPTER 9

THE BACKBONE AND THE BREADBASKET

'Unnnnnnnknoooooown Fla-sherrrrrrrr!!!'

I scream, bringing on the first featured act in the show.

He careens onstage to the classic 'Stripper Theme,' clad in ratty raincoat, tattered gloves, size 27 clown shoes, and a brown paper bag over his head with holes for eyes. His character is loosely based on the Unknown Comic, a stand-up who performed with an eye-holed paper bag over his head and became a minor celebrity on the *Gong Show*, the great-grandfather of *American Idol*.

I prattle on about how he's actually some horny homeless guy living in Central Park. Not in those words, of course, but that's the gist. Walking by the real homeless guys under the Fifty-ninth Street Bridge, it had occurred to me while memorizing this part of the script that making crass little jokes about some homeless hobo 'jumping out of the bushes and into your bush,' was very bad karmically, but like everybody else at Chippendales, I'm here to get P-A-I-D.

I feel someone staring at me. I jerk my head up to the crow's nest, which looms twenty feet up over the far end of the Pit, and there he is: Nick de Noia. He's a silver fox in cashmere clothing, combination queen mother and charismatic dictator. His stare bores a hole in my forehead, then he locks into my eyes, and shoots me an almost imperceptible nod of confidence. If you weren't looking for it you woulda never seen it, but he effortlessly communicates that I can be the Master of Ceremonies at Chippendales. At the same time, there's also a terrible threat lying under it all. That's how it is with Nick. *I'll be watching you.*

Suddenly the Unknown Flasher's naked but for the paper bag over his head and the lightbulb-bedecked G-string covering his jewels, which lights up in the blackout, as I scream:

'Whattayaaa-wann'emmmmmm-to-do?'

'TAKE IT AWWWWWF!'

Lights come back up, and when the Unknown Flasher removes the paper bag from his head, revealing a face full of dappley apple cheeks, and shining bright eyes over a giant sparkly smile, this elicits the biggest power surge yet. Revealing the face. Not the chest or the thighs or the ass. The beaming boyish man face of this truly beautiful male stripper next door.

When I'm in strip clubs where females take it off, seems like it's all about the ass and the tits and the vagina. At Chippendales, it's the face.

Observe the de Noia magic. There will be bad boys later, but first we have a sweet-faced lad you could take home to Grandma. Nick lets the Ladies enter slowly, opening them inch by inch.

Kiss & Tip is next. It's the climax of every featured act, in many ways the backbone and breadbasket of the Chippendales experience. This is when everything gets up close and personal, hands-on, lip-to-lip, cheek-to-cheek, in your face, and in your lap.

When the Flasher turns to face the left side of the house, $ waves over Lady heads like green leaves in the garden of Chippendales. Instigators all over the room wave $1's, $5's, $10's, $20's, and even the occasional $100 over shy friends' heads while everyone else in the pack howls in booze-fueled delight. Of course, many Ladies also shake $ over their own heads, happy to pay for their kisses.

Crazy Eddie, the redheaded fun-loving alcoholic DJ, ends the Flasher's song abruptly, thus concluding his Kiss & Tip. There's cash yet to be harvested from the fields of green, and the Flasher shoots Crazy Eddie a little pissed-off face. But Nick de Noia's in the house, and Nick wants the Ladies to believe that they're more important than their cash. So Crazy Eddie can't care whether the Flasher's mad about his missed simoleons. I've already been told five or six times that Nick's the kind of boss who'll chew you a new ass if you don't do exactly as he says. And if you screw up again, he'll fire you and your chewed-up ass. From the looks of him. Crazy Eddie's ass can't stand another chewing.

In the blackout, five smallish Ensemble Dancers enter in mangy monkey masks, furry arms, and loincloths. In the dark I can't tell which one is Arnolpho d'Alencar Araripe Pimenta de Mello. Two hosts whisk me quickly into a khaki jacket and pith helmet while I boom into the priceless mic:

'The Barrr-barian…arian… arian … arian … arian … arian …'

The echo was not in the script. I added it during rehearsal, and Nick loved it. Yet another thing to like about Nick. When he hears a good idea, he doesn't care where it comes from; if it makes the show better, bring it on and keep it in.

The spotlight shines on the crow's nest, twenty feet above the Pit, where the Barbarian is poised, in Viking-horned helmet, fur leggings, fur forearms, and newly repaired loincloth.

The Barbarian leaps off the crow's nest and flies through the air towards the Pit, as six hundred lady lungs gasp. As he sails down, it becomes clear, if you know what you're looking for, that he's holding a stick connected to a rope hooked to a pulley. The effect is stunning nonetheless: Tarzan in Manhattan swooping down from the treetops to ravish the sophisticated Ladies with his savage monkey love. When he comes to a running halt in the middle of the Pit, yet another primal animal din erupts.

The Ensemble Dancers pirouette, grand jeté, swirl, twirl, and pose Fosse-style with breathtaking synchronicity. It's as if they got kidnapped on their way to a Tony Award-winning production of *Oklahoma*, thrown into nasty monkey masks, and set loose in the Pit. They move with the beautiful fluid muscularity of trained gymnasts, and their perfect, compact mini-bodies mesmerize as they cut and thrust around the burly beefy Barbarian beating his chest and aping around crudely in the center of the Pit.

Ah yes, there's Arnolpho d'Alencar Araripe Pimenta de Mello. A little longer and leaner than the others.

The Barbarian suddenly hunkers, scurrying like a beast to the fringe of the Pit and burying his face in Big Alice's crotch. She grabs his head and pulls his mouth into her vagina while screaming:

'Yer an animal!'

Already I love Big Alice.

The Barbarian bangs into a fiftyish woman and bites her bosom, while snatching the $ her friend holds over her head. She recoils in pain, and takes off for the bathroom, her two dismayed friends following.

Seems more disturbing than sexy fun.

A fat-faced Lady in a too-tight vinyl candy-ass red dress grabs the Barbarian's hard monkey butt with her sharp pointy nails while she bites him viciously in the chest. He instinctively pulls away. Anger flashes but passes quickly as he grabs her $ and grunts away like he really is a monkey.

The Barbarian presents himself to model-hot Ebony and Ivory, who barely look up from their monumental make-out session with each other. At the female strip shows I've been to, I've never seen any model-hot men making out with each other.

Crazy Eddie cuts the music, and I bellow:

'The Barrr-barian…arian… arian … arian … arian … arian …'

The Barbarian simians to center stage, bows barbarically, and exits stage left.

Johnny's Velcro holds up like a trooper.

Next up: the Construction Guy. Ensemble Dancers in blue jeans, work boots, and hard hats strike construction poses: balling a jack, sawing a board, hammering a nail into a stud, while lip-synching to prerecorded dialogue:

'Yo, Mama, as long as I gotta face, you gotta place to sit!'

During the show I get one nine-minute break. This is it. I catch my exhausted breath, grinning as I watch Arnolpho and those fabulous Ensemble Dancer boys, who look much more like extras from a Village People video than construction workers.

Tenderly, lovingly, longingly, the tough Construction Guy lip-synchs the haunting Lionel Richie classic, 'Hello', to the red rose he holds.

A big beautiful babe wails like she's just seen Jesus in a G-string. He parades her to the middle of the Pit, gets on one knee, and right into her eyes he lip-synchs the chorus of 'Hello', asking the musical question: Is it me you're looking for? She screams and pants and Lawd Almightys. Naturally this ignites the moist center of the crowd, which goes from a 10 to an 11.

This is Chippendales at its best: A thick beauty gets to be all sexilicious in public, safely and sweetly, with no danger or shame. She really does seem to be releasing centuries of pent-up lust. She really does seem to be having the time of her life. As do her friends. Looks like they'll be telling this story for a very long time.

Ahhhh, yes, now I understand.

CHAPTER 10

$250 AN INCH

Leaving the Pit I take a moment to regather my wits. So far so good: no blood has been shed, no bones broken. But the night is yet young, my mind reminds me – still plenty of time for lots of disaster.

As I sigh, trundle, and harrumph across the carpet toward the back bar, a big-boned mule-toothed bleached-blonde babe blocks my path. She has her hooks into one of the hottest of the hotshot Men. In his mind at least.

Large Mark is über-huge and ultracut, head, neck, and chest all swolled up, with a washboard man-rack belly. He's a huge Terminator-type bodybuilder, complete with mammoth swept-back jacked-up hair. On Large Mark's vast tanned back lives a constellation of angry little zits, an Orion's Belt in pimples. Steroids: This dude is juicing big-time. Perhaps this would explain his black manic menstrual-like mood, and the muted but palpable diamond-hard rage shooting out of him. I shudder at the thought of his poor wee testes shriveling like grapes being dried into raisins.

Bleach Blonde blocks Large Mark's way, places her hand provocatively on his arm, glares hard into his eyes, and spouts, loud and proud, so everyone within earshot can hear:

'I'll pay ya five hundred bucks to snort a line of coke off your dick.'

This is officially my welcome-to-Chippendales moment.

Large Mark pulls out of her grip, curls a lip, and with a massive blast of snarling testosterone, he growls:

'Get da fuck awffa me!'

Large Mark gives Bleach Blonde the big-time brush and zooms away, leaving her standing in a cloud of his foul fumes.

Bleach Blonde's face falls, and when she looks around with shame in her eyes to see if anyone is watching, I can tell exactly what she looked like as a little mule-toothed kid. I can see her getting teased in school, screamed at by her callous fat mother, slapped by her cruel father, the latest in a long line of thoughtless angry careless men. I want to give her a big hug.

I have two thoughts, which I carefully formulate with the hope of getting a big laugh later from Johnny and Arnolpho:

(1) $500? Large Mark shoulda let her do it – that's $250 an inch!

(2) I'd pay good money just to watch her chop it up.

After I get a glass of ice water I retreat to the large public men's bathroom in the back. It's empty, all cool and quiet after the too-loud heat of Chippendales. My skates roll so easy on the tile as I slide into the final stall. I shut the door and lock myself in, take off my jacket, hang it on the hook, and plop down. In the distance I can barely hear Lionel crooning 'Hello.'

This will become my in-show sanctuary, where I go to recharge, reflect, and reenter my body.

I draw a deep breath.

Ahhhhhhhh.

The ice water feels good in my mouth. So cold. My God, there's just so much $ out there. Was there always this much money around? I just read about some benefit Willie Nelson's putting together for these farmers who are starving in the Midwest. What kind of a world have we made where male stripping is more valuable than food? Or is this just another version of Rome burning, with me fiddling away while the disco inferno flames on?

This leads me to a profound realization: I need to come up with a scam. Gotta get me some of that do-re-mi.

Wiping the sweat off my face I have a vision of my coal miner grandfather wiping the sweat off his sooty brow as black lung disease tries to plant its seed in his chest. There's sweat and there's *sweat*, I smile. I'm grateful to be working in the Pit of Chippendales instead of the Pit of the Coxlodge Coal Mine. Grateful I'm not begging someone to let me snort a line of coke off their genitalia for five hundred dollars.

CHAPTER 11
TICKLED PINK

Sitting in the bathroom at Chippendales, my mother pops into my mind. My mom's an immigrant, a feminist, and a lesbian. What will Mom think of Chippendales?

Maybe, as an immigrant, she'll be proud that I, her first-generation son, am living the American dream, getting paid big dough to scream my head off while skating around in circles as beautiful men strip and women from all over the world go nuts and throw money at them.

Maybe, as a feminist, she'll think that Chippendales empowers women, helps them to aggressively embrace their sexuality, become the predator instead of the prey. Will she think that this is a happy by-product of the Women's Liberation Movement, that burning bras, marching on Washington, and demanding equality have led women here, to Chippendales, to pick the fruit of their labor? Yes, women are still making sixty-five cents to a man's dollar, but at least in 1985 they get to give their dollar to a hot man in exchange for kisses and copped feels.

I flash back to when I was a kid and I asked my mom what she wanted me to be when I grew up. She said she wanted me to be happy. I wonder what she'd have said if I told her I wanted to be the Master of Ceremonies at a male strip club. I wonder if this is going to make me happy.

In fact, in about a year, my mom will come to see the show, with my brother in tow. They will sit behind the black glass of the VIP lounge. When I announce that night that my mother is in the house, the Ladies give her a big huge cheer. Afterward, when I ask her what she thought about the show, she doesn't mention the feminist politics or the sociosexual economics of Chippendales. She's tickled pink at how sweet the Ladies were for giving her such a nice round of applause.

I will then ask my brother, who's getting his PhD in mathematics at Berkeley, what he thought of Chippendales, and he will confess that he slept through most of the show.

CHAPTER 12

SLICK RICK'S SOCK COCK

Rehydrated, lizard drained, I try to slide by the Grand Central Station-packed lady's loo, with the show blaring as the Construction Guy does his Kiss & Tip.

I spot the Snowman in the Pit with the much-ballyhooed twins: They're a pair of early-twenties blondes, blue-eyed, bustier-bustin' babes. The Snowman's flexing his ripped-to-shreds abs for them. One twin has a hand on the three left belly muscles, while the other has her hand on the three right belly muscles. They smile eerily identical, toothy, tonguey smiles.

It hits me that being a great Master of Ceremonies at Chippendales is like being the greatest downhill skier in the Sahara Desert. You may be the crème de la crème, but who cares? It hits me even harder: I am never gonna get laid here. The competition is too stiff. Literally.

As if in reply, the universe shoves into my path a Lady with a buzzcut, crazy blazing green eyes, *Little House on the Prairie* dress, and army boots that look like they've been to war. She looks to be somewhere between eighteen and thirty. She grabs my arm and leans in. 'Arrrrre you the, uh, guy out there?' She sounds like a radio station that's not quite tuned in, and her wobbles make it clear that she's quite blotto. 'I mean, arrrrre you the guy in the, uhhhhm ... roller skates?' She looks down at my roller skates. 'Hey, you *are* ... the guy in the roller skates.' She totters and teeters. Leaning in farther, she loses her balance and falls into me. I catch her and slide my arm around her hip bone, while her hidden breasts press into my chest, and a jolt of excitement bombs through me. Now she's right in my face as she smiles sweet and says:

'You're the uh ... guy ...'

I'm the guy. Can you imagine? Me? The guy? Then it dawns on me: I'm Average Joe, the pleasant fellow who sits behind you in homeroom, the one you can confide in about the ludicrous theater of lust and cruelty as you crave the badboy.

Hold the phone, maybe I can find some love at Chippendales after all.

'I didn't waaaaaanna come here,' Buzzcut slurs. 'My sister made me. She thinks I'm a dyke. A DYKE!! Isn't that riiiii-diculous?'

I can hear my cue coming. In about twenty seconds it's going to pull into the station, and if I'm not at the platform to welcome it, there's a distinct possibility that Nick de Noia will feast on my ass before he fires it.

'That *is* ridiculous. Listen I gotta go.' I try to pull away, but Buzzcut won't release me.

I have to be in the middle of the Pit by the time this song ends. I'm never gonna make it. The show is gonna grind to a halt because of me.

Thank God the Snowman struts up and shoves Buzzcut off, then propels me into the Pit just as the Construction Guy's Kiss & Tip ends.

As I start to intro the next act, the long, lean, and lanky Tom Cat stumbles out in huge high heels and a giant curly blond wig, with half coconuts attached to a burlap bikini top where his breasts would be if he were a woman. He carries an array of Chippendales merch: Chippendales calendar, Chippendales playing cards, Chippendales T-shirts, and a Chippendales G-string.

I see again that the key to succeeding at Chippendales is coming up with some way to milk the cash cow. This is Tom Cat's scam, pimping the merch.

'Excuse me, miss,' I mock flirt, 'you've got a lovely bunch of coconuts.'

'Why thank you,' Tom Cat lisps into the priceless mic like a caricature of a homosexual. Not a woman, which is what is called for in the script. A gay man. Seems an odd choice, but the other Men of Chippendales are laughing like they're gonna piss themselves. Apparently Nick also thinks it's the height of hilarity. But I've been told that Nick has his own agenda, gay-wise.

Me and limp-wristed Tom Cat hawk the merch, then he wobbles off.

Two more acts to go, then the finale, then it's home again, home again, jiggedy jig. As I begin introducing the next act, the Snowman struts into the center of the Pit, like he wants to have a word with me. When he leans his lips in, the overpowering odor of baby oil, bad cologne, chemical hair products, and man-sweat swaddles me, and his 'stache tickles my ear.

The Snowman's supposed to say:

'Our next performer is out sick, what are we gonna do?'

Instead he whispers:

'You love sucking big fat cock, don't you?'

He barely suppresses a giggle, as he glances at Large Mark in the corner of the Pit. When Large howls with laughter, his steroid-bloated head bobs up and down and his colossal chest bounces.

I actually enjoy the hazing. As someone who feels like an outsider in every group, I love being one of the gang, in on the joke, even if I am the butt of it. Feels good to be part of a long tradition of ritualistic, sadistic, homoerotic male bonding that's been part of men welcoming men into fraternities, guilds, clans, and tribes since we've lived in caves.

Luckily I trained in much tougher rooms than this, so I breeze right on through, turn to the Ladies, and play to the front and the back rows with as much sparkle as I can muster:

'I've just been informed that our next performer is out sick. What are we gonna do?' I make a shoulder-shrugged, bug-eyed, palms-up, whattayagonnado? face.

The Snowman looks around, then points to Slick Rick, who's walking along the edge of the Pit:

'What about him?'

Slick Rick, the newest star in the Chippendales galaxy, looks like a cross between Prince and Michael Jordan, with a shining to-die-for light brown body, and the classic-smile and chiseled-cheekbone combo. He shyly smiles, white teeth shining in his beaming black face. He clearly indicates that he's far too bashful to dance in front of all these Ladies.

I turn to them, pause, then teasingly scream:

'What do you think, Ladies, do you wanna see Rick take it off?'

'YEAAAAAAAAAAAAH!!!'

Oh God that feels good.

Slick Rick looks at the Ladies all cute and coy, flashing a bashful smile as he protests:

'Noooo . . .'

Naturally this just makes them want it more, as the pot goes from lightly bubbling to boiling.

Slick Rick's a guy who was born to wear the spandex and cuffs'n'collar, but he's also good at his job. He really really looks like he's too modest and scared to dance for the Ladies. Professionally, I'm impressed.

I fill my lungs with oxygen, throw my hand up like Joel Grey in *Cabaret* and scream:

'Whattttayaaa-wann'immmmmmm-to-do?'

'TAKE IT AWWWWWF!'

The Snowman, Large Mark, and Tom Cat drag Slick Rick kicking and screaming into the Pit and dump him there. He tries to break away and run off, but they restrain him.

Suddenly the loopy hypnotic bass line to the seminal rap classic 'White Lines (Don't Do It)' kicks in. Slick Rick stops protesting and pauses in the middle of the Pit, listening intently to the music.

BAM!

He strikes a hot, cocky Fosse Princey pose, and the Ladies go crazy again. Slick Rick flips off his shoes, sits on the steps of the Pit, and starts to take off his socks. Now me, I've taken off my socks hundreds of times and never thought much about it. But as Slick Rick removes a sock, he grips the top of it with his toes and pulls the bottom of it toward his groin. He then moves his hand up and down, over and over, yanking it in time with the music, magically turning that sock into a cock while jacking himself silly.

Squeals reach Beatle-mania levels.

The song climaxes – as does Slick Rick, his perfect, sweating, wet chocolate body contracting in orgasmic rapture as the Ladies bliss out.

It's can't-take-your-eyes-off-it theater, and suddenly Slick Rick's nekked in a G-string, a Chippendales Calendar Man of the Year come to life. He grabs a bottle of champagne and playfully shakes it, then glances glowing up at the crow's nest with flirty twinkly sparkle.

And there he is: Nick de Noia, standing with erect spine, a dapper demigod eye-locked on Slick Rick from his perch up in stripper heaven. Nick throws him a tiny but highly satisfied nod, happy daddy to star pupil, with a jolt of what looks like some I-wanna-fuck-you thrown in for good measure. Or is that just me?

As Prince sings, 'Let's go crazy!' Slick Rick sprays champagne all over the Ladies, and they do in fact go CRAZY! I look up at Nick, and I can practically see his erection through his charcoal tailored pants.

Prince screams that he's a star, and when Slick Rick lip-synchs it, he looks a lot like a bigger, buffer, more-manly Prince. He totally sells it. And the Ladies totally buy it.

Slick Rick's really into his Kiss & Tip. Hundreds of greenbacks sprout up and wave in the wind. Slick Rick harvests the cash crop with kisses. A beautiful bride-to-be shoves bills into his G-string like it's a bank and she's making direct deposits.

Mama didn't raise no fool. Slick Rick floats straight to Big

Alice's honey. She buries her face in his G-string, nose-deep in dick. With a huge Richard Pryor *commedia dell'arte* surprise face, he plays the whole room as the roar deafens.

Classic de Noia: the bawdy, lip to lip with the silly, ends up being naughty instead of graphic, teasing instead of sleazy. Nick in a nutshell.

Slick Rick rubs up against Big Alice like a housebroken three-balled black cat, and the place goes ballistic. It's like I'm in the cockpit of a rocket fueled by pure Lady love.

When Big Alice shake'n'bake shimmies, the magic dollar peeking out of her cleavage takes on a life of its own. She plants Slick Rick's face like a flag in the continent of her décolletage.

When Slick Rick moves his head away from Big Alice's heavy cleavage he has the magic dollar clamped in his teeth. It's actually attached to another dollar with tape you can't see. And that dollar's attached to another dollar. Which is attached to another dollar. As he pulls on the line of dollar bills they snake magically out of Big Alice's cleavage. It's the old endless-handkerchief gag, only with money and breasts instead of kerchief and pocket. Looks like a moving Escher painting.

The Ladies give Slick Rick much love as he takes Big Alice back to her seat on the Pit bench, and kisses her hand like an old-fashioned chivalrous gentleman in a G-string.

This is the philosophy of Nick de Noia. Don't bring the thin beautiful babe out into the Pit. Bring on the large Lady live wire, the Big Alice. Celebrate the sexiness of the fat and the homely and the old and the lonely.

As Slick Rick bows and trots off, his two beautiful butter-scotch ass cheeks disappear into the dressing room.

Time to run these horses round the mountain and bring this show home.

CHAPTER 13
PRINCE CHARMING

Prince Charming is the hottest star in the greatest male stripper empire on the planet. He's the last act in the show, and his appearance means my opening night's so close to being over I can almost taste it.

Prince Charming is impossibly beautiful and impossible to dislike. Even as he grabs center stage he retains a modest vulnerable sweetness. He just seems so nice. And even though charisma drips off this spectacular bastard, he's one of those guys who makes it look like he isn't even really trying.

And oh my God! do the Ladies go crazy for Prince Charming.

I look up at the crow's nest to see Nick de Noia. But he's gone. I'm beginning to realize that this is part of his power. The man seems omnipotent. He's not there when you think he is. And he's there when you think he's not. No wonder everyone's so busy watching their backs and covering their asses.

When Crazy Eddie kills the music I scream:

'Priiiiince Chaaaaarming!!!'

His ovation is standing.

Finally it's grand finale time. I introduce the stars. When I get to the Ensemble Dancers I yell:

'Ahhhhhhnolfo Djallenca Arraripe Pimenta di Mello!'

Just like he told me. He shoots me a lovely thank-you smile, and a warm buttery feeling flows through me. I shout out to the insane Crazy Eddie and thank Johnny.

Naturally, Nick de Noia's in the crow's nest for the big finish, basking in all he has created. I make a big point of throwing him an extra dollop of thanks as he waves down at all of us peasants. I do feel a great and genuine gratitude to the man, like I've just gotten a master's degree in Performing at Nick de Noia University.

Nick makes my night when he gives me a little nod and demisalute. I'm suddenly awash and aglow from knowing I've succeeded in pleasing this extraordinary taskmaster. And I never once looked at my cue cards.

I did it. I have become the Master of Ceremonies of Chippendales Male Strip Show.

Now all I have to do is become the Master of Ceremonies of the David Henry Sterry Show.

CHAPTER 14

THERE'S NO ESCAPING THE JAWS OF THE ALIEN INSIDE

Dramatically I turn to the Hosts and Waiters, ready to be hailed a hero, hoisted up on boulder shoulders and carried out to the chants of:

'Da-vid Sca-ry! Da-vid Sca-ry! Da-vid Sca-ry!'

Imagine my surprise when I find that I've become completely invisible, right here in the middle of Chippendales Male Strip Club.

The men are still posing, macking, selling kisses, drinks, pics, weed, speed, whatever ya need, trying to get S-E-X, and get P-A-I-D. But no one seems even remotely aware of me.

Crazy Eddie cranks Michael Jackson's 'Thriller' at nut-crunching decibels. On the video screen a gigantic Michael turns into a monster.

Ladies leave in chick packs or groove out onto the dance

floor where they shake their moneymakers or hunt Chippendales man-meat.

The air slowly leaks out of me, and I'm coated in a thick
layer of black despair, as the Pit rapidly fills with women.
Dancing alone, dancing together. A Lady in a mauvish clingy
dress thingy with round salad-plate-sized holes all up the side
walks right toward me. She wears dozens of plastic bracelets
that spastically twitch. Her eyes seem a little too small and a
little too close together, and her teeth seem a little too big for
her mouth. I don't care whether I'm attracted to her; the
important thing is to make her want me. That's my aphro-
disiac. Yeah, baby, bring it on! The Master of Ceremonies is
gonna sex you up. Wait a minute. She's not looking at me.
She walks right through me. I *am* invisible. I have no substance.
I am a ghost of myself.

Exhaustion so deep seeps into the soul of my bones. Shaky
on my skates, I'm pingponged and pinballed by the suddenly
thick-packed full-contact hustle of humanity in the Pit. Please
God, you evil bastard, just let me get the fuck outta here so
I can go lick my wounds, since clearly no one is going to lick
them for me.

My head tightens as I wade through the Pit. Slammed by
a hard hip, I grab a shoulder to stop from falling, but a flat
hand slaps mine away. Sweat pours outta me and my skull
throbs. An elbow slams into my ribs, and the bony shard hurts
like shit.

'Sorry,' I say, even though she can't hear me, and I'm not
really sorry.

The music feels like it's coming from inside my head, and
someone's turned up the volume to 15, as Michael Jackson
screams about how there's no escaping from the alien inside.

When I spot a crack in the crowd, I speed up some steps and out of the Pit, part the red velvet curtain and roll through the dressing room door.

Sweat-drenched, swamp-hot, and steamy-mirrored, the dressing room is filled to the rim with exquisite sweaty naked maleness. Everyone's high from the show, and a wonderful buzz bubbles in the sticky air. There's much counting and sorting of much $ in this tiny fetid hot-house of a room that smells like a huge pair of testicles at the end of a muggy summer day.

The Ensemble Dancers wipe down their tight, tiny, pumped-up jockey bodies before changing into their street clothes. They're the only real professional dancers at Chippendales. They've trained at places like Juilliard and danced on Broadway. So Chippendales is a step down for them in the show business food chain, but it's only four shows a week here, as opposed to eight on Broadway, for about the same pay. It's a good living, but they're certainly not getting rich. They're chitting and chatting and dishing and being silly with each other, but they seem anxious to get on with their nights, their lives. They, like me, have no tip $ to count.

The stars have dumped all their Kiss & Tip $ into high piles on the counters. It's a pretty picture: a mountain range of greenbacks with mountainous men harvesting them. A thousand dollars cash money on a good night, for thirty minutes work.

Prince Charming's Money Mountain is the largest of all. As he meticulously dewrinkles his bills and irons them with his hands into their proper stacks, he looks like a little kid making sand castles, and I'm mesmerized by his gorgeous intensity, totally unself-conscious about his nakedness. Not all stuck up cuz of what a hunk he is. He seems like the guy you'd want to be if you could choose who you got to be before you were born. Nick de Noia may be the czar of Chippendales, but the star is gorgeous goldilocked Prince Charming. And Sleeping Beauty has to pay to get a kiss off him.

My eyes wander down to his perfect ass. Oh, sweet Jesus. Teeth marks: uppers and lowers, deep red and angry. Some lady really locked her jaws onto his cheek. You could identify her dead body with those teeth marks.

The bite mark. The mound of $.

America, wot a country!

I notice Slick Rick for the first time. He's off in the corner, a towel around his waist. I don't even remember seeing Slick Rick before the show. Now I see why. He lives alone on Slick Rick Island. No bantering with the boys. Aloof? Or painfully shy?

Too early to say.

CHAPTER 15
WHATEVER FLOATS YER BOAT

Johnny doesn't notice when I trudge my puffy white ass back to the costume room and plop myself into a chair there. This is a very difficult time in her night. It's her job to collect all the nasty funky steamy stinky men's costumes and get them looking good-to-go-sharp by showtime tomorrow.

'Come on, man,' Johnny barks at the Men as she gathers sodden codpieces, soggy jockstraps, and mangy monkey masks, 'I asked you guys to put that shit in the basket, that's why I *got* the goddamn basket. What the fuck!'

Deaf ears these words fall upon. Apparently there's no diva quite like a beautiful man diva. They just dump their filthy shit anywhere. If you don't like it, fuck you, I'm a star, baby!

I love how Johnny takes no shit from these palookas. She just dishes it out to whoever deserves it, doesn't care how gorgeous or hot or perfect they are. Could I do that? I don't think so. I want them to like me too much. And of course the irony is that they like Johnny and don't give a shit about me. Of course it does help that she's twenty and has all that curly brown hair and those thick pink lips. But she's a looker who doesn't just trade on her looks, and I like that. She busts her ass, busts their chops, and takes no prisoners. As I watch her being the costume mistress, I find myself imagining her naked. Flat belly, maple syrup skin, flammable eyes. Yeah, there's heat coming outta her. But it's got cool over the top of it.

A deep fuckit sigh heaves outta Johnny. It's easier in the end to just do it all herself than to try to get the Men to cooperate in any way, shape, or form.

'Motherfuckin' piece-of-shit dumb-ass douche-bag cocksuckers can kiss my mutherfuckin' ass . . . ,' Johnny mumbles and mutters as she gathers and sorts the stinky stanky costumes, then puts them into piles to be cleaned, folded, and sparkled.

I can't get my skate off. I tug, I grapple, I snatch, but the fucker's stuck and it won't come off.

'Cock-bitin' mutherfucker, what the hell is wrong with this piece-of-shit goddamn-it son of a fuck face . . .'

Suddenly I realize I'm muttering and mumbling just like Johnny.

Suddenly Johnny realizes she's mumbling and muttering just like me.

We both stop muttering and mumbling. I chuckle. She chuckles. Then there is smiling.

The Snowman struts into the room. This is one truly toocool-for-school dude. He's got this little insinuating smile on his face, like he knows something I don't know, and I'm sorta stupid for not knowing it. He's the kinda guy who swaggers even when he's standing still.

The Snowman looks at me lasciviously, raises his eyebrows comically, and mimes getting fellatio from twins, complete with a little whistle each time his hand thrusts the back of an imaginary female head toward his penis:

'Doubleheader, man, djoo check out the twins? They're gonna suck the chrome right off the Snowman's bumper. Prime cut, baby, USDA-inspected killer twin pussy. It's a Doublemint doubleheader, motherfucker.'

Johnny scowls a curly smirk:

'You're such a pig.'

'Yeah, you love it, don'cha, you saucy wench?' The Snowman nods his head like he thinks he's the sexiest bitch on the planet.

'No,' she sneers. 'I don't love it. It's disgusting. You're like a bad joke, man. No, actually, you're like the butt of a bad joke.' She stares hard, then says: 'So whattaya want?'

'Gimme five dimes of the A, and uh . . . ten dimes of the B, and, let's see . . . fifteen nickels of shake . . .'

Johnny turns around and bends down, and her kurly krazy mane disappears into a canvas bag where she rummages. Reemerging, she slips a bunch of small bags I can't quite see into the Snowman's hands. He slips them into a Chippendales fanny pack.

The Snowman hands Johnny what looks like a bunch of $.

So this is Johnny's scam. Marijuana distribution specialist.

The Snowman turns to me, looks down, and smiles with those Paul Newman-blue eyes and those absurdly perfect teeth, dazzling and intimidating.

'Hey, uh, lookin' fer some tootski?'

'Uh . . .' I stammer, 'no, uh . . . thanks, though.'

The Snowman smiles sardonically, rearranges his package, gives his head a cocky little tilt and says:

'Hey, whatever floats yer boat.'

The Snowman turns on his boot heels and blows outta the costume room like he's gotta coupla twins to do.

CHAPTER 16
MANGY MONKEY MASKS

From deep in the costume room, I hear the dressing room door open and a blast of 'What's Love Got to Do with It' crashes into the room. Then the door shuts, and the music goes away, as does the manly banter, bragging, ragging, and ranting.

Quiet.

Dead quiet.

That can mean only one thing: Nick de Noia is in the house.

'I am not happy!' I hear him bellow. 'Helloooooooo?! That show tonight was sloppy. Sloppy sloppy sloppy! I've told you a million times. We're the foxes.' Nick claps. 'They're the lambs.' Nick claps twice. 'And why is the Construction Guy so FAT! It's disgusting. If you can't get rid of that blubberbutt, I've got a hundred hungry studs just waiting in the wings. And believe me, we won't miss a beat, mister. Rick, you were fabulous tonight. *Faaaaabulous!* I want everyone in here to watch his act tomorrow. He was fresh, he was real, he was spontaneous, he was crisp, and he had a sparkle that knocked my socks off. He put his heart and soul and cock into it. He's cut, he's ripped, and he just looks like he's having a blast out there. A blast! Mark my words. If this show doesn't shape up, there will be some major changes around here. Now, I've got some big news. Big! A young woman by the name of . . .' Nick de Noia lets his pause linger, and it's so quiet you can hear a prick drop. 'Ms Brooke Shields is going to be joining us to celebrate her twentieth birthday.'

An appropriately excited buzz hums through the room. Brooke Shields, supermodel, sexy movie star, and It girl, is, according to the June 17, 1985, edition of *People* magazine, 'the most famous teenager in the world.'

'Naturally,' Nick continues, 'there will be lots of very important people here. Media, managers, producers, agents.' Nick pauses. Silence. The buzz stops. 'And Ms Brooke Shields is going to see the greatest show we've ever done. I want everything crisp. I want everything clean. I want everyone to sparkle. No excuses, no ifs, ands, or buts . . . Well, maybe a few butts.'

Nick de Noia pauses to let everyone laugh.

Everyone laughs: half blowing-off-steam and half ass-kiss.

As the jocularity fades I hear Nick's expensive Italian shoes headed our way. I can feel the man coming closer and closer, like he's a superhero whose energy field precedes him.

My balls freeze into ice cubes.

Johnny does a very impressive, I'm-over-the-whole-thing eye roll.

Nick's big, thick, salt-and-pepper eyebrows seem to enter the room before he does. He glides like he's moving on air, parks himself in the doorway, and poses regally. His skin is so smooth. He's an excellent shaver. I hope someday to be as good a shaver as Nick de Noia. His nails are very well mani- cured, and his hair looks so soft and sits so nice on his head. I bet that haircut cost him a bundle. If I live to be 120, I will never look that put-together. But beneath all that Rico Suave you can feel he's spring-loaded and ready to pounce.

Nick takes a moment to survey the room and registers my presence. When he beams at me I bask in that Nick de Noia smile, happy to be well-loved by the most powerful man in the building. On the Upper East Side. In Manhattan. In the galaxy.

I stand up. Nick reaches out his hand. I give him mine. He squeezes while he shakes it, incredibly intimate yet deeply manly. He looks into my eyes, and nods his head while he says:

'David, you were fabulous. Helloooooooooo?! Your energy, your pace. I just loved how you grabbed this show by the balls and made it your own. You did it: You drove those Ladies hard, and you put 'em up wet, as they say.'

Nick smiles like he's made a funny joke.

Cue for me to laugh.

I laugh.

I'm pathetic, I know it, but there's nothing I can do about it.

'I just have a couple of notes, why don't you come in Tuesday about four-thirty and we'll do a little rehearsal. As I'm sure you heard, Ms Brooke Shields will be attending the show this Saturday night. I talked to her people and Brooke is very excited. It's going to be a very important night. And I just know you are going to be faaaaaaabulous!'

Finally, someone who understands how faaaaaabulous I am.

'Wow, thanks, Nick,' I say, much too happy. 'I just wanted to tell you how much I appreciate the opportunity. And . . . well, I wanted to thank you for everything. It's just been . . . fabulous.'

I've never said the word *fabulous* in my life. But that's how it is with Nick de Noia. You hang out with him long enough, all of a sudden you find the word *fabulous* coming out of your mouth.

I'm aware that I sound like a big brownnosing suckass bumkisser. Still, I mean every word.

That doesn't stop Johnny from pulling a you're-such-a-loathsome-toady face at me behind Nick de Noia's back.

Which makes me like and want her even more.

Naturally Nick de Noia eats up my praise with a fork and a spoon.

'Well, thank you, David, it has been an absolute pleasure working with you.' Nicks leans in intimate. 'And I'd love you to come up to the VIP lounge to celebrate your fabulous debut.'

My fabulous debut. That's what I'm talking about. This is what I've been waiting my whole adult life for. Happiness washes warm over me. If Nick de Noia loves me, and I can get Brooke Shields and her people to love me, I'll be well on my way to getting everyone on the planet to love me; then everything else won't matter.

'Thanks, I'd love to.' I smile.

Then Nick de Noia turns ever so slightly to address Johnny. Amazing how much grace he can put into such a tiny move-ment. He makes a point of slowly pronouncing every single syllable, so there's no room for misinterpretation:

'Those monkey masks are hideous. HIDEOUS! Helloooooooo?!

I can't stand to look at them one more night. I want all the monkey masks replaced. I want everything crisp, I want everything clean, I want everything perfect.' Nick asks like he's talking to a six-year-old who's a slow learner, 'Are we clear?'

Even though I barely know Johnny I can see that having to just stand there and swallow all that shit from the Man is pissing her all the way off. If she were a cartoon character her whole head would be filling with red, and steam would be screaming from her ears.

But to her great credit, she's a model of restraint. She takes a breath, lets it out, and with a smile that lives right on the border of Submission and Fuck You, she says:

'Absolutely, Nick, no problem.'

Nick looks like he can't decide whether she's making fun of him or being a humble servant. Or both. He seems to weigh his options. Make her pay or walk away.

Nick pirouettes with practiced elegance and slides out of the costume room, leaving relief, exhilaration, and extreme annoyance in his wake.

Johnny whips around, makes intense eye contact, and with earnest urgency, she says:

'Lemme ask you something. Honestly. Do you think Brooke Fuckin' Shields is gonna come to Chippendales and go, "Well, I really woulda enjoyed it, except the monkey masks got in the way of me looking at all that naked ass!"?'

Having just witnessed firsthand how little the Ladies seem to care about the monkey masks, I utter with confidence:

'No, I really don't.'

'Then why the fuck am I gonna have to drag my ass all over town, trackin' down some stupid-ass monkey masks that nobody gives a shit about?'

I'm not sure if that's a rhetorical question, so I don't answer. Wait to see if she just busts on through. She does.

'Miserable fucking cockswallowing closet queen bitch.'

I deadpan:

'I hear ya.'

Johnny stops what she's doing, and everything changes in the costume room. I watch her step outside herself and take me in fully.

'Shit, I'm sorry, how was your first show? Were you ... ,' Johnny does a spot-on impersonation of Nick: 'faaaaa-bulous?'

She gets a nice laugh outta me. Personally, I like somebody who can stop midtantrum and ask you how your night went.

'Well, I didn't ... fuck everything up. There was no blood shed as far as I know.'

Surrounded by the Barbarian's fur loincloth, the Construction Guy's soiled hard hat, the Prince Charming tunic, and the Unknown Flasher's light-up G-string cockholder, Johnny and I laugh together.

Deep in her cave, Johnny has made me feel finally at home in my twisted new family.

Then the moment is over and she goes back to being the hard-bitten Costume Mistress.

'Fucking monkey masks,' Johnny bitches and hisses through clenched teeth. 'Are you kiddin' me? Anal retentive bitch can suck my dick! What the fuck is that cocksucker's problem? I should do us all a favor and put that bitch out of his fucking misery.'

This is the first time I hear someone say they'd like to kill Nick de Noia.

CHAPTER 17

WHAT MAKES BILLY CHEEKS SO FUCKABLE?

Billy Cheeks is the prototypical Chippendales Man. Just over 6', shoulder-length angel hair and dreamboat eyes surrounded by soft extralong eyelashes. Olive skin, athletic, lanky, easy on his feet and your eyes. There's always one of these guys in every high school. Everybody gravitates toward him, not because he's the smartest or the strongest or the sharpest, but because he's so unbelievably handsome and charming.

These Host/Waiter guys don't make that much salary, but the perks are insane. Mad cash, crazy sex, and 15 minutes of fame. Hustling drugs, hugs, and kisses. Selling off the best Pit seats, pimping pictures with the stars. I hear $100 is the going rate for cunnilingus, $250 to go all the way. But at Chippendales everything's negotiable.

Reagan really is a genius – he's got all this disposable $ trickling down in Chippendales. They're dying in droves in Ethiopia, but thank God at Chippendales we get to partyallthetime.

When Billy Cheeks oozes smooth into the room, he makes me, the white puffy Marshmallow Man, go: Wow, I wish I hadda body like that. I'm definitely gonna start working out. Hard. Tomorrow. If not sooner.

Naturally Billy Cheeks has a smile that makes him even more handsome. Shit, what would it be like to be that handsome? Seems like everything would be so much easier. People just like you if you're really really handsome. But Billy Cheeks does seem nice, too. His is not a mean, condescending, snarky smile, like the ones some of these sickeningly handsome fuckers flash at you.

When Billy Cheeks enters the costume room, all of a sudden, Johnny's not looking at me anymore. She's making unmistakable goo-goo eyes at Billy Cheeks, and he's giving as good as he gets.

I try to put my finger on exactly what makes Billy Cheeks so fuckable. It's not just the physical beauty. He's confident without seeming cocky, charismatic without seeming narcissistic. Would he be that confident and charismatic if he weren't so fucking handsome?

'Hey, babe.' Billy Cheeks twinkles easy at Johnny.

'Hey.' She gives him back half a wet smile, a blend of I-don't-give-a-shit and I'm-the-greatest-piece-of-ass-you'll-ever-have.'

'How's your night, babe?' Billy Cheeks really does seem to genuinely care.

Johnny shrugs with disgust and says:

'Nick's all the way up my ass 'cuz Brooke Fuckin' Shields is coming. Like she gives a shit about some stupid dumb-ass monkey mask—'

'Fuck Nick.' Billy Cheeks seems funny, sympathetic, and sensitive.

'Exactly.' Johnny appears happy that this radically handsome man is being so nice to her.

And I am invisible once more. Watching the two of them do this dance is fascinating, disturbing, and confusing. Is this sexy, happy, jump-your-bones banter? Or flirtation-that's-going-nowhere banter? With all the faux sex at Chippendales, it's hard to tell.

Billy Cheeks feels me staring at him like I'm trying to decode his DNA. He turns and observes me with a look, like: Shit, I didn't even see you sitting over there. Then, real friendly, he sticks out his hand.

'Sorry, uh . . . I'm Billy, nice to meetcha.'

His handshake is a little loose for my taste. But he has very long fingers. Unfortunately, I can't stop my mind from picturing his long penis, and it makes me uneasy in a way I can't quite explain.

'Hey, man,' I say, trying to look as long-penised as him. 'I'm David, nice to meet you.'

'Cool,' he says and nods. Billy Cheeks then refocuses every ounce of his attention back at Johnny, who seems to really like it. Then, way casual, like he's asking, What time is it? or, Can I borrow a pencil? he says:

'Hey, uh, you wanna hang out later?'

What exactly does *hang out* mean? Go for a beer? Or fuck like love monkeys?

'Sure . . . whatever,' Johnny replies with unconvincing nonchalance. Seems to me she's doing a bad job of hiding how much she wants to sex up this Chippendales Man.

Slow and sensuous, Billy Cheeks moves his all-star lips closer and closer to the soft of her neck. Johnny opens to let him in, and the temperature rises in the costume room.

Johnny puts her hand on his naked olive shoulder. She has very small hands. Before I can stop it, my mind is picturing his long handsome penis fitting into her small Latina vagina.

Billy Cheeks's lips whisper what seem like extremely sweet nothings into her very receptive ear. Johnny school-girl giggles. It would be totally adorable if it were me instead of him. She gives him a smirky smile and moves in for a moist, lingering kiss. Oh, she's a sexy one, our Johnny. And they're definitely doing it.

Johnny reaches down into her canvas bag and extracts something I can't quite see. She hands it to Billy Cheeks, who says:

'Thanks, babe. See you later.'

Unlike the Snowman, Billy Cheeks does not pay her. Apparently this one's on the house. He looks down at me, raises his eyebrows a demiscintilla, and gives me a tiny little head nod, saying good-bye with as little effort as humanly possible.

And Billy Cheeks is gone.

Johnny sighs and stars fill her eyes.

'Is there a factory where Nick has these dudes constructed?'

Johnny chuckles:

'Not that I'm aware of.'

'Well, like, where's he from? How did he get to be a Chippendales dude?'

'He's from, uh ... Sheepshead Bay, Long Island, someplace. Nick found him in Central Park, he was playing Frisbee with his dog.'

'Wow, so Nick's just cruising 24/7 for hot dudes,' I smile.

'Yeah, that's about the size of it,' she says, laughing back.

'Did he go to college?' I ask.

'Uh,' she says, 'I think he did a year at some junior college or somethin' . . .'

'Does he have another job?'

'No way.' She shakes her curls. 'He makes, like, two grand a month here, and he lives with a bunch of his buddies in Brooklyn, he rides his bike everywhere . . . he's got, like, no overhead.'

'*Hhm* . . .' I take it all in. I'm tired of talking about Billy Cheeks. 'So I saw the weirdest thing tonight, this woman said she'd pay Large Mark $500 to snort—'

'Coke off his dick, yeah, I heard,' Johnny cuts me off, like, this is so yesterday's news. 'He was such a sick pig when he was talking about it.'

I've been waiting all night for this moment. I pause to make sure I get it right.

'Yeah, I think he shoulda done it. The way I figure it, that's $250 an inch. And personally I'd pay good money to watch her chop it up.'

Johnny laughs out loud, good and hard. I may not get to make love to her, but at least I can make her laugh.

My skate slides right off, and I reassemble myself in my black, balloony drawstring pants and my Popeye 'I yam what I yam' T-shirt. One sock red, one sock blue. I face Johnny, who's intent on bringing order to this chaos so she can finish costume mistressing for the night and start her second job: marijuana distribution specialist at Chippendales.

I don't quite know what to say. Seems like I should say something. So this is what I pick:

'Hey, thanks, uh . . . see ya.'

Johnny stops.

'Oh yeah, sure. Listen I'm glad it went OK, maybe I'll see you later.'

Should I shake her hand? Should I go in for the hug? Perhaps a peck on the cheek?

Not knowing quite what to do, I do nothing except say:

'Yeah, maybe.'

Then I walk out of Johnny's costume room, hungry to see what Chippendales has in store for me tonight.

CHAPTER 18
LOOOOOOOOSERS!

Stepping out of the dressing room into the deafening smoke of the club, my whole body revolts: Lungs, tongue, blood, heart, nerves, and brain scream: GET ME THE FUCK OUTTA HERE! I swear if I don't get some fresh air I'm gonna keel. Unfortunately I'm in Manhattan, where the air reeks of bus farts and crusty piss, so fresh air is out of the question. But as I bust out of Chippendales Male Strip Club my lungs thank me profusely.

A line of men snakes up First Avenue, bends around the corner onto Sixty-first Street, and ends somewhere near the East River. Brooklyn guidos in shiny suits; Springsteen wannabes from Jersey in work boots and greasy hair; Harlem homeboys in killer shades; pachucos from Spanish Harlem sporting postmodern pompadours; farm boys from Oklahoma in decades-out-of-fashion blazers; and boozed-up Brits singing

dirty songs. All are lined up outside Chippendales Male Strip
Club with two things in common:

(1) They're willing to spend fifteen dollars to enter the club
    after the show's over.
(2) They're expecting the Ladies inside to be premoistened
    and likkered-up, craving Chippendales love but willing
    to settle for an average Joe like them.

The first time I saw all these guys I thought:
Loooooooosers!

But having just done my first show, I find myself in quiet
kinship with them, wondering if Buzzcut, the cute tipsy chick
in the *Little House on the Prairie* dress, is still drunk enough to
want me.

As I slide back in to Chippendales, my eyes get stuck on a
raven-haired Vampirella-looking chick hitting on the second-
most handsome Man at Chippendales. Pretty Peter is his name:
showstoppingly beautiful and sack-o'-hammers stupid. He's
also a male model, so he's been highly styled – spiky dyed
blond hair and tight jeans that look like he lives in them.
Leather sleeveless vest and no shirt reveal a perfect tan torso,
all supple ripples of muscle. Sweeping cheekbones make him
look like a statue carved by an Italian grand master from the
Renaissance. Pretty Peter would be handsome anywhere in the
world, any time in history. He's actually prettier than
Vampirella, who's pretty damn pretty, in a scary way. She's
doing the talking, which is good, because Pretty Peter can
barely talk and stand still at the same time. Vampirella looks
like she's selling hard. And Pretty Peter looks like he ain't
buying. But then again, as far as I can tell, Pretty Peter has

only one expression. It's either cool removed or stupid vacuous. Depending on your perspective. Pretty Peter and Vampirella seem like they deserve each other.

'Like a Virgin' blasts at a staggering volume as a gigantic Madonna tarts it up in a wedding dress on huge video screens. I read in *Rolling Stone*, I think, that she's making a point about religion and sexuality, but I can't quite figure out what that point is.

Before I go find Nick in the Very Important Person lounge and plant my nose up his ass, I scan Chippendales for Buzzcut. No such luck. I broaden my search to include anyone unattractive and/or drunk enough to give a hoipee-lipped puffy white Master of Ceremonies a tumble. The Pit's stuffed beyond the gills with air-humping, hip-pumping, butt-shaking, head-bobbing, cleavage-jiggling, white-man-overbiting everyday people, decked out in their going-to-the-strip-club finery. White folks and black folks and brown folks and all kindsa in-between folks.

Anchored in each corner of the Pit is one big huge speaker. Perched on each is a dancer. It's a coveted spot, actually, as the Ladies wave greenbacks for little kisses long after the show is over. Large Mark is up on the north speaker. I wonder if the coke-on-cock babe is watching him, hating him for being so nasty. Or is she even now sucking drugs into her nostrils off some other random but handsome penis?

'(You Gotta) Fight for Your Right (to Party)' by the beastly Beastie Boys busts a huge move through the speakers. A fine-featured blonde with long hair and a shocking body is up on the south speaker nearest me, go-go dancing in a cleavage-revealing bikini. I walk over to the speaker, and when I look up at her, she seems about eight feet tall, with gazelle legs that go on and on and meet at a heavenly intersection where thin pink material hugs her vagina so tight that I can practically see her lips blow me a kiss. Gazelle's eyes are half-closed, off in a personal pleasure trance, tongue peeking out the corner of her fire-engine-red lips. I can't stop my mind from picturing her naked, I'm making her sigh and writhe and squirm, she's calling my name, looking up at me with hungry eyes. I see Gazelle pregnant with my child, in our giant exquisitely appointed apartment in the Dakotas, Francis Ford Coppola calling to ask if he can come hang out with us.

Someone bumps into me from behind, the spell is broken, and I'm dropkicked out of my spectacular fantasy, landing with a dull thud back in Chippendales. A badly balding polyester-clad medicine ball of a man smacks into me as he bumrushes the speaker. He plants himself fat and squat, staring up at Gazelle, googly-eyed and moony-faced. His mouth hangs open like his IQ is plummeting by the second, drool practically dribbling down his chin. He is a caricature of a loser. And he looks exactly like I did about fifteen seconds ago. Am I this guy? A hopeless dolt, a clueless rube, worshipping like an idolater at the shrine of beauty, lusting for love from a goddess who will never know I exist?

I wish I were a drinker. Then I could go get drunk. Just my luck, the taste of liquor repulses me, the direct result of getting alcohol poisoning as a young man, when I drank nineteen pints of Newcastle Brown Ale at a going-away party that my lily-skinned, thick-skulled Geordie family threw for me.

I retreat to the perimeter of the Pit and survey Chippendales, my new professional home. I soak in the overpowering mojo of sex, drugs, and $. Did fate bring me here to turn me into a star? Or keep me a houseboy? Just as I realize I'm kinda nervous about my rendezvous with Nick and all the Very Important People in the VIP Lounge, my eyes take me to the DJ booth, where I see Johnny and Arnolpho d'Alencar Araripe Pimenta de Mello hanging out with Crazy Eddie. Without thinking about it my legs spring to life, and suddenly I'm headed up the steps to meet another man who will change my life forever.

And, as usual, I'm completely clueless.

CHAPTER 19

WHAT THE FUCK, LIFE IS SHORT, RIGHT?

'Money for Nothing' thunders as I enter the DJ booth. Johnny smiles and says:

'Hey.'

She seems reasonably happy to see me. But maybe I'd just like her to be.

'Hey,' I say. I am very happy to see her. More so than I'd like to be.

'Well, hello, Miss Thing!' Arnolpho tilts his head gaily and gives me a jaunty kiss on each cheek. His lips feel good on my skin and his snappy natty Brazilian joie de vivre immediately lifts my spirits.

'Hey,' I say with a smile.

'Congratulations,' he purrs. 'You got my name right.'

'It's the least I could do,' I grin.

In the DJ booth a massive console of knobs and buttons

and levers lives behind a large rectangular hole in the wall through which you can view the action in the Pit down below. It's much less noisy up here than it is on the floor, but it's smokier and smells a lot worse. In one chair sits a long woman in a short skirt with waist-length wispy thin hair and gangly legs dangling underneath her. She's an Olive Oyl-on-coke type, looks to be about 5'11" and 55 lbs. Her long skinny toes tap incessantly at a much faster rhythm than 'Money for Nothing.' Even in this low light I can see her wild eyes are wired, and if you listen close enough you can hear her teeth grinding.

Crazy Eddie, the Man himself, sits in the power chair, with a big shock of messy mad red hair that looks like it just caught on fire. He's got superwhite superthin see-through skin with a kazillion redhead freckles dotting it, decked out in a violently paisley polyester shirt over designer denim.

'Hey,' he booms in a voice full of broken glass, craggy gravel, and rusty razor blades, 'look what the pussy dragged in, it's the mouth that roared! What a fuckin' night! Look at this shit, huh?' He gestures to the dance floor, which looks like a many-celled organism happily writhing and multiplying. He raises a glass full of alcohol, air-clinks, and chugs a buncha booze, then screams:

'Party, baby! Paaaaaaaaaa-ty!'

Crazy Eddie's, for those who didn't live in NY, NY in the 80s, was an electronics chain that sold shitty discount-stereo supplies. They flooded the airwaves with a stream of schlocky, kitschy, immensely popular, no-budget commercials featuring a character named Crazy Eddie, an all-the-way-over-the-top pitchman who would scream at the screen like an escapee from a mental institute for the harmlessly insane:

'I'M CRAZY EDDIE. HOW DO I DO IT? MY PRICES ARE IN-SAAAANE!'

Crazy Eddie the DJ doesn't look or sound anything like Crazy Eddie the TV pitchman, yet they share an infectious, maniacal exuberance that makes the nickname an apt fit.

Crazy Eddie lights a cigarette off the one he already has going and flicks the old one hard against the wall, sparks shooting off the hot cherry, falling like meteors to the floor, the butt crashing and burning close behind. He turns to me and shouts with his scratchy shredded vocal chords:

'Hey man, good job tonight, you fuckin' rocked hard, man!'

Caught off guard, I'm lifted high by Crazy Eddie's kudos.

'Thanks man, I appreciate that.'

Again, I'm aware that I'm way too happy that somebody said something nice to me. Like a plant in a drought sucking at a drop of moisture.

Olive Oyl's eyes dart frantically, like a spooked cat that just heard a big dog growl. Popping knuckles, licking gums, and squirming like a worm with ants in her pants, she leans her anorexic lips into Crazy Eddie and whispers into his freckly ear.

'Excellent suggestion!' Crazy Eddie turns to us and screams in his damaged, ravaged voice: 'Any of you kiddies want some of Uncle Eddie's tootski?!'

'Yes, please, sir!' Johnny says like an enthusiastic nine-year-old hungry for a sweet treat.

'That would be lovely, thank you ever so much.' Arnolpho smiles graciously.

Swept up in the excitement of the moment, I forget to just say no, as this slips through my lips:

'Uh, sure.'

I'd snorted some college-caliber coke in my younger days, and it was kinda fun, a minor rush, but nothing to write home about. I'm anticipating more of the same.

'Would you do the honors, baby?' Crazy Eddie asks Olive Oyl. He extracts a thin mirror from under the console and takes a small, dark, thick glass vial from a pocket, dumps a nice-sized snow mountain on the mirror; then from a drawer he removes a razor blade, and places it gingerly on the mirror. He gestures for Olive Oyl to get the party started.

Crazy Eddie whips around in his swivel chair, and with the hands-quicker-than-the-eye alacrity of a master magician, he presses buttons, flips switches, turns knobs, and VOILÀ! 'The Power of Love' screams at an obscene volume. The massive crowd lets out a mammoth blast and changes rhythm with the music.

Olive Oyl begins chopping the drugs into easily sniffable powder, and channeling her manic energy into the task, she looks like a high school student dissecting a frog.

Crazy Eddie bops to the beat, turns, and says:

'Djoo hear some skanky heifer asked Large Mark to snort blow off his dick for five grand? Can you believe that shit?'

Me and Johnny exchange an eyebrow-elevated glance: Word sure gets around fast, and the truth sure gets battered in the process.

Arnolpho shrugs coquettishly with a twinkly little eye roll: 'Nothin' says love like a line of coke an' a snort of cock, don' you think?'

Johnny and I laugh.

Crazy Eddie, on the other hand, roars like this is the funniest thing he's ever heard. It's a laugh ravaged by years of hooch, smoke, and coke, but it's so saturated with joy. This is one man who truly seems to love life.

'Actually, I was there,' I say, 'and just to set the record straight, it was *500* dollars, not *5000*.' Pause. 'I thought he shoulda done it, I mean what the hell, that's $250 an inch, and personally, I woulda paid good money just to watch her chop it up.'

Johnny smirks at me: You're getting alotta mileage outta that material.

I shrug back: Why not?

Arnolpho lets out a droll smirky chuckle.

Crazy Eddie bellows more uproarious laughter. 'Me, too, man. I woulda totally given the fucker five hundred bucks to watch her chop that shit up. Large Mark and his bloody cock. Hey, weren't they a punk band?' Crazy Eddie chortles like a naughty schoolboy at a dirty joke, chokes down more cigarette smoke, chases it with a huge swig of booze, and says:

'What the fuck, life is short, right?'

'Live fast, die young, leave a good-looking corpse,' Olive Oyl says without even looking up from her cocaine preparation.

Johnny, Arnolpho, and I exchange surprised faces: I beg your pardon?

'What's that, baby?' Crazy Eddie croaks.

'Uh,' Olive Oyl says, without looking up, 'some rock-star fucker said that . . . Live fast, die young, leave a good-looking corpse . . . Uh, that's . . .'

It sounds like Olive has more to say. So we all wait for her to finish her thought. It's a funny silence in all that noise. Finally it's clear Olive Oyl is never going to finish that sentence, and this squirts out the side of Johnny's mouth:

'Hope I die before I get old.'

'Live young, die old, leave a big tip,' I say.

'I'll drink to that! Fuck yeah!' Crazy Eddie raises his glass and clinks with no one, then guzzles more booze.

Olive Oyl artfully guides the razor's edge, lengthening and smoothing the chopped coke crystals until she's laid out five white lines about four inches long and sufficiently thin to be easily snuffled up a human nostril.

'Five hundred fucking bucks to snort some tootski off that big bonehead's dick!' Crazy Eddie's voice grinds gears as he shakes his red head in amazement. 'Nice to see the economy's coming back, ain't it? Reagan's the greatest fuckin' president in history. The man may not know when he's been shot, but he's a great fuckin' president.' He turns sharp to Olive Oyl as Huey Lewis sings about the p-p-power of love. 'Hey baby, how we doin'?' He looks like he's really ready to do more drugs.

'Almost done.' Olive Oyl finishes finessing the lines until they contain exactly the same amount of coke. This, I will learn, is an important element of coke etiquette. All lines must contain the same amount of coke.

Crazy Eddie whips around in his chair and his magic fingers digitally manipulate the console at the speed of sound, segueing expertly into 'Ghostbusters.' The mood on the floor changes instantly, as the bobbing and jerking of the dancers takes on yet another rhythm, and the energy bumps up a notch. When the chorus asks the audience who they're going to call, the partiers scream:

'GHOSTBUSTERS!'

Crazy Eddie springs up out of his chair like a jacked-up jack-in-the-box, moved by the juice of the wild crowd, feeding off their frenzy as they feed off the musical love he's feeding them. He shakes out his arms, shoulders, neck, and head, then yells: 'Fuck the fuck outta me!'

Crazy Eddie's a crazy dancer. All freckled elbows and knees, he waves his hands in the air like he just don't care, eyes rolling madly around in his head, pelvis pumping, ass waggling, Irish-American funk flying off him.

Arnolpho, the dancing queen, joins in immediately, breaking into a samba shuffle, as smooth and controlled as Crazy Eddie is wild and out of kilter. Arnolpho's pelvis moves at a different speed than his shoulders, but somehow both are in synch with 'Ghostbusters.'

Johnny breaks into a swivel-hipped coochie dance that I find mad sexy. One small hand is on her belly while the other mambos through the air, her lips in the kissing position. She's a genuine force of nature, this chick.

Crazy Eddie plops back down in his chair, throws his red head back and yells:

'PAAAAAAAAAAAR-TAY!!!'

As Olive Oyl bends down to suck up some coke, she looks like a kid who's about to open a Christmas present she knows she's gonna love. With great gusto she hungrily hoovers up her rail, relishing every grain of cocaine. Her long body shudders, she rolls her shoulders, stretches her neck, and luxuriates like a cat in the sun.

'Baby,' Crazy Eddie wheezes to Olive Oyl, 'will you go get me a drink? Pretty please?'

'What?' When Olive Oyl reenters her body, she looks like she has no idea where she is.

'I need a drink, baby, will you go get me a drink, please?' Crazy Eddie repeats in his deep rasp.

'Oh uh . . . sure . . . yeah, that would be great, a drink . . . yeah, I'll get us some drinks.' Olive Oyl heaves herself up and dabs at her long nostrils with her long fingers to make sure there's no coke residue, then does a lanky jangle across the DJ booth and disappears down the stairs.

'How long you been goin' out with her?' Johnny asks with Southern politeness.

'Goin' out with her?' Crazy Eddie laughs loud. 'I just fuckin' met her an hour ago. I spotted her on the floor and I waved her up. She's fuckable, don't you think?'

'Definitely,' Johnny agrees.

'Uh . . . sure . . .' I'd fuck her, whispers a voice in my head.

Arnolpho snaps fingers on both hands while moving his head rhythmically. Johnny joins him as they deliver his signature phrase, the basic philosophic principle by which he lives his life:

'Honey, when you cum, it don't matter who's on the end of your dick.'

It's a wonderful performance and I enjoy it.

Crazy Eddie turns to me with mock gravity, and smiling like the ambassador of Fun Town, he motions to the coke and croaks:

'Welcome to Chippendales, motherfucker.'

'Thank you,' I say with a smile. 'I can feel the love all around me, and it's a beautiful thing.'

'Amen, Brother,' Crazy Eddie nods.

I lean down toward the mirror. Up close these lines look longer and fatter than they did from far away. This seems like an awful lot of tootski to be shoving into my face. Ah, well, what the hell, I didn't get where I am today by looking before I leap.

I hover over the mirror where my first taste of professional cocaine awaits. I love seeing myself reflected under those white lines. I heave in a big stiff sniff, and when the nose candy hits me, bells chime and whistles blow, my heart thumps and blood heats as excitement fills me and my pleasure center writhes exquisitely. A delicious delirious shiver chills down my spine, hits my tailbone, spreads through my coccyx, and ricochets around inside my nut sack, then shoots down my legs and up through my heart, bounces around behind my eyes, then seeps deep into my brain. It's like when you first fall in love and have sex with someone you're really hot for.

But the real selling point of dyn-o-mite blow is the almost unspeakably pleasant feeling that floods through me, in me, out me, and all around me. I read about some nuns who live in the middle of nowhere. They go into a heavy, deep, religious prayer-type trance, where they become one with the universe, time loses meaning, and a deep, peaceful, easy feeling envelops them in a profound, transcendent bliss. This sounds pretty much like my first line of high-end gourmet Chippendales coke.

I want to kiss someone! I want to take a bath in warm spumoni! I want to make love to Johnny! I want to make love to every lady at Chippendales! I want a beverage!

Suddenly I can see that tonight was actually my first big step toward that best supporting Oscar. The worm has turned. At last, my life is finally happening, unfolding like a beautiful flower, which is opening in slow motion.

I need a beverage.

Arnolpho quivers deliciously, turns to Crazy Eddie, and purrs:

'Thank you, Mr DJ.'

'Yeah, thanks, man,' I add.

'Gracias, señor,' Johnny says with a little curtsy.

Olive Oyl reenters with alcohol.

'I'm gonna get a beverage,' I say.

'Yeah, beverage,' Johnny agrees.

'A beverage would be lovely,' Arnolpho concludes.

As we walk out, Crazy Eddie shouts:

'Catch you fuckers on the rebound!'

I glide highly behind my two new best friends, toward what I know will be a wild and exciting coke-fueled adventure, as Frankie Goes to Hollywood blares.

I don't know who Frankie is, or why he's going to Hollywood, but I'm completely in synch with him as he tells me to relax when I want to come.

CHAPTER 20
RISK AND REWARD

Large dark-suited men protect the portal to the VIP lounge like three-headed attack dogs, in charge of preventing dull, boring, unexceptional, unattractive, short, fat, ugly, plain, or regular people from getting in and gumming up the works.

Kite-high and tightrope-wired, I feel Very Important as I enter for my date with Lady Luck, in the person of Nick de Noia.

The Old Gray Man's in the corner, lurking and smirking with rich, sinister condescension. Attached to him like a colostomy bag is the little, bony, heroin-chic dirty blond girly who looks 13 going on 30. With her pouty lips, teenybopper 'tude, moves, and bangs, she'd look right at home on the box of a porn movie in the Barely Legal series. Or is that just me being me? Teen Queen leans in and nuzzles the Old Gray Man's wobbling wattle, then whispers into his death-gray head, while her skinny little hand brushes up against his zipper suggestively.

I can't stop picturing her icy teen-queen lips laboring, slobbering, working overtime to get some blood into the old man's ancient gray member. Is all that great coke really worth it? Risk. Reward. I see her taking him home. Mom and Dad, this is my new boyfriend. He may be thirty years older than you and fifty years older than me, but he's very rich.

When you're this high, everything looks crisper, brighter, and sharper, and the pretty people are that much prettier. I enjoy the sparkling water with lemon washing the coke down my throat so much that I instinctively sigh:

'Ahhhhhhh!'

In the corner Large Mark holds court with his Tonto, Tom Cat. Prince Charming stands next to a farmfresh young woman in a ponytail. Not a ponytail on the side, not a ponytail sticking straight up, an old-school ponytail. No neon or crazy colors, just a simple peach cotton dress that stops a couple of inches above the knees. The front is cut so that just a little glimpse of breast peaks out. Compared to the massive racks and gigantic hairdos on display in the VIP lounge, she's refreshingly old-fashioned.

Large Mark and Tom Cat are decked out in pastel-colored jackets with sleeves rolled up to the elbow, pastel-colored T-shirts, and pastel-colored pants. They're dressed like the heroes of the wildly popular TV show *Miami Vice*. On the show a cool black guy and a cool white guy dressed in fashionable pastel colors chase down bad-guy drug dealers in Miami, while never breaking a sweat. I love the idea that Reagan is funding all these drug-dealer dudes in Latin America, and they end up getting busted on *Miami Vice*.

Cat's standing between Large and Cotton Dress, so it's hard

to tell who's the couple by their body language. Is she with Large Mark? Is she with Tom Cat? Actually, with their matching his 'n' his outfits, Cat and Large look like they're the happy loving couple. Maybe she's with Prince Charming. If I were her, that's who I'd be with.

Large Mark is talking with his huge arms and massive hands, hard and animated, like a cartoon He-Man, regaling the beautiful people with his tale, face lighting up as he acts out the story of Bleach Blonde and the coke cock incident. Tom Cat is a very enthusiastic peanut gallery: laughing and hooting, agreeing and encouraging.

Prince Charming has his large arms folded across his chiseled chest. God, he's pretty. Yet manly. He's smiling but not laughing. Not nearly as into Large Mark and his story as Tom Cat is. There's something either Zen peaceful or not too bright about Prince Charming. Hard to tell. Cotton Dress is smiling at Large Mark, too, but it looks to be a pained, forced, brittle smile, like it might crack if it got any bigger. She's leaning away from Large Mark, and her body language says she's just not that into him. Or is my coke-crazed brain projecting?

I really wanna hear what Large Mark is saying, so I ease in behind a couple of neon-panted bustier-topped huge-haired babes. Their teased-up porn starlet dos are excellent camouflage to hide behind.

'A pig dis bitch was – a total heffah,' Large Mark says in his thick mooky Brooklyn accent. 'I swear ta Christ, I wouldn't fuck dis fat bitch wit' Nick de Noia's dick. An' when she says' – Large Mark goes into a bad falsetto – '"I'll give ya $5000 to snort a line awffa your cock,"' – back to his normal voice – 'it was so fuckin' pat'etic. Seriously. It woulda been sad if it wasn't so fuckin' pat'etic. You shoulda seen dis fat piece o' shit.

Seriously, I mean, if she was hot an' shit, dat woulda been one t'ing, I could see doing dat, right?'

'Absolutely,' Tom Cat chimes in with an egging-on laugh. Prince Charming almost chuckles but doesn't say anything. Cotton Dress nods her head but moves farther away from Large Mark. Her left forearm covers her breasts, and her right forearm intersects it, right hand covering her mouth. Her body language says she's repulsed by this 'roid-bloated braggart but doesn't feel comfortable saying anything.

Large Mark's swollen head bobs. 'So I says, "T'ank you very much, but I respectably decline yer awfa, have a good night," ya know, 'cuz I di'n't wanna make 'er feel bad. I shoulda introduced her to Slick Rick, dat fat pig coulda snawted lines awffa his dick fer the rest of 'er life fer five grand.'

Tom Cat snorts a harsh hard coke laugh. Prince Charming sorta chortles and nods. Cotton Dress shifts and shuffles, then sucks hard on her drink.

'Look at that prick,' Tom Cat says. He looks like he's had a very good nose job. 'Can you believe what a suckass that cocksucker is?' He points surreptitiously with his highlighted head to the corner of the VIP lounge, where Slick Rick, the newest stud in the Chippendales love farm, is up close and personal with Nick de Noia. Slick's in tight-waisted pants that get baggy as they go down, then taper down around the ankles, with zippers at the bottom. Nick has his hand on Slick's neck, looks like they're having an incredibly intimate, intense, important conversation, their faces inches apart. Nick's doing the talking and Slick Rick the listening. Slick tries to break in and say something, but Nick stifles him. Nick gently touches Slick Rick on his bare brown chest, exposed by a studded, open half jacket with nothing underneath.

'I think Rick is sweet,' says Cotton Dress, 'and he's got a great act. The women really love him, and—'

'Sweet? Ah you fuckin' kiddin' me?' Large Mark scoffs with a steroid-sharp exhalation of breath. 'Guy's a total skank. He'd fuck his own muthah if there was a buck in it, no bullshit. Dis guy's a total douche bag. Dat act he does was supposed to be fer somebody else, I'm not naming names, but dat Slick sonafuck got de gig 'cuz he's Nick's butt boy—'

'Oh yeah, he's definitely Nick's butt boy, look at him, Nick's practically sucking his big black cock over there—' Tom Cat puts on his gay falsetto voice. 'Oh Rick, you're sooooo talented. Shove that big fat talented dick down my throat! Helloooooooooooo!'

Cat and Large laugh loud enough to turn several Very Important heads.

Prince Charming does not laugh. Cotton Dress moves in to him, and he puts his large arm around her with easy blond sweetness, pulling her in to him and holding her there. Her whole body relaxes. Looks nice. Turns out her name is Betsy. She's Prince Charming's girl. God, they make a handsome couple. I, on the other hand, will never be handsome. That thought hits me hard and fast and I plummet blackly. Fortunately, recovery time is instantaneous, because my coked-up attention span is so short.

Nick de Noia finishes with Slick Rick, who beelines toward a miniscule miniskirt with a pair of fishnet-clad legs, spiky black heels beneath it and heavy heaving cleavage up above. This chick's hair's piled skyscraper high. How much time and product does it take to get it to stand straight up like that? my brain asks me.

Man, this coke is fun.

Slick Rick leaves with Miniscule Miniskirt. This is clearly
my opportunity to pounce on Nick de Noia and enter as far
as I can into his inner sanctum. I slither through the fabulous asses, and the breathtaking barely covered breasts. I
wonder what I'll look like standing there talking to Nick de
Noia intimately in the shadows of the VIP lounge. Will
everyone assume I'm Nick's butt boy? What if that's the deal?
I'll make you a star if you become my butt boy, David Scary.
What am I willing to do to get what I want? Plastic surgery?
A blow job?

Risk. Reward.

Another benefit of top-drawer coke: I don't really give a
shit what happens. Whether I'm able to infiltrate Nick de Noia
Land or not. Normally I'd be a little shy and nervous about
approaching a man who could conceivably make me wildly
successful and therefore utterly lovable, but not now. In this
coked moment my feet are loose, and my fancy free.

When Nick de Noia spots me, his face lights right up. And
what a smile he has. 'And he really likes you,' the coke whispers, flooding me with a powerful surge of well-being.

'David,' Nick gushes, 'I'm so glad you decided to join me.'
He thrusts an enthusiastic hand out for me to grab and shake.
His touch feels so intimate and connected. Or is that the coke
talking? Do I care? Absolutely not!

'Thanks, I, uh, really appreciate getting this opportunity, I
really do, and I feel like I've learned—'

Nick cuts me off, as he leans in and whispers in my ear:

'Many are called, but few are chosen.'

Nick's hot breath flushes my skin. Does he want to have sex
with me? I doubt it. With all these beautiful dudes here, why
would he? What *does* he want from me? Maybe he just enjoys

the power of being a puppet master. Or maybe he's just a nice person who likes to help people.

This close I can smell Nick's cologne. He smells sexy. I should smell like that.

Nick de Noia looks off into the distance, gestures with beautifully manicured hands, and two champagne glasses appear. He hands me a glass and holds his up for a clink and toast.

I raise my glass. Nick clinks me.

'To my new Master of Ceremonies!'

My heart beams warmly and radiates through my whole body. I nod my head deferentially, in thanks to the great and powerful Nick. I pretend to drink some champagne, touching the liquid to my lips like I'm taking real sips. Bubbles explode onto my skin in delicious pinpricks, and my oh my, it's so good to be alive!

'I want to thank you again—'

Nick cuts me off again cold—

'I hope you understand how important someone like Brooke Shields is to Chippendales.' Nick is so earnest that this seems like the most important thing anyone has ever said. Yes, Brooke Shields is vital, I can see that now. 'Not only for the club and the media and the exposure that someone like Brooke Shields can give us, but for you, too, David. I mean, my God, hellooooooooo?! The place is going to be crawling with industry people: producers, managers, agents, directors. And I'd love to introduce you around after the show. Provided it's a great show, of course. Not a good show, a GREAT show. Yes, it was wonderful tonight, but there's LOTS of room for improvement. I want to take this show to the next level. Yes, of course, the asses are what everybody wants to talk about, but it's the showmanship, the craft, the passion, the sparkle that get a Brooke Shields coming down to Chippendales!'

At that moment I love Nick de Noia more than I've ever loved anyone. He's gonna grease the wheels for me, introduce me into the circle of power, my God, I can practically feel the Oscar in my hand.

'Sure, I know exactly what you're talking about, and—'

'I'd like to introduce you to Robert Wayne, do you know him?' Nick raises his eyebrows a little, indicating that I should know who Robert Wayne is. And, in fact, I do. Robert Wayne is a BIG agent who owns his own BIG agency: movies, TV, theater, commercials, BIG offices on West Fifty-seventh Street in Manhattan and Sunset Strip in LA. Robert Wayne is a star maker, a rain maker, and from what I hear, a horny old goat, of the man-on-man persuasion.

'If everything goes well,' Nick continues, 'I'll make sure you meet him after the show. He'll love you. How could he not? You're faaaaabulous.'

'Thanks so much, that really—' I'm so overcome by my own fabulousness, so stunned that someone besides myself recognizes just how vast my talent is, that I am rendered speechless.

'Of course, don't mention it, I'm happy to do it.' Nick looks into me and I feel the most profound simpatico with this man. He doesn't want to fuck me, he wants to help me. Large Mark is full of shit. Slick Rick's not Nick's butt boy. Neither am I. He's a guru, we are his student pupils, and I'm very grateful.

Someone behind me catches Nick's eye. He smiles, waves, then says:

'I've gotta take care of something. Will you excuse me?'

Nick de Noia seems to slide away without moving his legs.

How does he do that? Am I supposed to wait here? Are we done? I watch as he settles in beside a brunette stunner with freaky full lips and a hips'n'tits-hugging red dress that screams: VA VA VOOM! Nick kisses her on the lips, like a lover. Like a lover whose gonna have sex with her tonight. Now I'm all confused. Nick has a girlfriend, a woman, with a vagina. But I thought Nick was queer as a three dollar bill. Is Va Va Voom the most attractive beard in history? But why would Nick think he needs a beard? It's the 80s for God's sake. No one cares if you're gay. Not in Manhattan anyway. Not in the VIP lounge at Chippendales. Be gay. Relax, don't do it, when you wanna cum.

I ditch the champagne and step out onto the crow's nest, twenty feet high overlooking the Pit.

'Everybody Wants to Rule the World' is so loud, my knees buckle a little. Years later I will see some schmaltzy movie in which some pretty boy movie star poses on the mast of a ship with some gorgeous movie star chick by his side. With a look of handsome manchildish happiness and satisfaction he will proudly proclaim, 'I'm king of the world!'

And when I see the movie, I'll remember this moment, standing in the crow's nest looking down at the massed rabble, twisting and writhing to the beat, on the night of my faaaaaabulous debut, with my future shinning bright right in front of me, wired to the eye teeth on fairy powder and giddy with congratulations.

CHAPTER 21
HOLY MOTHER OF FELLATIO!

Midnight has descended on the evening I have become Master of Ceremonies at Chippendales. 'Hold Me Now' booms as I cruise through the Pit looking for Johnny. I don't know what exactly I'm gonna do with her if I find her. I haven't thought that far ahead. But something is compelling me to find Johnny.

No luck. As I part the red velvet curtain that separates the club from the lobby, I spot a mass of curly hair leaving with a taller, equally curly partier. They're vacating Chippendales together. Maybe it's not her. Maybe it's somebody with hair exactly like Johnny's. I step around two huge women in too-tight stretchy Day-Glo dresses, and I arrive near the box office door just as the two curly revelers bust out the front door.

It's definitely Johnny. My narcotized heart, already racing, pumps into overdrive. She's leaving for the night. Without saying good-bye. Why shouldn't she? She doesn't know me. Who am I? Nobody.

Billy Cheeks is the owner of the curly hair on the head next to her. He's with her. She's with him. With his flowing locks and silky Olympian gait, and her feline grace and great mane of hair, it looks like they should procreate and produce their own tribe of graceful exotic sexy beauties, with the greatest hair in the galaxy. They look excited to be going off to have hot sex with each other.

What goes up must come down. It's simple physics. As high as I was, that's how low I go, free-falling, knowing as I plunge that I'm gonna splatter when I hit the cold hard floor of reality. Buzz-kill is the technical term for it. When I crashland in my skeleton closet, where it stinks of rotting monsters and beasts screaming to be fed, all I want is to be somebody else. And high again. Yeah, that's what I need to dig my way out of all the shit. World-class coke. I'll find the Snowman, buy some blow, and snort it. Then I'll go find a woman, give her some of the drugs, and persuade her to be with me. There are still hundreds of Ladies in this club. Many of them saw me in the Chippendales show, roller-skating in my tux and top hat. Many of them are full of alcohol, which will greatly expand my chances of generating interest.

I immediately feel better once I have a plan. It's important to have a plan when you're crashing. I will go into the dressing room, splash water on my face, pull myself together, and execute my plan. Johnny's not the only fish in the woods.

It's nice and quiet in the dressing room when there aren't a dozen gorgeous nude men in it. But it smells bad. I unclench as I collapse in a chair. I hadn't even realized I was clenched until I unclenched. My jaw is sore from all the unconscious tightening, so I work the hinge a little in the mirror, all bug-eyed and sweaty. I imagine people doing exactly the same thing in lunatic asylums all over the world. That makes me chuckle. In the mirrored wall the puffy white Marshmallow Man chuckles at himself in the empty dressing room.

Smiling, I hoist myself up, walk to and open the bathroom door, excited about beginning my odyssey to get much mo' higher.

Holy Mother of Fellatio! My brain can't quite digest the information my eyes are feeding it. My first instinct is that I'm hallucinating. I blink, cleansing my visual palette so I can see what's really in front of me in the bathroom of the dressing room at Chippendales Male Strip Club.

The Snowman and his 70s pornstar mustache stand facing me. The two identical, wing-haired Doublemint twins squat in front of him with his naked penis at the tips of their lips. He wears the beaming smile you'd expect on a man getting head from pretty twins. And the weird thing is, they don't bat or blink an eye or a lash. They pause, glance up at me, and grin coquettishly. They seem to be posing for me, exhilarated by the exhibition of their sexual daring and skill, getting off on being watched as they share a cock.

The Snowman's chest swells peacock proud, as he puts one hand on each hard-haired blonde head, nods at me, and grins wickedly. I've never understood the expression, *shit-eating grin*. Who would grin when they were eating shit? I now under-stand. Even eating shit wouldn't wipe that grin off the Snowman's face.

You'd think that when a person walked in on such an inti-mate yet kinky act, he would politely excuse himself and leave, closing the door behind him. I'd like to blame the drugs for my failure to follow proper blowjob etiquette, but I don't think that would be fair to the drugs. I just stand there, staring at the intersection of his pecker and their sisterly lips. It's not that long, but it's pretty thick, and you could definitely hang a hat on the Snowman's hard-on. Are they porn stars? Paralegals gone wild? Or second-grade teachers letting their hair down? Is the Snowman gonna have intercourse with them? Certainly seems likely, given the physical evidence. Is that technically incest? Sharing a nice penis with your twin? Dear Abby, I like performing fellatio with my sister. Does that make me a bad person? Should I tell my mom and dad about this?

The Snowman jauntily cocks his sexy head and says:

'I like being a man at Chippendales.'

It's a line from the song in the Chippendales show.

I laugh really loud.

Laughing snaps the trance I seem to have fallen into. I should go. Or should I? I'm enjoying the show. It's like watching very attractive animals mating at the zoo. And it's free. Plus they seem to be enjoying me watching. Maybe the polite thing would be to keep watching. Maybe proper blowjob etiquette dictates that I whip myself out and put myself in the mix. Probably not a good idea. But that leads me to this thought: I'm not gonna get any love at Chippendales tonight. Certainly not from twins. Suddenly it's not so fun watching all that oral intercourse. I've become too emotionally involved.

'Well,' I say, 'it looks like you've got everything under control here, uh ... keep up the good work and have a nice day.'

The Snowman gives me a wink and a wee nod. The twins look up at me with a sweet, eerily identical cock-eyed smile. 'Nice to meet you,' I say with a smile.

The twins nod back.

I slide out and shut the door behind me. Suddenly I'm alone in the dressing room. I look in the mirror, and I see me at 17. The dread twists my guts, I'm swallowed into that black hole, my body's shaking I wanna smash the mirror with my forehead shatter myself watch the blood spurt out of my cut-up face, I'm sweating cold and hot at the same time my heart races face bloodless white I can feel hot breath on my neck as my tormentor calls me a punk! and a bitch! and a faggot—

Tom Cat and Large Mark burst in, laughing, carrying on, and cutting up, being Homo Chippendalus.

They jolt me right back to 1985, Sixty-first and First, the dressing room of Chippendales, where I'm trying not to look as freaked out as I feel.

'Hey it's the masturbator of ceremonies!' Tom Cat cracks.

'Ya know, I got t'ree-ta-one odds you woul'n't make it t'rough da show widdout fallin' flat on yer ass,' smirks Large Mark through his muscle mass.

'Lost a bundle, man.' Tom Cat joshes.

'Seriously, ya din't suck dat bad,' Large Mark jokes.

'That's what she said!' I say.

This makes them laugh. I knew it would. Yes, it's crude, it's rude, but at that moment I so desperately crave being part of anything that doesn't involve me tormenting myself. I've heard laughter can cure cancer. I don't know if this is true, but it sure can pick you up after you've had a coke crash flashback. My brain screams: Get me the fuck outta here!

'Uh,' I sputter, 'see you guys later.'

Large and Cat throw me a grunt that serves as good-bye.

I exit the dressing room, walk to the edge of the Pit, and stare out at the dancing masses, the huge hair bobbing, the bouncing mounds of round flesh, the ass-grabbing pants, the funk thick as Chippendales pulsates with Sly, singing about wanting to take me higher.

That's when it hits me: in all the fellatio-related excitement, I forgot to get some drugs from the Snowman. Oh well, fuckit. What do I care? It's 1985, $'s everywhere, sex is all around me, Nick de Noia's gonna hook me up with übersuperstar Brooke Shields, and I'm the Master of Ceremonies in the hottest show in New York, New York: today, Chippendales, tomorrow, the world!

PART II

SEX CHANGES EVERYTHING

CHAPTER 1

PLANET RAGE AND THE ANGER ORGASM

Today is a great day to be an actor in New York City: I have not one but two callbacks. Fram oil filters and Dial soap. Fram is looking for a young Tom Hanks/Steve Martin/Martin Short/ Robin Williams/Michael Keaton/David Letterman type. Dial's looking for a young dad. I've never been a dad, but I'd love to play one on TV.

The agent who took me on from my mailing has been sending me out on three or four auditions a week. All commercials. I booked a coupla little piddly jobs but no nationals. Fram and Dial are worth serious $.

That's the good news. The bad news is that Fram is at 4 P.M., on Canal and Broadway. Dial soap is at 4:30 on Fifty-seventh and Broadway. If I had a jet pack I could get there in about a minute and a half. But in midafternoon Midtown Manhattan traffic, in a cab it could take anywhere from ten minutes to a month. Forget the subway, you could get stuck down there and never be heard from again. So I decide to use my newly acquired roller-skating skills. I'll bomb up Broadway, take a chillpill, get myself feminine fresh, and book both jobs.

Nine other guys are called back for Fram. One's in a 'Where's the Beef?' spot. These are very famous hamburger commercials in which a cranky old lady opens up a hamburger bun, sees a pitiful little patty of meat, and snarls at the camera: 'Where's the beef?' In fact, Reagan will use this as a campaign slogan for a while. I guess that's why they call him the Great Communicator.

As I look around the waiting room, I notice that one of the other actors has a whole series of diarrhea commercials that are huge, my favorite involving a donkey ride down into the Grand Canyon. As I wait and wait, my mind keeps asking, Who are you to compete with the diarrhea guy?

I ask the casting director, a very charming but abrasive and pockmarked man, if I can go first. I explain my situation. He reminds me of how lucky I am to be here and implores me to sit down and shut the hell up. But he does it very charmingly, 'cuz he likes me. I'm not sure what his sexual orientation is, but he seems about three-quarters gay, so I ask him if he wants free passes to Chippendales, and his eyes light, while he inhales sharply, then says:

'I'd love it.' Pause. 'I'll see what I can do about getting you in earlier, but these clients are a HUGE pain in the you-know-where.'

Each moment is somehow loooooooooooooooonger than the one before.

Seconds pass like days. Minutes like months. Finally, at 5:15, I'm in. The director, a jaded-faced fellow with a Spielberg

beard, puts me through my paces. Do it faster. Slower. Friend-
lier. Edgier. More attitude. No attitude. At one point, after a
long conference with the clients, he says:

'I want it friendly but edgy, a little less Tom Hanks and a
little more Michael Keaton. It needs more greens and reds in
it. *Really* have fun with it, but not too much fun, OK?' I have
no idea what he's talking about, but I nod my head like he
said something incredibly profound.

Finally they're done with me. I look at the clock: 5:50. Holy
shit! I thank everyone profusely, throw on my roller skates,
bust outta there, and blaze up Broadway. I manage to catch
the lights, and get a good head of steam going, flashing past
all the standing-still rush hour cabs, pedestrian commuters,
and befuddled tourists. As I cross Fifty-fourth Street, I make
a mad rush to beat the light, and I'm sprinting hard, legs
pumping fast, sweat pouring, heart racing.

MAYDAY! MAYDAY! MAYDAY!

Out of my eye corner I spy a bicycle messenger bombarding
straight toward me on a collision course: Oh, sweet Jesus, he's
gonna smash right into me.

Time stretches again, slows till it crawls, and finally stops,
while I clench everything hard and tight, turning myself into
a solid mass. Here he comes. He's coming. He realizes he's
going to hit me and pulls frantically on his front wheel, while
slamming ferociously on his breaks.

When we collide, he's sideways, and I'm all balled up like
a human brick wall, so the bike bounces off me and the
messenger crumples to the street.

Suddenly I am a colossus, looming huge over the fallen
bicycle messenger and his steel steed sprawled all over
Broadway. Anger courses slow and red through me. I'm mad

at this bicycle messenger moron for running right the hell into me. Mad at the Fram people for not letting me go first so I had to rush like a loon uptown. Mad that I'm not rich and famous and popular. Mad that everything is always so fucked up. But I'm trying hard to be at peace with the universe, to connect harmoniously with the life force that flows through all living things, to be the gentle Zen warrior and master of my ceremonies. So I look down at this pathetic messenger and say:

'I forgive you.'

He mumbles something I can't quite hear, and I skate away, feeling like an indestructible Jesus-like superhero that bullets and bikes alike bounce off. Finally I'm at Fifty-seventh and Broadway, sweat-drenched, furiously waiting for what seems like the slowest elevator in the galaxy. It's 6:05. Could the Dial soap people still be here? Of course they could. They've gotta be.

When the slowest elevator in the galaxy finally arrives, many humans pile out. I'm the only one who gets on. Lugging my skates, with my pack on my back, I occupy the otherwise empty elevator and press 10.

Nothing happens. Damn this elevator! I press 10 again.

10. 10. 10. 10. 10.

Like that'll help it get there faster. Finally I push the button with the arrow that looks like this: ><. Slowly the doors close. Slowly the elevator lurches upupup.

2.

3.

4.

5.

6.

7.

8.

9.

At long last, 10.

As soon as the doors open, I gush out of the elevator like water from a clogged hose that's just been unkinked. The casting office is empty. Don't panic, maybe they're waiting for me. They could be waiting for me. Yeah, they're probably waiting for me.

I charge up to where the receptionist sits. She's still here all right. Thank God. I'm gonna book this Dial spot, mark my words.

'Hi,' I say, 'I'm David Sterry, I'm here for the Dial callback.'

The receptionist is a gerbilly, earth-toned, early-twenties chick with limpish dishwater hair.

'Oh, uh, sorry, they're done. They left about half an hour ago.' She glances at a sheet in front of her. 'Your time was four-thirty . . . It's, uh . . . six-ten.'

'I know what time it is,' I'm barely able to contain the seething rage that's scything through me. 'I had another call-back, my agent called and said I'd be late.'

'Riiiiight . . .' she says, like, I don't give a shit, you're late, you're a loser, we're done, and I'm trying to get the hell outta here.

'Well, are they gonna have more callbacks? . . . Sometime?' I'm trembling with the effort of keeping all this fury contained inside me.

'Uh . . . they don't exactly consult with me on these decisions.' Snide snarky sarcasm saturates Gerbil's voice. She's dropped all pretense of being a professional and treating me like one. I have clearly become the late, pushy, dumb-ass actor.

'Of course, I realize that, but I raced to get over here, and . . . is there anything I can do?' The pathetic desperation in my voice just makes me more angry.

Gerbil's voice is all condescending dismissal:

'No.'

I am a mad camel, and this word is the straw that breaks my back. Apparently all my Zen is gone, because I hiss between clenched teeth.

'Goddamn motherfucking piece o' shit!'

Then I scream, not directly at Gerbil, but close and loud enough to terrorize her:

'What the **FUCK!**'

I fling my backpack as hard as I can and it slams into the wall with a gratifying **THUD!**

Gerbil flinches backward. I like that rush of power. I pick up the clipboard/sign-in sheet from the table and throw it with all my might down onto the hardwood floor, where it hits with a satisfying **THWACK!**

Gerbil jumps out of her chair and takes a step away from me, like a victim-to-be in a horror flick moving away from the maniac/slasher/killer.

It's so good, the physical release, making her suffer as I suffer, forging another link in the chain of abuse. But in the end it just makes me want more.

'FUCK!'

When I scream I can feel my facial veins pop as my head reddens with hot blood.

'Sir, uh . . . you're gonna have to . . .' Gerbil doesn't know how to finish that sentence, but it's clear she's gonna call security if I don't cease and desist.

Luckily her voice brings me back from planet Rage, and I see myself standing there in the afterglow of my anger orgasm. I think there may be something seriously wrong with me. Reuniting with my senses, I gingerly put the clipboard back on the table, pick up my backpack and skates, and say to Gerbil:

'Sorry, it's, uh . . . been a rough day . . . I'm really sorry . . .'

She doesn't exactly accept my apology, heartfelt though it is. But she doesn't reject it either.

Later that week my agent calls. I got the Fram job. Who needs to be in a Broadway show? Or Martin Scorsese's new movie? I'm gonna star in the new Fram oil commercial.

CHAPTER 2

CALIFORNIA, RICKY RICARDO,
THING 1 AND THING 2

It is a very special time at Chippendales: Nick de Noia is auditioning a new batch of Men. Upscale casual in his Calvins, Nick stares at the wannabe Men like a hungry hound dog eyeing a juicy bone. Or a horny cock hound eyeing a juicy boner.

It's three o'clock in the afternoon a few days after my triumphant, albeit barely noticed, debut. The club seems so small and ordinary when it's not dark, full of sexed-up people and really loud music. It's empty but for janitors and cleaners, janitoring and cleaning, the sound of a vacuum cleaner competing with the hum of ice machines. I showed up mired in the middle of some listless anticlimax after-debut blues, but the human dramedy of these auditions has taken me right out of myself, and I'm riveted, skulking unseen in the black shadows of Chippendales.

Five nearly-nude dudes are lined up in the Pit. Two huge Terminator-type bodybuilders: Thing 1 and Thing 2. Two long, lean, and lanky types: a California blond surfer and a fellow with a tremendous black pompadour and soft bronze skin. And one 80s-style Ricky Ricardo Latin lover, who's shorter, with some pudge.

I catch myself judging him like a rump roast. As I really look at the guy, I realize that he'd be a hot body around normal people. And compared to me, the puffy white Marshmallow Man, he's got a Greek god bod. But compared to a perfect specimen of manhood, he looks lumpy and dumpy. Chippendales has already infected my brain.

Thing 1 and Thing 2 are stiffly bound, flex-posing as if they're in a Mr America competition. California has a cocky half smile. At first blush he looks relaxed, but upon closer inspection seems coiled too tight. He's more average-looking than the pompadoured fellow, who is truly beautiful, a pre-Vegas Elvis, with wicked brown eyes, a jawline you could slice paper with, and thick lips that tend to the pout position. But Young Elvis looks uncomfortable in his soft skin, jittery and skitty, like he's got the big-time fidgets. Ricky Ricardo, on the other hand, looks very happy to be strutting his almost naked stuff. He's got thick sexy-ass lips under eyes that seem to be doing the rumba. He's kinda dancing in place to some mariachi sound track in his head, bobbing and weaving his hips all syncopated so his swinging G-string looks like the clapper of a bell being rung by a Latin love machine. He looks like he could fuck you all night long.

'Many are called, but few are chosen,' Nick de Noia pronounces as he moves smoothly off the bench, floating over to the line of men like a flamboyant General Patton addressing new recruits. 'Chippendales isn't just a show, it's history. And when a Lady comes to Chippendales, she knows she's getting only the best of the best. Yes, of course, hot and handsome, that's a given. But I'm looking for a few good Men who know how to please a Lady, to make her feel special, make her feel like a sexy, hot, liberated babe who's not afraid to say, "I like beautiful, young studs! Where's the beef?"' Nick de Noia smiles, clearly expecting a laugh. Ricky Ricardo laughs first, and the others follow. Nick looks like he's totally getting off on the whole thing. 'I'm looking for guys who know how to say please and thank you and "Yes ma'am, it would be my pleasure." Fat girls, grandmothers, housewives from Iowa with little piggy noses and buck teeth, it's your job to make them ALL feel like a ten, like Bo Derek.' Pause. 'Like Brooke Shields . . . who, by the way, is coming here to celebrate her twentieth birthday.'

The boys nod, sufficiently impressed.

Lurking in the shadows of Chippendales, it strikes me as kinda funny, how star-fuckery Nick talks about Brooke Shields. Why does he need to impress these dudes? They're here to impress him.

Nick de Noia walks the length of the line, looking into each and every eye of each and every guy, relishing how eager they are to please him in their near-naked state.

Nick flows slow behind the wannabe Men, drinking in the curves of their buttocks, the hard muscles running down their backs, the knotted calves. If he were a cartoon character he'd be a drooling huge-toothed wolf, rubbing his hungry paws together.

The discomfort level of the guys in line rises palpably. A man is sexualizing their asses, judging them, invasive and predatory. Since Nick is behind them, there's no more poker-facing from the boys who would be Men. Unease fills their faces. Especially Young Elvis, who sighs and clenches: he looks like he's fighting the flight instinct.

Ricky Ricardo is the only one who seems completely unfazed. In fact, he's even working his ass a little, arching and wiggling for Nick. Wait a minute. Is Ricky Ricardo gay? He looked so perfectly straight thirty seconds ago. But now he looks so perfectly gay. About 60 percent of the Men of Chippendales seem that way to me. Like, if there's a buck in it, or they're horny enough, they'd fuck pretty much anything that moves. In fact, it doesn't even have to move – they'll fuck it. About 25 percent seem completely gay. And maybe 15 percent seem like no-questions-asked breeders. But these figures are based on my own survey, which, frankly, did have some methodological problems.

Nick de Noia finds these Men everywhere. He cruises the crowds after the Chippendales show, of course, but also at restaurants, laundromats, and health clubs, in Times and Union Squares, on Coney and Fire Islands; Nick is indeed a 24/7 hunter of beautiful men. And yet he's banging the beautiful and über-feminine Va Va Voom. Or is he? As I watch Nick de Noia inspect the absurdly handsome men he collects, a theory begins to form in my head. Perhaps the hostile, toxic explosions that erupt out of Nick's sweet, charming spread-the-love persona are a result of this conflict between his man-sex craving, which he keeps secret, and the need to seem like a womanizing breeder, which he pushes so hard in public. And at the moment that nasty rancor seems to be radiating outta Nick onto these guys in the Pit. You put out enough of that shit, it's gotta come back sooner or later.

Nick moves close in behind Ricky Ricardo, and a naughty smile curves on Ricky's lips. Right behind him I can see Nick's face, eyes narrow with a darkness dancing in them. He grabs a handful of Ricky's chubby tummy love handle and pinches it very hard. Ricky Ricardo tightens unconsciously, then seems to force himself to relax, to let Nick de Noia have his way with him.

'That. Is. Un. Acceptable.' Nick overenunciates. 'The Men of Chippendales are not fat. It's disgusting, it's laziness, it offends me. Do you think a Lady wants to come to Chippendales to see a pudgy, fat little fuck? Helloooooooooo?!'

Nick de Noia keeps squeezing Ricky Ricardo's flesh. You can see it hurts, but Ricky doesn't react at all. He just waits until Nick lets go, then smiles, does a little hip shake, and with his Latino-New Yorky accent says:

'I say, "Hhhey, tha's jus' more of me to lub!"'

It really is funny. The other auditioners seem too emotionally involved or too dense to appreciate the comedy, but I sure do, and I have to stop myself from laughing out loud in the cover of my corner shadow.

Nick throws back his salt'n'pepper head and laughs right out loud, full of joy. It's a sweet laugh that makes his face loosen and ends in a chuckle, and I remember again how easy it is to fall in love with Nick de Noia.

This allows the nearly nude boys to express a little merriment, which they all do, except for Young Elvis, who's a study in sullen discomfort.

'Spunk,' Nick exclaims with jaunty good humor. 'I'm a big fan of spunk. I'll tell you what. You go away, lose that nasty baby fat, and you've got a job, mister.' Nick says all this to Ricky Ricardo's ass.

Which seems extremely odd, yet perfectly normal.

'Wow, rilly? Sirriously?' Ricky Ricardo is over-the-moon,

totally focused on the good – you've got a job opportunity – and not the bad – you're a fat fuck. I love this guy. I hope he does get a job here.

Vintage Nick – he'll rile you, ride you, deride you, make you feel like a heaping steam of shit, but if you can take it, he'll give you the opportunity to shine, and he'll encourage you to work your ass off so you can be all that you can be.

Nick moves around front of Ricky Ricardo, sparkling with rakish raffishness:

'Yes, of course I'm serious. Are you serious?'

'Oh, I'm siiiiiii-ree-us!' Ricky Ricardo smiles free and cocky, easy as you please and eager to do what needs to be done.

Nick sticks out his hand good-naturedly, and Ricky Ricardo shakes it, holding Nick's stare, giving as good as he gets. Nick releases with a flourish:

'Go. Leave. Make yourself beautiful. Call me.' Nick hands him a card.

'Wow, cool, thanks, uh—'

'Go. Now.' Nick cuts him off with a stiff little smile that says: Get the fuck out, while the gettin's still good.

Ricky Ricardo takes his cue and exits stage left, his plump bottom jiggling deliciously.

Nick now stands in front of the naked-but-for-a-G-string Young Elvis, scrutinizing him up and down, nodding and murmuring:

'Hhmmmm . . .'

Elvis's foot taps unconsciously, and he exhales a small, sharp snort of exasperated, ill-at-ease air.

Nick's eyes settle on the guy's sizable and well-packaged package. Young Elvis glares at Nick with barely disguised disgust. Nick feels the heat of the stare and looks back up into the guy's eyes, to meet the challenge, to cross swords. This seems to be what Nick lives for. With a jerk Young Elvis looks away. Nick sneers, feeding on this young man's fear and anger.

Young Elvis will not meet Nick's eyes. He looks left, looks up, looks down, looks right, looks left again, anything to avoid Nick de Noia, who is literally right in his face.

'What the hell are you doing here?' Nick sneers dismissively.

'You saw me at China Club and you told me—' Young Elvis defends himself too hard and harshly.

'No, no, no,' Nick cuts him off, pauses, and manages to finally catch Young Elvis square in the eyes, turning him into a beautiful bunny caught in the highbeams. 'What the hell are you doing here?'

'Well, uh . . .' Young Elvis seems to be torn between wanting it and wanting to tell Nick de Noia to go fuck himself.

'Well, uh . . . what?' Nick's relentless, he's got his teeth into Young Elvis, and he won't let go.

'I don't, uh . . .' Young Elvis stops and exhales. 'Fuck it, man, this is bullshit.'

Young Elvis breaks Nick's stare like a strong-willed mouse escaping a snake. He starts to say something that looks important but stops himself. Disgusted, he turns and clomps off, disappearing through the red velvet curtain.

Nick nods and tosses off a grin full of sweet satisfaction:

'Many are called, but few are chosen.'

And then there were three. Maybe I'm just prejudiced against huge mutant 'roided-up muscle heads, but Thing 1 and Thing 2 look like equally stupid and grotesque carica- tures of Men to me. They *are* interesting to look at, these extreme humans, with their muscles popping through dark taut skin, giant vein-engorged legs, teeny tiny waists, vast expanses of pec land, and nuclear gunboat biceps that make you want to poke them and ask, 'Are these real?' But the muscle neck collars they've made for themselves are truly hideous. Frankly, I find the whole cinderblockhead look the opposite of sexy, and with their water-retaining bloated faces, it's kinda hard to find their eyes, they're so small in the middle of those swolled-up heads. Even after studying them, I can't even really tell if they're handsome or not. And my mind keeps picturing their shriveled little testicles hanging in the midst of all that sculpted pop-veined twitching hulkiness. I read in a leading national magazine that steroids make your boys shrivel but your hammer bigger. So at least they've got that going for them anyway.

Nick takes his sweet time eyeballing Thing 1 and Thing 2, who flex and muscle-pose with as much subtlety as two huge brutes can muster. Nick, so close he's practically sniffing them, seems unconvinced. Shaking his head, he sits his ass gracefully on the bench along the edge of the Pit, and crosses his legs with royal savoir faire. His eyes move on to California, who curls his sexy lip and nods straight back at Nick. He's not as pretty as Young Elvis: eyes are a little too far apart, teeth gapped and crooked, nose bumpy, but not in a good way. His hair is not shaped quite right for his kinda-crooked face, but he's got a top-drawer body, with very little fat. He's more graced than bound by muscles. He's well over 6', looks like an Olympic swimmer with an attitude, and there's a poor-man's-James-Dean feel to the guy.

'You,' Nick points at California. 'Come here.'

There's no hesitation in California, who parades right over and plants himself directly in front of Nick. Definitely seems like a breeder. But possibly one of those straight guys who could be 'had,' as Arnolpho is fond of saying.

I've noticed that at Chippendales the notions of hetero-, homo-, and bisexuality seem hopelessly outdated. Gay? Straight? Seems like under the right circumstances, everybody's capable of doing anyone.

Nick de Noia is now sitting inches from California's fully loaded G-string. If he wanted to, he could lean forward a little and bite the head of the guy's penis. Nick uncrosses his legs as his gaze rides around the neck, chest, and hardbody belly of this tall blondy and rests lovingly in California's eyes. Like so many of the actual Men of Chippendales, California has that nasty, knowing, nodding grin. Where do these Men learn that exact same I-don't-give-a-fuck face? That same cocky body language? Why wasn't I smart enough to learn how to do that? To be that guy? Maybe you can only be that guy if you're that handsome.

'And what are *you* doing here?' Nick de Noia asks, like the answer will go a long way toward deciding whether California becomes a contender or a bum.

'I want to be a Chippendale,' California says simply. It reads real.

'Excellent.' Nick says, like California has successfully leaped through the first burning hoop and is moving rapidly toward a prosperous and exciting future. 'And what does that mean to you?'

'Well.' California puts on a thoughtful face as he pauses. 'Like you said, it means being the best of the best. Like, the cream on the crop.' California says this with absolutely no irony, like he has no idea that he just said something howlingly malapropish.

Nick smiles and nods: He seems to know exactly how silly

and stupid it was, but it's also clear that Nick doesn't care if California is as dumb as a bagful of hamsters. Could be California's just as smart as he needs to be. He does seem like if he were a canine he'd be lying on his back displaying his dog balls, making sure everyone knows that he knows Nick de Noia's the alpha.

Nick purses his pensive lips, thinks, then says:

'Turn around.'

California turns around. Nick moves his face forward just a hair and says into California's double-scoop-of-vanilla-ice-cream ass:

'Bend over and grab your ankles.'

Is Nick de Noia slightly breathless and enjoying this way too much, or is it just me?

There is no hesitation in California. He just bends over and grabs his ankles. His cheeks open slightly, and Nick looks like he'd love to insert his nose into the brown rose winking at him, dive face-first into California's beautiful blond ass and swim around in his hotness.

'You're gonna need to work on your flexibility.' Nick says gravely. 'Are you ready to work for it?'

'Yeah, sure, you just show me how.' California's voice sounds muffled and weird 'cuz he's upside down, but there's no mistaking his kiss-ass ability, top to bottom.

'Excellent.' Nick sounds highly satisfied. 'Straighten up.'

California bends back to upright, and before he even knows what's hit him, Nick de Noia whacks his ass, a loud

SMACK! of palm on unsuspecting buttocks. California
jumps and flinches, shocked by the sudden resounding surprise of it. But he doesn't say a word: Here's a guy who clearly knows where his buns are buttered.

'When you're a Chippendales Man, you've gotta be ready to get your ass slapped, you have to take it with a smile and love every second of it. Can you make a sixty-five-year-old granny from Peoria feel sexy?'

Nick stops. California looks unsure whether he's supposed to answer this question.

'Well,' Nick prods, 'turn around. Can you?'

Eager-beaver California turns and answers:

'Yeah . . . I mean, I'll try as hard as I can, and . . . uh, I'm a quick learner, I am, really . . .'

California is playing his cards just right. And they're good cards.

'Excellent,' Nick purrs. 'Come back here at seven tonight, ask for Vicky, and we'll get you started.' Nick extends his manicured hand magnanimously.

California shakes Nick's hand with undisguised glee:

'Thanks, I really appreciate this. Really . . . I do.' California lets Nick keep pumping his hand.

Finally Nick de Noia releases California's hand.

'We'll have to do something about that hair. Tell Vicky to make an appointment with our guy.'

'Hey thanks again, uh—' California shuts up when Nick raises a hand to mute him.

'What's your name again?' Nick asks, all charm and light.

'Barry . . . uh, Buck Evans.'

'All right, Buck. When Vicky gets you situated tonight, come find me, and I'll give you a little crash course on the . . . ins and outs of Chippendales.' Nick enjoys his double entendre, as he beams that 20-megawatt smile.

California nods ecstatically while walking away psyched and stoked.

Nick de Noia now turns his attention to the hugeness of Thing 1 and Thing 2, who lunk in the center of the Pit. Nick ponders, sighs, tuts, sighs again more dramatically this time, then shakes his head and *phumphs*.

'No, I don't think I can use you right now. But make sure you leave your number with Vicky. She's upstairs – have her take a Polaroid.'

Thing 1 and Thing 2 look stunned.

'Helloooooooo?!' Nick rolls his eyes impatiently. 'Good-bye!'

When Thing 1 & Thing 2 finally get it, they waddle like fleshy rocks away from Nick de Noia and disappear.

As I'm about to step out of the shadows and claim Nick's attention, Slick Rick springs into view from nowhere, in tight blue jeans and a puffy silver, shiny rock-star shirt unbuttoned so his smoking chocolate torso is exposed. He seems so clean and he moves beautifully, exuding easy powerful grace. He smiles nice at Nick, a good smile, a real smile. But his face looks like it contains a dark tension just under the surface, worry and trouble at the edges of his eyes and the corners of his mouth.

Nick lights up when he sees Slick Rick. Nick's so handsome when he smiles. He walks forward to greet Slick Rick like he's his son. His son he'd love to fuck. Or so it seems to me. They shake hands, and Nick touches Slick Rick with intimate familiarity. No wonder everyone thinks they're doing each other.

Nick and Slick Rick work hard on one move. It's a high leg kick that leads to a kind of backward swan dive. They do it over and over and over. Nick demonstrates, then physically takes Slick Rick's leg and moves it up, getting the toe to point. He puts his hand on Slick Rick's back and shoves it forward, then moves the arms backward, with the fingers pointing out.

Nick's a great teacher; he cajoles, humors, inspires, snaps, goads, encourages, and rewards. And Slick Rick seems a great student, ultra-attentive, no ego, hungry to learn. And a marvelous mimic, molding his body to Nick's exacting specifications.

Slick Rick finally pops the move perfectly: chest out, leg kicking up, toe pointed, head back, arms popping while fingers point. What an athlete this guy is.

It's a very cool move.

Nick and Rick share the joyful satisfaction that comes from working hard on something, then succeeding. They come together and congratulate each other, completely connected.

Slick Rick says good-bye and leaves, as Nick gives him a playful pat on his magnificent black ass.

When Slick Rick walks past me, he catches my eye. He doesn't know I was watching. He stops and smiles nicely, relaxed, having just been put through his paces by Nick. As opposed to how he so often presents in public: slightly wary and removed on Slick Rick Island.

'Hey,' he says, 'how's it goin'?'

'Good, man. That's a cool move,' I say with a small smile of my own.

'Thanks . . . Nick's great,' Slick Rick says, nodding.

'Yeah, he is,' I say.

'Hey, I never got the chance to tell you, but you're doing a great job, man.' Slick Rick says this like he really means it.

I've so hardened myself to the idea that none of the Men care about me and/or my performance, that this gentle, generous, and genuine compliment stuns me into silence. When I realize I'm standing there like a village idiot, I regain the power of speech:

'Oh, uh . . . thanks, man, really . . . thanks.'

'Sure,' he smiles with no guile. 'See ya, man.'

Then Slick Rick is gone.

Nick looks at his fancy-schmancy watch. He turns around to see if I'm ready and waiting. Not a good idea to make the emperor wait, so I stride forward with vigor:

'Are you ready for me, Nick?'

'Yes.' Nick smiles, motioning me forward. 'Now, the first thing I want to go over is the opening. You were a smidge late coming in, and you peaked too soon. Remember, I want you to stop at the p – "Chip-" – and go up at the end – "en-daaaaales!!!" That's very important. You almost have it, but I need you to really let it out, make it go all the way up to the top of the rafters. Use your hand – I want you to invite every Lady in the audience into this show. You understand?'

I nod. I just love how serious Nick is, like a master explaining the secrets of the universe.

'Do it for me.'

I fill my lungs full of air. Concentrating hard as I can, I attempt to duplicate Nick's rhythms, intention, and tempo:

'The Men. Of. Chip-en-daaaaaales!'

'Excellent!' Nick nods with satisfaction.

As he pats me on the back, a satisfied happiness consumes me.

This is what people forget about Nick de Noia: how good he can make you feel.

CHAPTER 3
THE UGLIEST MAN AT CHIPPENDALES

'Chippendales,' announces the sign over the tight blond reporter beaming into a big camera, standing on Sixty-first Street in front of the club. She prattles on about how Brooke Shields is the most famous teenager in the world, how she's gonna try to find 'endless love' here tonight at Chippendales, how the 'pretty baby' from a 'blue lagoon' is here to celebrate her twentieth birthday with a bunch of her best friends. Brooke Shields, Tight Blond goes on, was the youngest model to ever appear on the cover of *Vogue* magazine, shot to fame as a twelve-year-old playing a child living in a New Orleans brothel, posing provocatively, and in the process, creating lots of white-hot controversy about child pornography. Then, when she was fifteen, Brooke starred in some sexy Calvin Klein commercials, with her famous tagline: 'Nothing comes between me and my Calvins.' People were furious at Calvin for sexualizing kids. And they bought lots and lots of his jeans. Many people have accused Brooke's mother of exploiting her daughter's sexuality to make a buck. In fact, her mom became a symbol for ruthless stage mothers to some, while to others, she was just helping Brooke live the American dream of fame and fortune. Brooke was the People's Choice Award-winner for Favorite Young Performer, 1981–1984. She was Michael Jackson's date to the Grammys in 1984, and she dated Prince Albert II of Monaco. And she's coming here to Chippendales for her twentieth birthday party, Tight Blond smiles tightly.

It's sevenish on this most exciting night, and a massive throng of Ladies-in-waiting mill outside, desperate to be in with the in crowd, hoping to beg, borrow, or steal a ticket. Many are called, but few are chosen.

It's my prom night, Super Bowl Sunday, and the premier of my Hollywood movie all rolled into one. I was already keyed up and wired tight before I arrived, but now I'm going outta my nut, trying to stay coolcalmcollected, a white-knuckling mixture of sick fear and mad hope coursing through me. When I picture Brooke Shields and her entourage, her manager, her agent, and her mom, all scrutinizing me, a clammy crazed agitation rattles through me as I scratch, claw, and paw my way through the lobby.

At the dressing room door I'm suddenly confronted by a supersized Lady with an orange, glow-in-the-dark, tight-as-skin synthetic top over a girls-just-wanna-have-fun skirt, orange tights, and high, hard orange hair. She's trying to sneak into the dressing room undetected. Given that she looks like a two-hundred-pound pumpkin, I don't know how she thinks she's gonna get away with it. We arrive simultaneously, and she shoves me out of the way. The Great Pumpkin is solid and packs quite a wallop. As I right myself, she glares, and for a second I think she's gonna take a poke at me. I picture her wrestling me to the ground and making me cry uncle in front of all the Men. The shame! The humiliation! But as she zigs, I zag and, grabbing the handle of the door, shoot myself into the dressing room.

It takes me a moment to get my breath together and establish my longitude and latitude. As I calm, I realize I'm already seriously sweaty. It's gonna be a wet night.

Slowly the dressing room comes into focus. First thing that hits me is the electromagnetic man-energy that's banging and crackling so hard I can feel it pinging off my skull. Mutherfucker, Brooke Shields has got the joint jumpin'! As I let my eyes wander over all these absurdly handsome, practically nude lads, I'm reminded once again how disheartening it is to be the ugliest man at Chippendales.

The Snowman struts in like a rutting moose with a pornstar mustache and proclaims:

'I'm bangin' Brookie baby *and* her ma – it's gonna be a Pretty Baby doubleheader, motherfucker.' The Snowman does his mimed fellatio bit, and he gets an even bigger laugh than usual. But it's less a happy-banter laugh than an edge-of-the-nerves laugh, tight and forced and clipped. Even the Snowman himself, the king of cool, the guy who actually does do twins, seems to be trying a little too hard tonight.

Only Prince Charming, methodically preparing his golden hair and blue G-string, while good-naturedly rolling his eyes at the Snowman, looks truly unruffled, a stunning oasis of sexy big easiness in the face of this Brooke Shields shitstorm. He's one of those guys who smiles at life and has life smile right back at him. In all the chaotic backbiting bickering, he's a friend to everybody. You can't not like Prince Charming.

At the other end of the dressing room it's all intense and wired on Slick Rick Island. His brown eyes dart here, there, and everywhere. In the mirror he checks his hair and makes a minute adjustment, undetectable to the human eye. He checks his package, rearranging his nutsack in its G-string. He puts on a cuff. Rearranges the cuffs. Re-rearranges hair, balls, and cuffs all over again. The obsessive-compulsiveness of it all is painful to watch.

'I got fifty bucks says I bang Brooke Shields tonight!' The Snowman swaggers.

'I'm in for fifty,' Tom Cat says and grins, all long and slinky and cute-haired.

'Count me in,' grunts the Barbarian.

'Oh, I def'n'tely wanna piece o' dat.' Large Mark, looking more huge and dangerous than ever, reaches over and slaps hands with Tom Cat.

'Hey, Rick,' Cat taunts Slick, 'you wanna piece of this?' He slips into a lisping caricature of a faggy nelly poofta: 'Or are you too busy getting a piethe of Nick, thweety?'

A big roar pours out of the Men who are actually paying attention, as all eyes turn to Slick Rick, who's jolted out of his OCD preparation ritual. His eyes squint and this slithers out low but lethal through his thinned lips:

'Fuck you.'

Tom Cat limps his wrist and makes a gay kissy face:

'Oh you wish, don't you, thweety!'

Much to the delight of most of the Men.

Large Mark pretends to be Slick Rick talking to Nick de Noia like a raving gay flamer:

'Sthay, Nick, doesthn't my cock look hot in yer mouth?'

Big laughs, particularly from Tom Cat.

Slick Rick snaps so hard you can practically hear it, like a bone cracking. Murder in his eyes, muscles taut and uncoiling, he lunges, hands rushing violently toward Tom Cat's white collar-covered neck, as if he wants to choke the life out of him.

Large Mark cocks a huge angry fist and starts to unload it at Slick Rick's nose.

But Prince Charming slides in front of Tom Cat, stopping Slick Rick cold, while nudging Large Mark out of his punch.

And who should pick this moment to come sparkling into the chaos?

Nick de Noia, of course.

All the ugly vanishes, and everyone goes back to their normal preshow routine: primping, preening, prepping.

The effect is startling.

Nick, in giddy preshow mode, doesn't notice anything askew. He's here to deliver the evening's win-one-for-the-Gipper speech, the gist of which is: Dare to be great, but if you fuck up in front of Brooke Shields, the biggest movie star on the planet, I'm gonna cut off your balls and feed them to my dog, blahblahblah ...

I slip undetected into the costume room, and as I step into Johnny's lair her tea rose perfume soothes me. She's standing in the middle of her queendom with misery plastered on her sad lost face. Because she looks so disturbed, I ask:

'Hey, you OK?'

When Johnny looks up and sees it's me, her face lights a little, and a decent-sized smile sprouts on her lips.

'Yeah, I'm, uh ... fine ...' She's not very convincing. But

she seems to not wanna talk about whatever's upsetting the hell out of her. 'How's it hangin'?'

'It hangs as well as can be expected,' I say and smile back, happy at how easy it is for me to converse with this beautiful woman I want so much, who will never want me.

'You ready for Brooke Fucking Shields Night?' Sarcasm oozes from Johnny, and as always, it makes me like her a little more.

'Oh yeah, I'm all aquiver.' I move in and lower my tone intimately: 'And how are those new monkey masks?'

'The new monkey masks are faaaaaaaabulous!' Johnny mimics Nick de Noia.

And we laugh.

Johnny displays the new monkey masks like she's Vanna White, glamorous TV letter-turner extraordinaire. Johnny does it well, and I laugh more, which is a blessed relief considering how tight I am.

I have to admit, the new monkey masks do look a lot better. The fur is way thicker, and the faces are much more monkey-like. I nod with exaggerated appreciation:

'Those are some nice-lookin' monkey masks.'

'They should be,' Johnny clucks with disgust. 'I dragged my ass all over town looking for the fucking things. And every step of the way, I'm thinking: Brooke Shields can suck my dick.'

'Funny, I was thinking the same thing when I walked in tonight.' I get a good laugh out of Johnny, and I'm flowing so easy with her, it makes me very happy.

As I change into tux, tails, top hat, and roller skates, she preps the costumes furiously. Both of us are acutely aware that as soon as Nick's done out in the dressing room, he's gonna be in here. When Nick's near, your antenna goes all the way up, and you're always half holding your breath.

Sure enough, Nick slides in, all silk and linen. The costume room is a little too small to hold all of Nick de Noia, and it suddenly feels very crowded in here.

'David,' Nick says as he settles into a masculine yet dancerly pose, 'remember, you're the locomotive that drives this show. So keep your hand on the throttle, but don't race – let them have their moments, then POW! you're on to the next bit. OK?' Nick beams his big grin at me, and I am a true believer: If I just do my job and worship at the altar of Nick de Noia, I'll end up in Brooke Shields's next movie with John Travolta, and that'll be my Big Break, and then it'll all be good!

'Yeah,' I murmur as my blood pressure lowers.

'Excellent.' Nick puts his hand lightly on my shoulder and leaves it there, so personal, while confidence infuses through my system.

Nick then demipirouettes fluidly toward Johnny and demands:

'So, where are my new monkey masks?'

'Uh.' Johnny's trying so hard to be submissive, and I can see it doesn't come naturally. 'Yeah, they're right here.' She points to the brand-spanking-new monkey masks, as she smiles all cute and pliable and obedient.

Nick picks up a monkey mask and studies it meticulously, as if it were a precious gem and he a jeweler appraising it for the royal family. Johnny holds her breath, but little gasps escape now and then.

I'm rooting for Johnny to avoid a tongue lashing, but I don't see anything I can do to help her.

'Hmmmm,' slides out of Nick's mouth. Hard to interpret. But, my God, this dynamic feels familiar. Nick seems to create these situations over and over: a heightened atmosphere of tense fear in which he has ultimate control and can vent whenever he pleases. Verbal violence seems perpetually a stone's throw away.

'They're not perfect, but they're a vaaaaast improvement. I hope it wasn't too much trouble.' Nick smiles at Johnny, sweeter than summer corn.

'No, no trouble at all,' Johnny says, practically batting her eyes like Little Mary Sunshine.

Nick studies Johnny, trying to decide whether she's mocking or bowing to him. Finally, he smiles and says:

'Johnny, you're a pain in my ass, but I can't help myself, you've grown on me, thank you, and have a wonderful show.'

Then Nick de Noia gives us each a nod and is gone.

'Whew.' Johnny does a big wipe-the-brow gesture.

'Well, I think Brooke Shields is going to be very impressed by the quality of monkey mask here at Chippendales Male Strip Club tonight,' I say with a nod.

'Oh yeah,' Johnny snorts derisively, then says like a Valley girl: 'Well the show wasn't that great, but the monkey masks were *totally* awesome!'

I laugh.

Johnny makes me glad I'm alive.

CHAPTER 4
TOO STUPID

'Fucking right I will!' Nick's voice booms out from under the door of the upstairs office, where the $ lives. The dressing room has thinned considerably, and the thunderous sound of 'Freeway of Love' by Aretha the Queen dominates. I can't quite make out all the words, but there's no mistaking the furious anger. I can only catch snippets and tidbits:

'Who the hell—'

'I will NOT—'

And his signature:

'Helloooooooooo?!'

There are other voices, two at least, equally agitated. I can't hear what they're saying either, but it's ugly.

The door upstairs slams open and Nick flies out, jaw tight, surrounded by a cloud of anger. Stay the fuck out of my way! seems to be the message coming out of Nick de Noia as he corkscrews down that metal staircase toward us. I take several steps back to avoid Nick shrapnel. No worries, he busts right out the door and into the club with no eye contact. Shoulders shrug and eyes roll. Business as usual.

Up above us on the landing, the Edwards brothers appear in their dark suits.

Plus a new presence: An Indian man with plain black hair and plain brown clothes joins them on the landing. Though he looks like an ordinary man, he is not. This is Steve Banerjee. He's Nick's partner, the man who financed the show from the git-go, supplied the $ while Nick brought the showbiz razzmatazz, as they built Chippendales from a rinky dinky little dive into the greatest male stripper empire the world has ever known.

Hhmmmmmm . . .

When I open the door to the club, the music hits me in the forehead like the flat end of a shovel. I arrive in the Pit with plenty of time to spare, buoyed and buttressed by Nick. I survey the masses of Ladies. Holy shit! They're crammed rafter-high, packed to capacity, and then some. Looks like there could not be one more lady crammed in to Chippendales tonight. There's an extra snap, crackle, and pop in the air, the alcohol flows as a sexy ripple floods, gushes, and squirts through Chippendales, where 650 fevered Ladies are waiting. And one of them is Brooke Shields, who, unbeknownst to her, holds the key to my future.

The Men are jittery, flitting about with jumpy eyes, but I feel good. It's almost time. I'm ready. I look up at Crazy Eddie. He flashes a big goofy thumbs-up.

Game on!

Lights dim to black, and the crowd explodes with pent-up

fem energy. I feel like that picture where the guy's sitting in front of a music speaker that's blowing him backward, and he's holding on for dear life.

Just as I'm about to shout my first line, the one that sets the Men in motion, someone large slams into me hard and knocks me flat to the floor. I look up pissed, only to find all 6' 2" of Pretty Peter, the second-most handsome man at Chippendales, standing over me, glaring down like *I'm* the asshole. Those big pretty eyes, that pouting mouth, that chiseled chin, the hair that falls so beautifully with no apparent effort – the whole package is utterly infuriating. Pretty Peter is *really* making me mad. He should be apologizing to *me*, helping me to my feet so I don't make the show start late on this, the night that Brooke Shields, It Girl extraordinaire, is here in her famous flesh. But apparently he's too stupid to understand that, at this moment, I, the Ugliest Man at Chippendales, am more important to the show than he, the second-prettiest.

Oh shit, there it is, my cue! I'm supposed to yell right now. But I'm flat on my ass, and I have no breath. I suck up as big a bellowful of air as possible, and yell as best I can from the seat of my pants:

'The Men of Chippendales!'

But it's all wrong: three beats late, squirted out instead of boomed, weak and ineffectual. The show's barely begun, and already I've fucked everything up. SHIT! As I drag myself awkwardly onto my skates, Pretty Peter shouts something angry at me, but I can't hear him as I roll into the center of the Pit. I glance up at the crow's nest above, and sure enough, Nick de Noia's glowering a sour scowl down at me.

Kool and his gang funk out a deep baritone about how it's Ladies Night, and another shout busts out of the Ladies, as the Men of Chippendales strut into the Pit. But I've thrown the show off by coming in late: Half the guys are clapping and marching to one rhythm; a quarter are on another rhythm; and the rest look like they don't quite know what the hell's going on.

It's a disaster, and IT'S ALL MY FAULT!

Of course, the Ladies don't seem to care one iota. The Men are all half-nude, they all have killer hair, killer pecs, killer abs, and variations of the same hot, cocky, sexy expression on their faces. And this seems to be all the ladies care about.

Big Alice, everyone's favorite überregular, is up and shaking her huge hooters. A whistling white-veiled bride-to-be screams, goaded on by her drunken hen friends. They look like this is the most fun they've ever had.

I sneak another peek at the crow's nest. Nick is livid, shaking his head and gnashing his teeth. I'm careful not to make eye contact. IT'S ALL MY FAULT. Shit! Why is it always *my* fault? Nick's gonna fire me. No, first, he's gonna chew on my ass like it's cud and he's a cow. Then he'll fire me. Shut up! Here comes my next cue. I'm where I'm supposed to be. Maybe I can get this train back on track:

'The Men of Chip-en-daaaaaaaaaaales!'

I hit this one square between the eyes and get a big rise outta the Ladies. The Men are marching in place now, they're not perfect, but they're closer to the beat. I glance up to check on Nick in the crow's nest, but he's already flown the coop.

I whip the show along with speed, but things keep fucking up all night. The Unknown Flasher's lighted G-string fritzes and blinks. The Barbarian stumbles when he lands in the Pit. During the Construction Guy number, two of the Ensemble Dancers smash into each other, and one of them bounces into the Construction Guy, who loses his place while doing his moony lip-synching of 'Hello.'

I'm extremely happy to arrive at my break in the show. I take a breath, step away, and clunk toward the chill of my bathroom cocoon.

CHAPTER 5
TRIPPENDICULAR

I roll off the Pit floor and thump unimpeded up the steps toward the back bar, but as I enter the overstuffed, undulating crowd, I'm jostled, jolted, shoved, bumped, and thudded. I keep on moving though, pushing ahead toward my tall cool glass of water.

As I claw past a stunning young woman in a Madonna-style bustier topped with fingerless lacy gloves and some second-skin-tight hothothotpants, a dense middle-aged female barrels into me with great urgency. I bounce off, as this flies out of her:

'Umph!'

I careen back on my rear wheels and throw my hands instinctively forward to maintain my balance. My hand hits her drink, which spills all over the front of her blouse.

I bump into the buttocks of a peroxided, curvaceous,

jumpsuited woman, who turns and growls, snapping something angry I can't hear in the din. But my momentum stops, and my front wheels return to earth.

The dense Lady regains her footing and bearings. When she looks at the liquor I spilled on her, a sour storm gathers on her face.

As I settle, my brain goes ballistic. Do I have a fucking target on my chest? Why does everyone keep bumping into my Marshmallow Man ass? My hands form fists without any conscious thought on my part. I see myself punching the Lady in her dense, middle-aged face, feel her nose crack under my knuckles, her blood wet on my hands. In my mind, it's so satisfying.

I'm jarred from my violent reverie by the unpleasant reality of the Lady stepping into my face, and breathing what smells like sour booze up my nose as she shouts:

'Heeeeeey!'

I try to recoil, but there's nowhere to go.

'What do you think you're doin'?' Granted, I'm in a state of agitation, but she appears to be dead skunk drunk. 'Youuuuuuu spilled my drink!' she screams, going up on her tiptoes so she's inches from my face and I can practically taste the sour second-hand alcohol fumes. Then she bellows:

'Do youuuuu know who I am?'

Oh great, she's SOMEBODY. Just my luck.

'Look, uh, I'm sorry but . . .'

'Do youuuuu have any idea who I am?' Her face goes from crimson to scarlet to purplish.

'No, but . . .'

'IIIIIII'm Brooke Shields's MOM, that's who I am!' She screams triumphantly, like it should all make sense now, and I should apologize immediately and profusely.

I can feel an are-you-out-of-your-fucking-mind? look take over my face.

'What is WRONG with you?' she screams, the fumes singeing my eyebrows.

I'm just barely evolved enough to take a mental step back, heave a deep breath, and glare furiously at her.

She doesn't seem to notice. She paws the wet patch of alcohol staining her blouse, looks back up at me, and spits:

'What are you gonna do about myyyyyyyy DRINK?!'

I go from pissed off to pity. What the hell happened to her? Poor thing.

Suddenly the sights and sounds of Chippendales come rushing back, like I'm stepping out of the Mrs Brooke Shields's cone of silence. The Construction Guy's still lip-synching melodramatically to the overamplified strains of Lionel Richie wailing, and Ladies are still screaming.

Even though she's still screeching at me, I walk away from Mrs Brooke Shields. I squeeze by two tiny thin spinner women who carry see-through purses, display midriff skin, and sport teased blond hair as big as they are. I shake my head all the way to the back bar, where absurdly handsome Hot Bob flashes his fabulous grin and says:

'Hey man, wuz happening?'

I blow out a blast of exasperated air.

'I hear ya, man,' Hot Bob chuckles. 'This is some totally trip-pendicular shit.' And with that he sizzles away in his spandex.

How many people will Hot Bob get the opportunity to sex up tonight? And again the thought smacks me right between the eyes: no way am I EVER gonna get laid at Chippendales.

Plus, now Brooke Shields's mom hates me with a fiery passion.

CHAPTER 6
THE WANK OF A LIFETIME

Slick Rick is literally on fire. Well, not literally, but by God, he might as well be, with all the white hot dark black heat he's generating. *En fuego*. It's not that the moves are any different. But tonight, there's something extra. Slick Rick is *on*. And the chicks are digging him the most: whooping, hollering, screaming, crying, and sighing.

When Slick Rick executes the kick-swan-dive move Nick taught him, the Ladies just freak the fuck out. When he does his masturbating sock/cock bit, I swear he really looks like he's having the wank of a lifetime. What an amazing show Slick Rick puts on.

I keep stealing peeks at the crow's nest to see what the king is thinking tonight. But Nick de Noia is nowhere to be seen. I scan again and again for Brooke Shields and her mom, but it's so packed they could be anywhere.

When Slick Rick's Kiss & Tip starts, greenbacks flash hand over fist, waving with frantic psychosexual anticipation. But he's not greedy about it. He could harvest the garden of $ for hours, but he takes his time and gives kisses and pats and winks and smiles, like a lover with a slow hand.

A square-shaped, Barbara Bush-looking, white-domed matron has three of her crone cronies holding $ over her head. Slick Rick gracefully grabs the cash while somehow not looking like a money glutton. He takes her hand the way a genteel G-stringed gentleman in an old-fashioned romance novel might and escorts her with playful respect right into the middle of the Pit. Her galpals go crazy, as their girl becomes the focal point of the whole show. This, of course, ignites the tinderbox all over again. Softly and tenderly the very black Slick Rick takes the very white Barbara Bush in his arms. She giggles like a kid, and it's so beautiful watching a sixty-year-old woman turn into a giddy schoolgirl getting wooed by the hot guy. Barbara Bush looks over at her *amigas*, and they shout out to her with much love. She beams back at Slick Rick with a silly yet sexalicious smile. Slick moves in slowly with his thick lips, and the din rises as her smile grows. His mouth lands lightly on hers: no ugly thrust or tongue probe. So it's easy for her to relax. Looks like she has a coupla drinks in her, too, which certainly doesn't hurt.

Whenever I'm in strip clubs that cater to men, it seems like so many lone wolves are prowling for solo pleasure. Or bachelor parties where there's often an ugly undertone of competition and degradation. I never feel that at Chippendales. These women seem to really be having the time of their lives together, experiencing the whole thing through and with one another.

When Barbara Bush reaches around and plants her hand on Slick Rick's nude chocolate cheek and gives it a cheeky squeeze, the crowd crescendos. He breaks the embrace and pulls a huge, wide-eyed, I'm-shocked-at-how-naughty-she-is face, which he shows to the whole audience.

Barbara Bush's posse erupts, clapping and cheering, leading the crowd in a rousing round of applause, as she waves in acknowledgment. At this moment, she's a bigger star than Brooke Shields.

When Slick Rick finishes his Kiss & Tip, there's still lots of cabbage out there. But he just walks away from all that cash, drenched in sweat, looking like he's had the time of his life as he bows deep, waves, and trots off.

Stress brings out different things in different people. Many of the Men seem off, inhibited, or like they're trying too hard. Slick Rick, on the other hand, gives his best performance ever.

And then there's Prince Charming. He's the only person who acts EXACTLY like he does every other night. Like he doesn't have a care in the world. Like he's just Prince Charming.

Then I spot her: Brooke Shields, the most famous teenager in the world! God, she's gorgeous. And so tall. Brooke and her galpals seem to be having a solid blast. When she gets scooped up by one of the dudes, her dress rides up high on her thigh. She yanks it right back down but in a cute, sweet way that makes me really like her.

And suddenly it's almost over. The Brooke Shields show may not have been a complete artistic triumph, but you'd never know it by the eruptive ovation as I end the show.

During the finale, Nick de Noia waves like royalty from the crow's nest. When I point up to him, give thanks, and acknowledge his genius, he smiles at me real nice, and that make me feel better. Crazy Eddie presents me with a great nod of his wild red head when I give him a shout-out, and all seems right with the world.

Still, as I scratch and hack my way back to the dressing room, an uneasy dread heads my way. Yes, I often have that feeling when there's no evidence that trouble is anywhere near, but when you work for a man like Nick de Noia, you always have a reason to be afraid.

CHAPTER 7

ARE YOU KIDDIN' ME? WHO? BULLSHIT!

The dressing room is as happy after the show as it was tense before. Sweat-drenched flesh, some welts, ruddy flush-faced cheeks, eyes alive with triumph, boastful man voices booming out. And most important: counting that cash crop.

The Snowman walks through me like I'm a puffy white ghost. As I bask in his tan, I can't help but think that he's gonna be one crusty craggy skin-cancery old dude. Would it be worth it to get fellatio from twins? Live young, die old, get lots of head.

'Yo dudes, you wanna go ahead and pay me now? 'Cuz the Snowman is bangin' Brookie to-night. Pretty Baby's gonna get some big-time Snowman bone, homey! Where's the beef? Right here, motherfucker!'

Prince Charming wears his tiny bemused smile, removed and engaged, happy and handsome, taking it all in without judgment as he sorts his vast stacks of cash.

Slick Rick's totally divorced from the testosterony horseplay and monkey business, relaxed now, completely intent on meticulously straightening his $ into perfect little piles.

Large Mark and Tom Cat laugh loud.

'You wanna go double or nuttin'?' Large Mark shouts at the Snowman.

'Double or nuthin' this, bitch,' the Snowman blasts back.

Sloppy Sam, the stage manager, and second-ugliest man at Chippendales, walks into the dressing room with a note in his hand and a smirk on his homely mug. You can feel he has some important news, and his cheeky sneaky little grin suggests that there is some special fun afoot.

Banter vanishes as quiet takes over and a muffled 'Thriller' pounds from inside the club.

Sloppy Sam holds the note aloft while he slowly surveys the expectant eyes in the tiny dressing room. After he's milked the moment for all he can, he says:

'I have a message from a *Ms* . . . ,' he says, hitting *Ms* hard.

'Brooke . . .'

Pause.

'Shields.'

Low wolf whistles, sexed-up exhales, and an:

'Oh yeah, baby!'

The Snowman cock-walks up to Sloppy Sam and rakishly goes to grab the envelope. Sloppy Sam starts to hand it to him, with a wide grin on his chubby face, but at the last second he pulls the envelope back, leaving the Snowman grasping air, while gleefully exclaiming:

'Psyche!'

Sloppy Sam will never be as handsome as this dude, but he

does occasionally get to prick the vanity of the Snowman and squash him like a bug.

Big laughs fly outta the captive Man audience, many of whom have $ riding on the contents of that note. Sloppy Sam grins impishly. Large Mark and Tom Cat are beside themselves, hooting and pointing, making mock of the Snowman, who takes his medicine good-naturedly.

'Ms' – again Sloppy hits the Ms hard – 'Brooke Shields wants this . . .' – he references the note – 'to get delivered to . . .' You can practically hear the drumroll . . .

'Slick.'

Pause.

'Rick.'

Sloppy Sam smiles big-time, as the Men say:

'What?'

'Ohhhhhhhhh, baby!'

'Are you fuckin' kiddin' me?'

'Who?'

'Bullshit!'

'No fuckin' way!'

Large Mark and Tom Cat slap-snap while taunting the Snowman:

'Da Snowman got awll froze out!'

'I want my mo-nay!'

The Snowman shoots them a classic doublehanded middle-fingered fuck-you bird.

Arnolpho grins at me like Pan, the god of naughtiness, and I laugh right back.

All eyes are on Slick Rick, who looks like he doesn't quite know what the hell's going on, as Sloppy Sam holds out the note. Slick opens and reads it slowly. You can see him get to the end, 'cuz his eyes get wide. Then he smiles:

'Thanks, man. Tell her I'll be up as soon as I'm done.'

But Sloppy Sam's already striding away. He seems to have equal disdain for everyone more handsome than he. Which is everyone in the dressing room. Except for me, of course.

I duck into the refuge of Johnny's costume room. It's so quiet and dark and peaceful in there. The intense tension and stress of the past two hours evaporate and I breathe easier than I have in longer than I care to remember. But here in the land of Viking horns, moneky masks, and sodden jock straps, something's off.

It's Johnny. She's what's off: subdued, subpar, no wise-ass sass.

'Hey,' I say, 'you all right?'

She looks up at me like she doesn't quite know where she is or who I am. Quickly she dials in and smiles. But it's a smile that looks like it's trying to convince you it's real.

'Oh yeah, I'm good,' she nods unconvincingly.

'OK,' I say. I start to pry deeper but she's already gone back to collecting and sorting the nasty pile of stinking costumes.

I wanna help, but I don't know how. So I change into my black drawstring balloon pants, my red high-tops, and my vintage bowling shirt that reads 'White and Tite' on the back. That's me. White and tite.

'Hey,' I say, 'is there, uh, anything I can do for you?'

Johnny looks back detached and distracted, and with a semiapologetic smile, she says:

'Naw . . . thanks.'

Looks like she wants to say something else, something important. But she doesn't.

I'm not smart enough at this point in my life to do anything but walk away.

CHAPTER 8
THUG BUSTER AND PAGEBOY

'Addicted to Love' is so loud I recoil as I part the red velvet curtain and move back into the club. An enormous Robert Palmer, the very model of a modern English gentleman rocker, lip-synchs in front of pouty pasty-faced heroin-chic super-model chicks with the same tragically bored expression on their placid yet exquisite faces. They're totally disengaged, making a mockery of pretending to strum and pluck their instruments, just holding guitars and drumsticks while they stare blank-eyed into the camera with bloodred lips in little black dresses. In 1985, you don't even have to play an instru-ment to be in the band; all you have to do is look really bored and hot.

A scrawny dude with a huge attitude busts past me wearing a T-shirt that reads 'THUG BUSTER.' On his back is a picture of Bernard Goetz, the 'Subway Vigilante,' who earned his

name by shooting four black men when they demanded $
from him on the subway. After Goetz gunned them down, he
stood over one of them and said, 'You don't look so bad.
Here's another.' Then the Subway Vigilante shot the black
guy again. It was all anyone could talk about in New York
when it happened, and a huge chunk of disgruntled white
people all over the country embraced Goetz as a genuine
American hero who stood up to the thug motherfuckers,
kicked their asses, and took no prisoners. The black men
Goetz shot had nine convictions and ten outstanding bench
warrants between them. Goetz was found not guilty on
seventeen counts of attempted murder and assault. I steer
clear of the guy in the Thug Buster T-shirt.

My eyes slowly adjust to all the wild lights gyrating and
strobing. Look at all these Ladies. Brooke Shields is somewhere in the house. Is Slick Rick hitting it off with Brooke?
Making out with the most famous teenager in the world?
Prince Charming, Large Mark, Hot Bob, Tom Cat – they'll
have their choice of Ladies. But where is love for the Master
of Ceremonies?

As if in reply, the universe places in front of me a blonde
with black streaks in a lacy teddy with long legs under a puffy
skirt. She is lovely. I'm gonna talk to her. I really am. I'm
gonna do it. Just as I'm turning thought into action, a hopelessly gorgeous man wearing a blue denim Calvin Kleiny shirt
stops in front of her. It's Pretty Peter, the second-most beautiful Man at Chippendales, who earlier this evening knocked
me flat on my ass. Lacy Teddy's body goes all melty, and you
can practically hear her vagina getting wet. Sure enough, Pretty
Peter puts his hand on her ribs, she touches his shoulder, and
away they go, to have fantastically good-looking sex together.

Before I even have time to feel sorry for myself. I feel someone staring at me. I turn, and a brunette with a pageboy-banged do and striped overalls over a bowling shirt seems to be giving me the eye. At first I think she must be checking out a Pretty Peter-type behind me, but when I look, there's no one there. By God, she's staring at *me* with her pretty moon face and her big starry eyes.

'Uh,' she starts, bold but shy, 'aren't you the MC? Of the show?'

'Yeah, I am.' Stay cool, my brain whispers to me.

'I thought so. You were really good, I was watching you . . . you were really funny.' Pageboy has a soft warm smile, and her mouth seems to be sending me an invitation.

'Thanks,' I say, as calmly as I can.

Pageboy takes a step into me and touches my elbow. Ohhhhh, that's good. I adore her overalls and her body underneath them. Plus, she's wearing a vintage bowling shirt, just like me. I think I'm in love.

'What's your name? My name's Karen.' Alcohol steams hot from her sweet mouth. Karen seems drunk. But how drunk is she? Drunk enough to know better? Or too drunk to take advantage of?

'My name is David. Where you from, Karen?' I mentally kick myself. We're way past the where-you-from questions. I should be asking her the your-place-or-mine? questions. Get with the program, motherfucker!

'Those guys seem kinda gay. Are they gay? I mean, uh, are most of them gay? 'Cuz some of 'em seem really gay.' Karen is so close to me by the end of her sentence that if I were to tilt my head down and forward just a little I could kiss her very sweet mouth. I have to resist the urge to do so. Maybe

I shouldn't have. 'Cuz just as I'm about to invite her up to the VIP lounge to meet It girl Brooke Shields, two women with severe hair, way short on one side, spiked and long on the other, bound up and pounce on Karen, jabbering at the same time over 'Addicted to Love.'

'We were *totally* lookin' all over for you.'

'We *totally* thought we lost you.'

'We were *totally* like, where's Karen?'

'We were about to *totally* freak.'

'We were *totally* looking, like, everywhere.'

'Totally.'

Karen turns to her asymmetrically headed friends and says:

'Oh wow! Hey! There you are! Look who I found! It's the cute guy from the show in the roller skates!'

That's *me*, my brain says excitedly, the cute guy in the roller skates!

Two lopsided heads register me, check me out, dismiss me, then pull Karen away. She resists and looks back at me with a 'Wait a minute!' face. Then Karen leans in to her friends and whispers something I can't hear.

'What-ever!' says one of them.

With a shrug Karen wordlessly apologizes back to me as her friends drag her away into the thick night.

'Wait a minute,' I yell like a million desperate men before me. 'Can't I get your number or something?'

But her overalls, her bowling shirt, and her pageboy have already disappeared into the Ladies.

Totally disappeared.

Shaking my head I trudge up the stairs to the VIP lounge. Maybe Lady Luck is saving herself for my introduction by

Nick de Noia to Brooke Shields and her powerful team of industry professionals.

Yeah, sure, that's probably it.

CHAPTER 9

FLESHY AND THE TALL DARK STRANGER

The VIP lounge is wailing as 'Kiss' by Prince (before he became the Artist Formerly Known As Prince) booms in from the club. I survey the Very Important People, looking for Nick de Noia and Brooke Shields. There's Prince Charming with his girl, Betsy. He's looking thoroughly tasty in his blue jeans and tight tee. But she's transformed. Gone is the cotton dress and the simple ponytailed look, replaced by blond hair, big and stiff, redder lips, bluer shadowed eyes, pinker cheeks, shiny white minidress with shiny white boots. The most handsome couple on earth is in the corner nursing drinks, while some late-thirties Lady wearing way too much gold with huge pointy fake titties is trying to wedge herself between them. Prince Charming subtly slides his arm around Betsy. Fake Tits looks put off, like she's used to getting what she wants. And apparently tonight she ain't getting any Prince Charming, so she and her artillery storm away. Betsy cuddles into him. He leans down and lays an affectionate, sexy kiss on her neck. It's nice to see some actual human intimacy at Chippendales.

Wait a minute, there's Nick de Noia, holding court in front of a coupla people. None of whom is Brooke Shields. Damn. I scan the room quickly. No Brooke. With a deep breath, I run my fingers through my hair, slither through the Very Important People, and plant myself next to Nick, who's waving his hand around with animated charm as he finishes a story:

'I said, "Helloooooooo?! That's no banana, I'm just happy to see you."'

His audience, three middle-aged Ladies and a fat man, roars with laughter. I laugh, too, even though I have no idea what's so funny.

Nick spots me:

'Ah, David . . .' He's gonna introduce me, it's actually happening, it's all so exciting. He turns to the middle of the middle-aged Ladies, a woman who has two chins and a gigantic forehead. 'This is David Sterry, our wonderful new emcee—'

Before he can even finish the sentence, she leans in to Nick, whispers, then points to something behind me. It's the Unknown Flasher, all charismatic with that handsome dimply smile, moving in as Nick gestures for him to join us.

'This is our Unknown Flasher,' says Nick de Noia. 'He's actually a very talented actor. Very talented.'

'Yes, I can see how talented he is,' Mrs Forehead says, mesmerized by the Flasher's dimples.

And just like that, I become invisible again.

I recede into the Very Important People as Nick de Noia says something that makes everyone laugh. I gotta get outta here. As I make my way to the door, the Old Gray Man walks in with a different blond great-granddaughter-looking chick, equally coke-eyed and clingy.

I drag my ass outta VIP, headed for some redheaded Crazy Eddie love. 'Walk This Way,' screechy white-wail-heavy-metal-meets-gangsta-street-beat rap, thumps as I walk into the DJ booth of iniquity. Two women with identical ratted black hair sit and drink. One is big and fleshy, the other, crazy emaciated. Emaciated has long black nails and a tiny pink dress that accentuates her concentration-camp body. Her eyes are sunken black holes in her bony face, with bangs hanging down to her severely plucked eyebrows. Fleshy and Emaciated are in large matching T-shirts. One says: 'Stop!' One says: 'Go!'

A tall dark stranger with long straightened hair and a fringed leather jacket lingers in the corner shadow. Under other circumstances, I would be leery and wary of a fellow such as this. But here in Crazy Eddie's House of Fun, it's all good, baby!

'Well, look what we have here!' Crazy Eddie croaks through a big grin with his shattered-glass voice. 'It's the baddest man in the whole damn town. Killer show tonight, my man.' He holds out his hand and I slap him some skin, white-man style. His welcome warms me, and immediately I forget my troubles and get happy.

'You, too, dude,' I nod. 'You rocked the joint hard, man.'

'Hey sweetie, set my man up with a coupla fat rails.' Crazy Eddie nods at Emaciated, who takes a vial from the console, pours out a lump of coke, and begins the chopping process. I glance at Fleshy and Tall Dark Stranger. No introductions are forthcoming and no eye contact made.

'What a fuckin' night!' Crazy Eddie barks like a dog that's recovering from throat cancer. 'Brooke Fucking Shields, huh? Jesus Christ, fuck me, right? Am I right?'

'Absolutely,' I smile, 'Fuck the both of us.' No matter what shit comes down, when I'm around this redheaded bastard, life is sweet.

'Yeaahhhhhhhh!' Crazy Eddie yells at the top of his damaged lungs.

I laugh. What else is there to do? Looking down at the club crammed with bobbing, rocking, pulsating partiers, it's hard not to believe that we're at the center of something exciting, wild, and historic, like the earth is quaking, and this is the epicenter.

But the more I look at it, the more frantic and desperate, unhealthy and excessive, fall-of-the-Roman-empirish it all seems. Congress just announced a deficit of $171 billion. The United States has become a debtor nation for the first time since 1916. British scientists found a hole in the ozone. Palestinian terrorists seized an Italian ship and murdered American Leon Klinghoffer. And Rock Hudson just died from the 'gay plague,' which is what they called AIDS back then. It all seems connected to me, but I can't figure out how. The only thing I'm certain of is that here at Chippendales, with Brooke Shields in the house, I really wanna do some of Crazy Eddie's crazy coke.

'Oh man,' I say excitedly, 'guess who I ran into tonight?'

'Lay it on me, motherfucker.' Crazy Eddie flashes his freckly grin, revealing a set of mossy teeth.

'So I'm taking my break during the Construction number, headed to the back bar, and this Lady, I swear she seemed drunk-out-of-her-mind, she smacked right into me and she went ballistic, man, so it turns out that she's the one and only mother of . . . Brooke Shields.'

'No shit!' Crazy Eddie roars. He's the greatest audience ever. 'Mrs Brooke Fuckin' Shields drunk as shit! Only at Chippendales, baby!'

As Crazy Eddie's laugh fades, Emaciated finishes her chopping and spreading and beckons with a rolled-tight bill to a hefty cocaine rail that's all mine. She keeps pressing her index finger onto the mirror where grains have strayed, rubbing the magic crystals onto her gums, and then running her tongue over her teeth over and over and over.

I take the $ tube from Emaciated and try to find her eyes so I can thank her. She hides behind her hanging bangs, but I keep hunting and eventually I find her pupils. They're hugely dilated, red where they're supposed to be white, and dead where they're supposed to be alive.

I turn to Crazy Eddie and point to him with my index finger while raising my eyebrows and saying:

'Thanks, dude.'

$ up my nose, I suck in the virgin snow, and power surges through me like somebody just plugged my ass into a 220-volt socket. DING! DING! DING! Oh Mother, what a fucking rush my skull's busting with love as the cocaine train slams into my brainpan. Like a soaking dog trying to dry off, my whole body does a crazy shake as I light up like the Christmas tree at Rockefeller Center.

Crazy Eddie's one of those makes-it-look-ridiculously-easy Michael Jordan types. He's not even looking at the console as he segues seamlessly into 'Everybody Have Fun Tonight' by Wang Chung. I suspect there is no real Wang or real Chung. But I really want to have fun tonight. Apparently so does the crowd, which surges and adopts its bop to the new rhythm.

Suddenly I'm bursting with smiles. I wanna go find Pageboy and her overalls and her bowling shirt and tell her I'm madly in love with her. No, no, I wanna go back to the VIP lounge and tell Nick de Noia that he needs to hook me up with Brooke Shields's management team so we can star in a movie together. No, no, I wanna go dance with the masses and drown myself in the boogie beat. No, no, I wanna go find Johnny and convince her to be my girl.

'I gotta go drain the lizard, man,' Crazy Eddie croaks, then turns to Emaciated and says: 'Hold down the fort for me, will ya babe?'

She barely nods as he bounds off. I try to imagine her holding down a fort. Frankly, it looks like the only thing she's capable of holding down is more coke. Speaking of which, I should buy some coke. I should get a beverage. I should—

Tall Dark Stranger is starting to freak me the fuck out: His stare has turned into a glare, and the vibe in this room has deteriorated badly since Crazy Eddie left. The whole thing is giving me the willies.

'Hey thanks,' I mumble through an attempted smile, then slide outta the DJ booth. I feel like a superhero bounding down the steps three at a time. I love how the loud music makes my nuts hum. I'm so happy to be alive, to be one of these writhing gyrating throbbing humans here on planet Earth, dancing the night away in the Pit of Chippendales. I dive into the kaleidoscope of pretty party titties, giant flying hair, big bracelets and huge hoops, too-tight shirts and too-short skirts. Everybody's havin' fun tonight!

Eddie Murphy is singing about how his girl wants to partyallthetime.

Me, too, I wanna party all the time.

A large brunette is directly in front of me, making fuck faces as she puts her hands over her head and shakes everything in rhythm to the bangin' beat. Her polyester tube top can barely contain all her sexy flesh, and I wanna plant my face into the middle of her cleavage and shake my head ecstatically in her milk pillows. Then she's gone. But I don't care, they're everywhere. Whirling dervishly I dance like no one's watching, my body so loosey and goosey, rubber band bones, skin all tingly. Suddenly I find myself in the middle of a Long Island-style bachelorette pack, it's a group drunk, and they're having a grand old time. They're fun, these babes, bumping, cutting up, being silly. They surround me, and a big one with canary yellow eyeshadow maneuvers the long-necked bride-to-be babe in front of me, like a sacrificial lamb.

Bride-to-Be dances stiffly with me; she seems self-conscious being the center of attention, her long neck locked into place like some giant flightless bird.

But I don't care. I do a shimmy-shimmy shake, smiling a mile a minute. The bachelorettes shake their shimmy right back, and finally Bride-to-Be breaks out of her protective shell and busts a shimmy of her own. And it's good: The girl can flat-out dance. When she spreads her arms out and gets her long swan neck moving, by God, she looks so happy and sexy, I wanna tell her to dump her husband-to-be and come with me and we'll make long-necked babies together, live happily ever after, with all her crazy friends.

The splendid Eurotrash of 'Rock Me Amadeus' blasts on,

and the girls return to their senses. They wave good-bye to me sweetly and rush off to their next adventure.

Drenched with sweat and parched desert-dry, I realize it's time to rehydrate and strategize. The buzz is thinning and I'm not quite so happy to be alive.

Gotta do something about that.

CHAPTER 10

FEELS LIKE RAIN

I enter the dressing room just as the soft Steve Banerjee is walking out. Suddenly we stand facing each other.

'You are the new master of ceremonies?' he asks me in a dark brown Bengali voice.

'Yes, I uh . . .' I'm too aware of how very very rich this man is, and it's making me shaky. I really really want him to like me: 'Yes.'

'I'm Steve,' he says, 'I thought you did a very good job tonight.'

'Oh, uh, thanks. I . . . it was fun . . . So, are you . . .' I have no idea where to go with this thought. Are you happy being the moneyman behind the greatest male stripper empire in history? Are you, in fact, very very rich? Are you getting sex hand over fist? Or are you a family man? Or both? Are you furious with Nick? I hear he's ripping you off – is that true?

Are you pissed off you have a partner who's a vicious charming bully who loves to publicly humiliate people? But most important, are you in a position to help me become a star? '. . . Are you staying long?' Oh God, what a moron thing to say! I'm discovering that coke can make you the most articulate man on the planet, or it can tie your tongue into nine kinda knots.

'No,' Banerjee says softly. 'I am leaving now.'

'Oh,' I say. 'OK, well, it was nice to meet you.'

'Yes, you, too.' Steve Banerjee reaches out his soft hand, and I shake it. It's a decent handshake, if a little on the soft side. When it's done he nods politely, then ducks out the door. I'm left with the impression that he is a confident, thoughtful fellow, quiet and respectful, well-mannered and decent. But not someone you could push around. He seems so average at first blush, not at all like a man who's selling a million calendars a year and is, in fact, the very epitome of the American dream come true.

I am now alone with the mirrors in the dressing room, and I really really wanna be as high as I was thirty minutes ago. Suddenly it dawns on me that maybe the Snowman is getting fellatio from a new set of twins in the bathroom ten feet away. Or maybe Slick Rick is kissing Brooke Shields in there. You just never know at Chippendales.

I walk quietly to the bathroom door, a bit tingly with the anticipation of seeing some illicit sex. Suddenly I realize I am fuck-an-inflatable-doll horny.

I open the door slowly.

Nothing.

I'm a little disappointed, actually. Maybe I should do an experiment where I go out into all those Ladies and ask them one by one to have sex with me. How long would it take for one of them to say yes? What if no one ever said yes? That would be too depressing. I abandon the experiment. I need a time-out. I need a plan. So I wander into the costume room.

I feel her before I see her. Johnny, sitting in the corner on a small stool down low like a little kid, is holding a monkey mask. When she meets my eyes, she tries to smile but fails. Her cheeks are wet, her eyes are red, and her face is splotchy: She's obviously been crying. And hard, too.

'Fucking monkey masks,' she sighs.

I don't know what else to say, so I repeat:

'Fucking monkey masks.'

In the silence that hangs after that, I wanna say, Hey, you OK? Or, Can I do something? I wanna put my hand reassuringly on her shoulder. Comfort her with a big, sympathetic asexual hug.

But I don't do any of those things. In fact, I don't do anything. I disconnect. I feel like I'm missing the part of me that makes a human capable of reaching out to another human who's in need.

'Billy really fucked me over,' Johnny says plain and flat. 'He's such an ass-wipe.'

Again I have no idea what to say. So I mutter:

'Well, that sucks.'

'Fucker can suck my dick,' Johnny spits.

'You said a mouthful there,' I say with a straighter-than-straight face.

Johnny laughs, which softens her face. Feels good to make her laugh.

'Hey,' she says as the laugh subsides, 'I gotta get the fuck outta here.'

Johnny packs up her stuff. I pack up my stuff. She's in old

tight ripped jeans with a wide leather belt and a small black T-shirt with 'THE RAMONES' on the front and 'I WANNA BE SEDATED' on the back. Brown leather boots that look like they belong on a Dickens character. Her hair is one massive tangle of brown curls that seems to have a life of its own, bobbing and weaving around her face and over her shoulders.

Without a word we duck out of the dressing room and slide undetected past the cashier's hole where yet more people are paying to partyallthetime. We slip out the glass doors, past the massive bouncer mountains in black jackets, and out into the warm Upper East Side night. The air's heavy and thick.

Feels like rain.

CHAPTER 11
A GREAT WAY TO NOT GET LAID

The pizza is most excellent at the Most Excellent Pizzeria across the street from Chippendales. It's hot and gooey and cheesy, and the sauce is zesty while the crust is crunchy. Johnny catches my eye and nods her curls while arching her eyebrows: 'Damn, this is a good slice!' I nod right back. She gets a slice to go.

Walking down First Avenue, the pre-rain air is good on my skin after the smoky claustrophobia of Chippendales. As we walk under the Fifty-ninth Street Bridge, Johnny spots a homeless hobo and shouts out:

'Hey, Chili Dawg, howz it hangin'?'

Chili Dawg has a wool cap pulled down almost over his eyes, while many layers of clothes float over his bones. Everything lights up at the sight of Johnny, and he practically dances over, eyes so wide they seem to take up half of his face, as he mumbles excitedly:

'Hey hey, Miss Curly Girl, tell me something good, tell me that you love me.'

'Gotta slice for ya!' Johnny smiles as she gives him the slice of most excellent pizza. 'You lookin' good enough to eat tonight yourself, Chili Dawg,' she drawls.

He howls like a happy animal:

'Oh yeah! The men don't know but the li'l girls understand!'

What would Chili Dawg think of the Unknown Flasher's homeless jokes in the show? All that $ people just throw away every night at Chippendales. In a month, five million Americans will form a human chain across the continent to protest the plight of the homeless and the blind eye turned by Reagan and his money glutton cronies. They'll call it 'Hands Across America.'

After we bid a fond adieu to Chili Dawg, we cruise down First Avenue past the UN, with the flags of many nations flying. I just love knowing that all those dignitaries from all over the world are here on this island. Diplomacy, G-strings, we're all doing our part for the evolution of the species. Then again, I read that when the UN recently celebrated its fortieth anniversary, they couldn't even agree on a declaration for the occasion.

It starts to rain a little, but it's a warm, soft rain, a Blanche DuBois rain. Feels like it's baptizing us, washing the slime and muck of Chippendales off.

'You suppose Brookie's makin' out with Slick Rick?' Johnny asks.

'Yeah, she probably got all turned on by those sexy new monkey masks,' I reply, and this gets a rich laugh outta her.

'So,' I ask, 'how long you been at Chippendales?'

'Well,' says Johnny, 'I started at the beginning, so I been here, like ... a year ... a little over a year ...'

'Was it, like, a big deal when it opened here?'

'Oh yeah, definitely,' Johnny nods, 'it was already a huge hit in LA.'

'And what are they all screamin' at each other about upstairs?' I ask.

'Well, it's not like anybody consults me on any of this shit, but I heard the Edwards Brothers think Nick's scammin', and Nick thinks the Edwards Brothers are skimming, and Banerjee thinks he's getting jacked by everybody. But who the fuck knows?'

I take it all in.

'Well, good thing they all have such wonderful conflict reso-lution skills.'

'Yeah,' Johnny laughs.

'But how,' I ask, 'did you get to be the costume mistress?'

Johnny gets very serious:

'Many are called, but few are chosen.'

On the muted TV some skinny little white wanker in stupidly tight black pants, a sleeveless T-shirt out of which pasty wasted chicken-wing arms protrude, and lacquered hair that narrows into a point between his eyes is flailing around and lip-syching into the camera. On her boom box Johnny is playing 'Brick House,' and Lionel is bringing the funk.

'She's a brick houuuuuuuuse! She's mighty mightay! Letting it all hang out!'

Johnny's skin is all browned butter in the soft light. I could just lean over and kiss her. That would be natural, organic. Wait a second, she just got dumped by some hand-some asshole. Men suck. The last thing she's gonna want right now is some sperm-loaded dude flying at her. No, I should wait and let her make the first move.

This, it turns out, is a great way to not get laid.

Suddenly the exhaustion of the whole thing hits me like a brick house. Damn, man, I went from wide-awake laughing to conflicted, irritable dead tired misery in half the blink of an eye.

'Wow, I'm tired,' I sigh.

I wait for: Why don't you crash here? Or: You can just sleep here if you want. Or: Why don't you stay and have sex with me?

Needless to say, none of that happens.

Standing at her door I have two vivid visions:

Johnny lying under me naked.

Johnny with my child inside her.

I hear that voice in my head:

BITCH! FAGGOT! PUNK!

'OK, well . . . ,' she says.

I have no idea what that means.

OK, well.

What does this woman want me to do? No clue.

'OK,' I say.

'Take a Chance on Me,' by a Swedish husband-and-wife team, starts playing on Johnny's mix tape. They're urging listeners to take a chance on love.

The Swedish husband-and-wife team are not yet divorced. But they will be.

I really want to kiss Johnny. I think she wants to kiss me, too, but the thing is, I just can't tell.

Suddenly I feel seventeen again.

'See ya,' she says.

'See ya,' I say.

Out into the crispness of the wee hours I stroll, lugging my load with me.

And thus ends Brooke Shields Night.

CHAPTER 12
BROOKE'S BRUTAL BLACKNESS

I didn't really think much about Brooke Shields for the next twenty years or so. I saw her occasionally on TV. Read about her getting married to tennis star, philanthropist, and TV huckster Andre Agassi. And I'd smile when I remembered getting spewed on by her mom that night, as young Brooke left her twenties at Chippendales.

Then one day in 2005, I was surfing the Web, and I happened to come across Brooke on *Oprah*. She was talking about the brutal blackness of her postpartum depression. She spoke quite courageously and eloquently about using antidepressants and psychiatry to fight her way back, and I was filled with a whole new respect for and deep kinship with her.

I had a vision of Brooke's mom barking venom all over me. The same mom who had her get all sexy and naked in front of the whole world for $, while she was still a kid.

As I relived that moment again, I didn't smile this time.

CHAPTER 13

1,000,000,000-POUND WEIGHTS

Walking in for my week's work, I stop dead. Hanging on the wall of the Chippendales dressing room is a picture torn from a New York tabloid. It depicts Slick Rick and It girl Brooke Shields beaming at the camera.

But someone has desecrated the photo by hand-drawing a penis, which appears to be crudely entering Slick Rick's mouth. A thought bubble drawn over his head says, 'I love cock.' The words 'IGNORANT SLUT' have been written over Brooke's head. My first thought: Wait a minute, isn't she going to Princeton or Harvard or some big-brained place? And isn't she a high-profile virgin? Methinks the grafitti-ists need to do a little fact-checking.

Large Mark and Tom Cat titter in the corner, carrying on like a coupla catty girls. No, wait. The way they're laughing, touching, and whispering so intimately makes these two butch Chippendales Men seem like a bitchy gay couple.

It's almost 7 P.M. on Wednesday night. Kind of a dull hangovery feeling after all the excitement of Brooke Shields Night. I guess starring in the hottest show in New York is like any other job. You get bored and cranky and take it for granted very quickly. As I look at the picture of Slick Rick with a dick drawn in his mouth, I realize I should have been more specific about the kind of success I wanted. Becoming a star seems even further away now that I'm entrenched in the Land of Chippendales.

The Barbarian, biceps quivering, pumps what looks like 1,000,000,000-pound weights; he's stripped to the waist, his bulgy bottom half stuffed into a pair of short shorts. Blood pumps, veins pop: ho hum. The Unknown Flasher stares into the mirror, utterly entranced by how beautiful he is, spears a square of cantaloupe and places it in his mouth as if it's the sexiest thing anyone's ever done. The Construction Guy looks extremely unhappy with his rose. I see trouble brewing.

Prince Charming sits, nude blond and still. What must it be like to be Prince Charming? To get paid a shitload of dough to flounce around nekked for half an hour, four nights a week, with your pick of the most gorgeous females on the planet to have sex with, in addition to a beautiful sweet girlfriend? And the best thing about Prince Charming is that you feel cooler and hotter when you are with him, not uglier and stupider. He begins carefully, meticulously, patiently applying flesh-colored makeup to the tattoo on his arm.

When Large Mark and Tom Cat catch me staring at the graffitificized clipping of Slick Rick with the cock in his mouth, they giggle with innuendo, like they want me in on their frat boy shenanigans.

I'm ashamed to say that I don't do what I wanna do, which is tear the desecrated clipping off the wall, crumple it into a ball and slam-dunk it into the trash. Instead I play along, pretend I think it's really funny. I make myself sick sometimes.

After they snicker like evil children and do their little handshake-slap thing, Glitter takes some fleshy makeup out of a small bag and, without hesitation or a word, starts covering the steroid zits on Large Mark's back with tender loving strokes.

Slick Rick busts in a little late, smiling and out of breath, looking like he's on a natural high. Everyone stops what they're doing and looks away from Slick Rick, which intensifies the tension exponentially.

'What?' Slick Rick asks suddenly suspicious.

Large Mark and Tom Cat can hardly contain their hysterical glee.

The Barbarian looks right at the clipping on the wall. That's how stupid he is.

Following the Barbarian's eyes, Slick Rick twirls and takes in the picture with the hand-drawn penis headed toward his mouth and 'IGNORANT SLUT' over Brooke Shields's head.

His face and neck tense and his fisted knuckles clench, while his mouth spasms involuntarily. He takes a deep breath and closes his eyes. It looks like he's making a tremendous effort to go deep inside and calm himself. One one thousand. Two one thousand. Three one thousand. He lets loose a long, slow exhale, turns, and says in a calm voice that belies his facial agitation:

'Who did this?'

Everyone looks down, looks away, or looks off. Except for two people: Prince Charming, who keeps patiently applying his makeup, and the Barbarian, who looks right at Large Mark and Tom Cat, silently indicting them as surely as if he'd pointed at them and said:

They did it.

'Did you do this?' Slick Rick accuses them, violent turbulence just below the still dark of his face.

Large Mark and Tom Cat completely ignore him.

'I said.' Slick Rick pauses, gets a grip on himself, and says directly to Large and Glitter, 'Did you do this?'

'Oh,' Large Mark puts on a big surprised face, looks around behind him, and says, 'Ah you tawkin' to me?' He's clearly mocking and goading, pricking and needling, furiously pushing Slick Rick's buttons and working his nerves.

'Yes.' Slick Rick's smile strains on his face. 'I'm asking you if you drew this shit on this picture?'

Large Mark and Tom Cat shake their heads with big innocent faces while saying:

'No, no way. Hell no.'

Slick Rick's brown eyes roll up in his head, like he's asking a higher power to give him the strength to suffer these fools. Then he softly says:

'OK. Whatever. I'm not gonna let you fuckers bring me down. Some people are just jealous assholes, and if you let the assholes fuck with you, then you're even worse than the assholes.'

Large Mark puffs up and takes a big dangerous step forward while he lowers his voice and says:

'You cawllin' me an aysshole?'

Slick Rick does not back down:

'Did you do this to the picture?'

'I tol'ja,' sneers Large Mark, 'no.'

'Then I'm not calling you an asshole,' spits Slick.

'Fine,' snarls Large.

'But I am calling whoever did this an asshole.' Slick Rick glares first at Large Mark, then at Tom Cat, clearly calling them assholes.

'Whatevvuh.' Large Mark shakes his huge hair and steps back with a chuckle. 'Kinda funny if ya ax me.'

'How was she?' Tom Cat raises his eyebrows rudely.

'D'jou fuck 'er, or did she strap it on an' fuck you?' Large Mark grins while Tom Cat giggles.

'By the way, do you let Nick watch?'

'Or did Brookie end up watchin' you an' Nick?'

They roar hooligan laughs.

'Very funny,' Slick Rick dismisses them. 'Brooke is too cool to even talk about with you losers.' He rips the clipping down off the wall and does what I couldn't: wads it into an angry ball and slams it into the trash. Then he goes to his locker and calmly goes about his business.

Large Mark and Tom Cat stride haughty out of the dressing room and into the rest of their huge night.

'Hey man,' Prince Charming says to Slick Rick, 'don't worry about those guys, they just wish *they* were going out with Brooke Shields.'

Slick Rick nods grateful at Prince Charming.

'Thanks.'

'No problem.' Prince Charming smiles back.

CHAPTER 14
THOU SHALT COVER THINE ASS

Construction Guy, half-clothed, enters the dressing room, clearly pissed, and thrusts his rose toward Johnny's nose. It's not the greatest rose I ever saw, but it's perfectly decent, especially considering that nobody even remotely gives a shit about it.

Except the Construction Guy, of course, who's really ruined the mood in the dressing room, where Johnny, Arnolpho, and I are carrying on gayly.

'Look, I don't mean to be a pain in the ass . . . ,' the Construction Guy starts.

It occurs to me that whenever someone starts a sentence like that, you can bet they're going to be a pain in the ass.

'But this rose is . . .' he urges us to look at it. 'Well, I mean, my God, the petals are wilted, it's just all . . .' The Construction Guy is so overcome by how pathetic his rose is, he doesn't have words to describe it.

Arnolpho and Johnny exchange eye rolls, not even bothering to disguise their disgust from the Construction Guy. I myself am having a hard time suppressing a derisive laugh, but I was raised by English people, so I keep the laugh to myself.

'Look,' Johnny says, like she's right at the end of her tether, 'there's nothing wrong with the rose, man, and besides, nobody gives a shit. If you have a problem, I suggest you take it up with Nick.'

'Nick's not here tonight,' says the Construction Guy, 'which—'

'He's not?'

'He's not?'

'He's not?'

Arnolpho, Johnny, and I sound like hopeful kids who've learned that their cruel teacher is absent for the day.

'No, he's not,' says the Construction Guy, 'and—'

'You sure?' Arnolpho, Johnny, and I ask simultaneously.

'*Dios mio*, tha's the bes' news I hhhad since Buddy's warts fell off,' sighs Arnolpho.

The Construction Guy shoots a withering glance at Arnolpho that doesn't wither him one jot, Arnolpho being basically unwitherable.

'Well, I'm definitely gonna talk to Nick about this,' the Construction Guy threatens lamely.

'Go ahead,' Johnny says, 'go fucking tell Nick, I don't give a shit.'

'Fine,' the Construction Guy says, like he's proven his point, when in fact he really hasn't proven shit, and seems like a half-nude prima donna prick who's the pudgiest, least talented, and most unstudly of the stars. Wow, working at Chippendales really does warp your shit quick. I try to imagine a society where being fat, ugly, misshapen, and brilliant made you desirable.

'What-ever!' Amazing how much attitude Johnny manages to load into those two syllables, as she dismisses the Construction Guy.

He sighs, then turns to me like I haven't been standing here listening to this whole lame conversation. His smile contains more smarm than charm as he says:

'So, I was thinking, when you introduce me, you should say, "And now, it's Chippendales's answer to Don Johnson!"' He being the hot pretty boy *Miami Vice* star. 'I think you should say it just like that. "And now, it's Chippendales's answer to Don Johnson!" I think that would be really good.' He has a deep voice. Combine that with the gravity he put into the sentence, and it seems like he's talking about how to split the atom or achieve world peace.

Arnolpho and Johnny do not stop their audible chortles.

I do.

'Hey look, we should clear this with Nick.'

First commandment of Chippendales: Thou shalt cover thine ass.

'I told you, Nick's not here tonight.'

'Yeah,' I say, 'but I'd really rather run it by Nick first.'

'OK, how about we try it tonight, and see how it works, and then I'll talk to Nick about it?' the Construction Guy says with utter sincerity.

'All right,' I shrug.

The Construction Guy smiles at me again, a little more natural this time, but still barely skin-deep.

Then he's gone.

Arnolpho waits exactly the right amount of time, then with jaded aristocracy he says:

'Mus' be her time o' the month.'

Johnny and I crack the fuck up.

'Mus' go. So many to do, so li'l time.' Arnolpho air-kisses Johnny on either cheek, does the same to me, then he, too, is gone.

Johnny immediately plunges into her night's work, and I begin my transformation into the Master of Ceremonies.

'How ya doing?' I like how easy and comfortable it is in Johnny's strange cocoon.

'I'm all right,' she says, casual as you please. 'How you doing?'

'I'm good.'

Everything is so much more relaxed when Emperor de Noia is in absentia.

The Snowman bursts in, hair all puffed hard and coiffed impossibly high:

'I hear Billy Cheeks dogged you bad.'

'Yup,' Johnny says.

'Beings how the motherfucker's a dog to the max, I'm not surprised. That dude is what my old lady used to call a mutt.'

'A mutt?' I ask.

'Yeah, a dog that comes from a bitch who got fucked by every Rover, Spot, and Fido in the neighborhood,' says the Snowman.

'Well, yeah, I guess that about sums it up,' Johnny smirks. 'Whattya want?'

'Lemme have three dimes of chronic and fifteen nickels of shakes.'

As Johnny retrieves the weed, the Snowman addresses me:

'You want some nose candy? Some Bolivian marching powder?'

My first impulse is to say no. I'm working. I'm a professional. But the more I think about it, the more it seems like it would be a lot more fun doing the show whacked and cranked. The cat's away, and I'm feeling like a very playful mouse.

'Sure,' I say. 'OK.'

The Snowman nods and a smile moves across his mustache. It's the first time I'm putting his blow up my nose, and he seems happy that I am joining his club.

'OK, listen, you know that intro with the bowler.'

'The sixteen-pound balls?' I ask.

'Exactamundo,' says the Snowman. 'I want ya to use that one for me. And really lay it on, will ya? I need some wamma lamma ding dong tonight, dude.'

So *that's* it. Here I am thinking the Snowman's giving me some coke outta the goodness of his heart. No, he wants a better intro from the Master of Ceremonies. He wants more juice, which will make him more $, and get him more sex. The old maxim 'There is no free lunch' is illustrated again and again at Chippendales.

'Sure,' I say, 'no problem.' I don't give a shit who has the sixteen-pound balls. Certainly willing to barter that for free high-quality coke.

'Cool.' The Snowman extracts a small glass vial from his little Chippendales fanny pack. When he shakes it and opens the cap, a little spoon hangs down – no fuss, no muss, an all-in-one mini coke snorting unit. Ingenious drug users are always pushing the envelope of design and function when it comes to imbibing their drugs. Gives me hope for the continuing evolution of mankind.

The Snowman digs the spoon into the coke and comes out

with a heaping helping of chopped-fine snow. I snuff it up hard into my blow-hole, and OH MY GOD, here we go again! He does not offer any to Johnny. She does not seem to expect any.

Breathing deep I revel in the heart bone blood mind blowing high and sigh:

'Thanks, man.'

'No problemo, dude. You ever wanna buy some, you come to the Snowman.' He winks big, makes a gun out of his hand, and shoots me with it.

Oh, I see, it's also a promotional giveaway, in the long and hallowed tradition of drug dealers doling out little bits of candy until they've got you frantically buying it.

Whatever, I'm really enjoying the perks of my new job.

Johnny hands the Snowman his weed bags, and he stashes them in his little Chippendales fanny pack.

'Later, motherfuckers.' The Snowman does a small salute and disappears.

'OK,' I say, trying to keep the runaway train that is my brain under control as I start to wander out.

'Wait a minute,' Johnny says, 'aren't you forgetting something?'

'Uh, I don't know . . . ,' I mumble, 'my head?'

'Here,' she tosses a half smile as she grabs my red bow tie and hands it to me.

'Shit,' I say, 'forgot. Damn.'

My hands are all thumbs as I fumble with the clasp like a pumped-up junk hound.

Johnny leans in and fastens the clasp easy as you please. We're standing so close, our lips are inches apart, the air crackles between us. The kiss is so close. And I want it bad.

But it seems like the wrong time, the wrong place, and the wrong drug making cotton grow in my mouth.

'Uh . . .' the coke cat's got my tongue. 'Thanks.'

Johnny grins:

'My pleasure.'

'See ya later,' I say.

'OK,' she says.

Excited by that prospect, I clomp on my skates toward the Pit, my brain on fire, looking forward to doing my greatest show ever.

CHAPTER 15

A TESTOSTERONE, ESTROGEN, ADRENALINE COCKTAIL

My ordinary Wednesday night is magically transformed into a wacky wonderland by the power of amazing cocaine. As I enter the Pit of Chippendales I can barely contain my glee: so many vaginas, all in one room! Makes me positively giddy. I rub up against a pair of bottom cheeks packed into tiny tight Guess jeans. Brush up against breasts bottled up in a tube top. Marvel at legs cascading out from under microscopic minis. My God I could just reach under one of those barely there skirts and grab a handful of vagina. Not that I would. But I could. And the possibility is utterly intoxicating.

In the Pit, I look up into the DJ booth and catch the blood-bank red eyes of the freckled Crazy Eddie, and he waves his arms around like the lovable loon he is. I shoot him a thumbs-up so big it becomes farce: He throws that red head back and roars. God, I love Crazy Eddie.

Testosterone, estrogen, and adrenaline make a crazy cock-tail, and with the loud pounding music, it's a total kick in the head, shot to the heart, and squeeze of the balls to be coked up in the seething bubbling Pit of Chippendales.

All the Men march and clap on the same beat, except for:

Pretty Peter, the second-most handsome man at Chippendales. He's too busy eyeing the ladies: winkin', grinnin', gettin' all sexy. His clap is half a beat behind every time, like it always catches him by surprise. And he gets away with it. This utterly infuriates me. It's not just that he's so stupid, although I do find that unbelievably annoying. It's not just that he doesn't give a shit about fucking up my show. It's also the fact that in spite of these first two facts, because of how stunning and hot he is, he not only gets away with it, he flourishes: money, love, and pussy thrown at him willy-nilly. I bust my ass every night, and nobody ever throws me any love, money, or pussy, willy-nilly or otherwise. I'm bothered by how incredibly bitchy the whole thing makes me feel.

It's very easy to get distracted when you're all jazzed on racehorse charlie, and I almost miss my cue. But when I fling my hand up into the air and the ladies scream, it's like my arm is a lightning rod that catches a blast of kinetic AC/DC, and I am a holy-rolling tent-show revivalist at the Chapel of Love.

When I intro the Snowman I lay it on extra thick:

'Our next stud is a big bowler in his *spare* time. And Ladies, it's no wonder, 'cuz he's gotta pair of sixteen-pound baaaaaaaalls!'

They roar like a chorus of horny angels as the Snowman struts his mustache center-stage, full of dangerous sex. He's been cultivating a whole circuit of Lady hotties he'll be macking and fucking and sucking $ from while he supplies stepped-on blow and three grades of weed at inflated prices, and they yell out from the crowd.

The Snowman gives me a nod with his astonishingly coiffed head. He likes me. He really likes me. I catch myself star-fucking, and I'm overcome with loathing – for this place, for a world where beautiful heroin-anorexia-thin supermodels and hypersexualized fifteen-year-olds are used to sell jeans, where Pretty Peter gets celebrated and Chili Dawg is homeless. But most of all I loathe myself for buying into the whole thing.

When I introduce the Construction Guy, I say:

'Next up is Chippendales's answer to Don Joooohnson!'

The overall response is decent, though certainly not over-whelming. But one big beautiful babe gets up in the left side of the Pit and screams in a voice so loud and piercing you can hear it over the madness.

The Construction Guy makes a special point of giving her a few sexy faces. She laps it up, as do her rowdy big beautiful babe friends.

During his showstopping Lionel Richie 'Hello' number, I pay special attention. He actually lip-synchs the cheesy drip-piness directly to the rose. As if the *you* in the song actually refers to the rose. The Ladies don't care; they go crazy when the tough, construction worker hunk reveals his tender senti-mental side, like they always do.

The much-discussed rose does look a bit weary. But I'm sure I wouldn't have noticed if it hadn't been a bone of such contention.

Naturally the Construction Guy makes a special point of throwing big beautiful babe the rose. After she catches it she goes into a state of ecstatic rapture. She practically starts fucking the thing, she's so turned on. The slightly subpar rose seems to have no effect whatsoever on her level of excitation. When he brings her into the center of the Pit, gets down on one knee, looks up into her eyes, and kisses her hand, she moans and screams and swoons. She grabs his head in both hands and bends down a little. All coked up, I think for a minute that she's gonna guide his big head under her voluminous dress so he can dine at her Y. That would be so cool if she actually did put his mouth onto her kitty and she came like crazy. Man, the roof would just blow clean off the joint. Instead she guides him into her big beautiful breasts. The Construction Guy shakes his head around in there, and the Ladies, how they scream while a field of green sprouts from the crowd.

The Construction Guy makes a killing in his Kiss & Tip. So, from his POV, the Don Johnson thing worked like gangbusters and got him maximum bang for his buck. But to me, MC Marshmallow Man, with no financial ax to grind, it seems a bit cheap, antithetical to the timeless, classic, Folies Bergère cabaret show Nick de Noia has worked so tirelessly to create.

As I slog off to take my break, I realize I'm not nearly as high as I was at the start of the show. And I find that incredibly annoying. My mood plunges fast into black. I want more coke!

I ease when I enter my bathroom sanctuary, where it's so cool and quiet. I remove my tux jacket and wipe myself down. I gulp icy water, chew a few cubes, and already I'm breathing easier. I push open the metal door of the last stall and start to roll in to drain my kidney through my lizard. I stop, popeyed, when I see:

Pretty Peter, leaning against the cool tile wall, with a woman's mouth attached like a barnacle to his pretty penis. She pumps her big mass of blond corkscrewed hair back and forth. She pauses, turns her head, and looks up at me. She's very pretty in an Ivy Leaguey, Jodie Fostery kinda way. She grins a wet smile that seems to say: Ain't I a lucky gal? Like there are hundreds of fellatio-starved chicks who'd die to trade places with her and have the opportunity to swallow a man as beautiful as Pretty Peter. Maybe there are, now that I think about it. I have not observed the same craving for puffy white Marshmallow Man cock.

Pretty Peter grabs the back of Jodie Foster's head like she's a ventriloquist dummy and starts jack hammering away while she makes sexy little suck sounds. He's not mean, mind you. Insistent.

'How's it going?' Pretty Peter asks me with no apparent irony.

'Good,' I reply. 'How you doin'?'

'Excellent,' he says. He looks down at Jodie Foster and asks, 'How you doin'?'

Jodie Foster removes the gorgeous Chippendales wangdangdoodlehammer from her mouth, looks up at him, looks up at me, and says:

'Excellent.'

All I can think is:

Why don't people ever lock the door when they're getting head around here?

CHAPTER 16

THE CASE OF THE MISSING G-STRING

Slick Rick is wet from his champagne/cum shower, naked but for one small shiny green G-string. He's on a platform above the Pit, looking down on the Ladies, dripping and radiating, his black body engorged and pulsing.

Frankly, I'm fading. My happy, I-love-everyone coke high has long gone bye-bye, replaced by a poisonous lockjaw that has my face frowning for no apparent reason. But I have free-form improv time coming up during Slick Rick's Kiss & Tip, and I'm determined to just let myself go and truly be in the moment and flow as I never have before.

Because I'm a bit preoccupied waiting for Slick Rick to begin his Kiss & Tip, I don't see exactly what happens next. But here are the facts as I've been able to reconstruct them.

When Slick Rick tugs at his G-string and threatens to take it all off, silently asking the Ladies with his face and body if they'd like to see his penis, like he does every night, the thin elastic that attaches the triangle of bright green fabric breaks, and droops forward.

Have you ever heard six hundred women gasp as one? I hope you have the pleasure of that experience, because all that startled female breath being sucked in at the same time is breathtaking.

Why the gasp? Because Slick Rick's cock pops out. By the time I see it, the penis is already exposed, swinging, big, black, and fleshy, about half-hard. I believe the semi-erection is an illusion created by a tie-off. The tie-off, as I understand it, was first pioneered in male stripperdom in the wilds of Canada, where men are allowed full-monty nudity. But it has certainly been used in various contexts for centuries and is, in fact, a cousin of the dick pull. It's a simple but potentially dangerous technique. A thin strip of leather or elastic is strapped around the base of the testicular/penal unit when the unit is engorged with blood. When you tie off, the blood is trapped in the unit. This creates the impression of an erection, even when there is no sexual excitation. The danger comes when you tie off too tight for too long. The penis begins to turn a frighteningly deep purple. Perhaps this is the origin of the expression *blue balls*. There's a male-stripper urban legend that one dim Canadian stripper woke up the morning after an alcoholic stupor to find his blackened cock popped off and lying like an andouille sausage on the floor.

I can't say for sure that Slick Rick tied off that night, but from the look of his engorgement swinging around in front of all those shocked Ladies, I'd almost bet my left nut on it.

Slick Rick's penis seems overjoyed to be released from its incarceration in that tiny G-string prison and looks like it's ready to be adored and loved by the fawning female fans.

Holy shit, Nick's gonna pitch a fit! That's my first thought. It's been drummed into us that any public display of one silly millimeter of penis could result in Chippendales losing its cabaret license. Which would mean closing the show, killing the cash cow, slaying the golden-egg-laying goose, and the unemployment of us all.

Bug-eyed jaw-dropped silence is followed by a piercing eruption of gleeful female screams. I still believe that pound for pound this is the loudest sound I've ever heard.

Slick Rick looks down at his unsheathed penis. Then back up in bug-eyed surprise. But the whole thing feels planned, canned, and reeks of premeditation. I have no evidence of this; it's just the feeling I get, like Slick Rick rehearsed the moment. He's always so obsessively meticulous in his preparation. Plus, he doesn't cover up right away. He milks the hell out of his shlong flop: Wow, I can't believe it popped out!

Finally, after what seems like about a month of Slick Rick's naked phallus flailing around, he hops off the platform, and disappears for a coupla seconds, then reemerges wearing a new, bright green G-string, and dives into his staggeringly lucrative Kiss & Tip.

Wait a minute. If Slick Rick didn't plan this whole fiasco beforehand, why was there a stashed G-string all ready for him to slither into?

'It's hide-the-salami night here at Chippendales!' I ad lib, and that gets a nice rise outta those who are paying attention.

As I roll into the center of the Pit my skate slips on a slick patch of oil from the smoke machine, and I almost land flat on my ass. I catch my balance at the last second and lurch forward like a drunk. So I roll with it, literally, and channel a teetering, tottering, wobbling drunkard, letting my skates splay farther and farther apart as I move forward, until I'm almost doing the splits, ranting like I'm intoxicated, under the superhuge musical din, while everyone watches Slick Rick Kiss & Tip:

'I used to beeee,' I slur like I'm nine sheets to the wind, 'the hottest dude at Chippendales! Ohhhhhh yeah, baby! I useta get blown in the bathroom, humped in the hhhhallway, boned in the balcony. Oh, you don't believe me? Watch this!' I perform several snockered, mock pelvic thrusts and do a cartoony imitation of Slick Rick's swan dive move, spin around drunkenly several times, arms and hands and feet and knees and wheels flailing, till I land flat on my ass.

'But one night,' I slur crawling besottedly on my hands and knees, 'my penis popped out. Don't asssssssk me how, but the old John Thomas, she just popped right out. Hey, can a pecker be a she? Maybeeee that's my whole problem. Ha ha haaaaaaaah.'

I flop down so I'm lying on my back in the middle of the Pit. Suddenly I feel like a deeply troubled mental patient on his shrink's couch. So I spout into the priceless mic:

'Well, doctor, on my third birthday, my dad, he gave me a brand new gun. He said, "Happy birthday, son, today you are a man." So I shot him dead. And SMOKE came out of the hole in his head!'

When I say SMOKE, the guy who's operating the smoke machine lets out a blast of dry-ice fog, and I disappear in a gray shroud of a cloud, and the crowd fades away. Oddly, the sounds of the show fade, too. Ah, it's so peaceful in there, like a little womb in the moist center of Chippendales.

As the smoke clears, Large Mark and Tom Cat are heckling

and jekylling over me, laughing at my mayhem. Apparently my madcap antics are a much-appreciated respite from all the naked boredom.

Large Mark is so huge looming over me, like a spandex-clad Mt Rushmore in cuffs'n'collar. Suddenly I feel like Chili Dawg hanging under the Fifty-ninth Street Bridge, so I look up pitifully, and with a gravelly, guttery voice, I say:

'Hey fellers, got a quawtah? You fellas sher are han'some hunks. Brothers, could ya spare a dime?'

Large Mark and Tom Cat shoot me twin middle-fingered fuck-you birds. As soon as they turn their backs, I growl loudly into the priceless mic:

'Stuck-up dumb-fuck ass-face butt-munchin' pretty boys!'

Large Mark and Tom Cat wheel around together, stride over and pretend to kick, punch, and work me over, professional-wrestler-style, while I grunt and groan and suffer their blows in my hobo voice:

'Owwww! Dat hoits like a bastard! Wow, dat's pain!' When they're done I moan and smile, while holding my injured parts.

Large Mark grabs one of my arms, Cat the other, and they drag me on my back across the floor of the Pit as I shout:

'It's a honnuh an' a pri'lege to get physical abused by dudes as han'some as youze.'

They twirl me around in a circle, faster and faster. I get giddy dizzy as the Chippendales merry-go-round spins deliriously: Lady faces, tits and slits, long legs and pretty shoes, round and round she goes, where she stops nobody knows.

Large and Cat release me and I continue to spin until I slowly lose speed and finally come to a stop. Then they preen around handsomely. Personally, I always found Large Mark more large than handsome, but Tom Cat sure is pretty. When they tug me up, Large Mark almost rips my arm out of its socket. To my surprise a lot of people are watching us and we get a very nice round of applause for our tomfoolery. We all take a little bow. Large Mark and Tom Cat nod and point at me. It's sick how tickled and thrilled I am to be acknowledged by the popular boys I despise.

And I understand even more profoundly that I can do anything I want here, because no one in the audience gives even the littlest shit what I say or what I do.

Slick Rick finishes his Kiss & Tip, which means it's time for Prince Charming.

By the time I finish slogging through the rest of the show I'm irritated, exhausted, disillusioned, dehydrated, and totally out of love with life.

When I enter the dressing room, Sloppy Sam, the stage manager and man ultimately responsible for the bolts and nuts of the show, is already grilling Slick Rick – much to the amusement of Large Mark and Tom Cat, who seem hungry for the blood of the man they love to hate.

Slick Rick defends himself vehemently. But it has a very methinks-the-Lady-doth-protest-too-much feel to it.

'No, I swear to God, the thing just came apart. I guess it was loose. I don't know, man, but I just did what I do every night, and all of a sudden, the thing just came apart.'

Sloppy Sam shakes his disgusted head:

'Look, all it takes is one chick to complain. Or one cop to be here undercover, or whatever, and they yank the fucking cabaret license, and they shut us down, and—'

'I know, man, but it's not my fault, the thing just came apart, it just came apart—'

The way Slick Rick keeps repeating the phrase *'the thing just came apart'* seems highly suspicious to me. But again that is strictly my own speculation.

'I don't give a fuck.' Sloppy Sam is seriously hot under the tux collar. 'It was *your* dick that popped the fuck out, and if it happens again, you're gonna get suspended for sure, and fired, and hopefully have it chopped the fuck off, if I have anything to say about it. You understand?'

'That's not fair, man. It wasn't my fault, the thing just came apart.' Slick Rick's all palms-up-shrugging, bunny-eyed innocence.

'I don't give a fuck. Don't let it happen again. Do. You. Understand?' Sloppy Sam looks like he's ready to rearrange Slick Rick's pretty Prince face.

'Yeah, sorry, sure—' Slick Rick starts to say something else, then thinks better of it and cracks several knuckles.

Sloppy Sam storms off into the costume room. Johnny's in trouble. I exchange a glance with Arnolpho, who does a little Brazilian headshake eye roll, silently indicating that he's not buying a word of Slick Rick's story.

Large Mark, all pumped up like a 'roiding blowfish, strides right into Slick Rick's face.

'If I find out you did dis shit on poipose, I'm gonna kick yer ass awll de way up Foist Avenue, you unnuhstand?'

'Hey man, I didn't—' Slick Rick gets shut down quick.

'Shut de fuck up!' Large Mark growls.

Slick Rick shuts the fuck up.

'If dis shit evvuh happens again, dat's it!'

Large Mark makes a massive fist and swings it at Slick Rick's jaw.

Slick flinches back into the locker behind him with a bang.

Large stops the fist an inch before it smashes into Slick Rick's face.

'Hey, what the hell!' Slick Rick protests.

But Large Mark is already gone. Tom Cat follows smugly, shooting a sneer at Slick Rick as he trails Large like the tail of a comet.

Danger momentarily averted, the Men go back to the task at hand: sorting and counting $, while I retreat to the costume room to see if Johnny needs the cavalry.

'No fucking way, man!' Johnny protests. 'I checked that G-string tonight, I swear to God. And before he went on, I saw Slick Rick fucking with the seam. I didn't think anything of it at the time, but now it totally makes sense.' She doesn't look like she's fibbing. But maybe Johnny's just an excellent fibber. Still, she doesn't have that shakiness that guilty people so often display – that Slick Rick just displayed. She has more of the I'm-being-framed-and-I'm-not-going-down-without-a-fight vibe about her.

Sloppy Sam purses his lips, shakes his deeply troubled head, then says:

'Where's the G-string?'

'He says it's *gone*.' Johnny nods her head like she's not buying a word of it, like in fact Slick Rick losing the G-string is more proof of her innocence and his guilt.

'What do you mean it's *gone*?' Sloppy Sam's making sure he has all the facts straight for the Nick de Noia inquisition he knows is on its way.

'As soon as I heard what happened, I tried to get my hands on that G-string, to see if he really did fuck with it, like I saw him fucking with it. And all of a sudden, it's *gone*. He can't *find* it. Yeah, *right*.' Johnny's face can barely contain her disgust.

Sloppy Sam mulls, gives a little tsk, then exclaims:

'Aw fuck!'

Then he blasts past me and out the door.

I can hear him demanding to know where the offending G-string is. I can't hear Slick Rick's response, but I have a good idea that no straight answers are forthcoming.

To this day, the Case of the Missing G-String remains unsolved.

Johnny shakes her disgusted curls and utters:

'Un-fucking-believable . . . un . . . fucking . . . believable . . .'

'Wonky G-strings, flopping cocks, mangy monkey masks, if it's not one thing, it's another!' I try to lighten the mood.

Johnny picks up some funky fur leggings and angrily dumps them in the fur legging box, then stops and proclaims: 'What the fuck am I doing here?'

'Looks like you're working your way up the male stripper food chain so that one day all this' – I motion around the dank man-stink-filled dressing room – 'can be yours.'

'Nick's gonna fucking ream me nine new assholes. I gotta get the hell outta here,' Johnny says with absolute certainty.

Arnolpho flits dramatically into the room.

'Ohhhhhh, you should hhhave seen Miss Thing!'

He launches into a spot-on Slick Rick impression:

'It wasn't my fault! I don't know what happened, really I don't. The thing just came apart, and next thing I know, my big black cock just popped right out!'

Arnolpho becomes Slick Rick standing there with his dick accidentally-on-purpose out, making a big-eyed face while miming an exposed penis so well you can almost see it.

Oh, how we laugh, Johnny and I, really let loose with a much-needed release.

'Ohhhhhhh bay-bee.' Arnolpho touches Johnny on her chest while placing his other hand over his own heart. 'You shoulda seen hhher, what a performance! Miss Slick better hope she never has to testify on hhher own behalf 'cuz hhhoney, it's gonna be, "Guilty! Guilty! Guilty!"'

'Oh my God!!' Johnny gasps through her laughs.

'By the way, we're goin' out tonight, so strap it on, hhhoney!' Arnolpho ends his proclamation with a theatrical flourish that suggests a night of madcap Manhattan high jinks.

'No, I—' Johnny's cut off by Arnolpho.

'Shhhhhh! No discussion. Buddy bought a new jacket, Princess Charming and hhher girlfrien' are comin', an' I simply will not take no for an answer.'

'But I—'

'Nooooooo, bay-bee. You get you' tired ass togethuh, put on you' party hat, an' let's go-go.' Arnolpho turns to me. 'You comin', mistress of ceremonies?'

I look at Johnny, who shrugs, like Arnolpho is a force of nature and it would be futile to resist. So I say:

'OK, sure, absolutely . . .'

'Chop chop, train's leavin', bay-bee.'

And with that we're swept up and away on the Arnolpho D'Alencar Araripe Pimenta de Mello fun machine, where it's all good, and it doesn't matter who's on the end of your dick when you cum.

CHAPTER 17

AN ANDY WARHOL WANNABE
AND A REAL-LIFE IDOL

Prince Charming leads us to the front of the line waiting to get into Zamboni, the white-hot club du jour for trendy Manhattan partyallthetimers. He walks like someone who's so perfect he doesn't have to prove he's perfect. On his arm Betsy is barely recognizable as the simple, girl-next-door, cotton-dressed cutie beauty I first saw him with. Tonight she's in a classic spaghetti-strapped little black dress that showcases her fabulous legs. Her face is all purples and pinks, and vampire-suck-blood red covers her lips. Her large, curled, teased hair creation has to be extension-based. Arnolpho is absolutely fabulous in a soft pink silk shirt open over a pair of loose linen white pants and two-tone brown and white shoes full of his talented feet. Buddy, his live-in lover, wears a pair of orange, pegged rockabilly pants with his new jacket, which is a beautifully cut black, pearl-buttoned, shoulder-padded number. They make quite the pair. Rounding out the sextet are Johnny, all curls and attitude, and me, baggy black drawstring pants, my 'White and Tite' bowling shirt and red high-tops.

We move past all the losers in the long line and get ushered right in, me and my posse. Of course, in reality, I'm the weakest link in the posse, and Prince Charming is clearly the alpha. Just basking in his reflected glow makes me more beautiful and fuck-worthy, and strolling into Zamboni, it's a strange and wonderful sensation to be the envy of head turners.

Electro-Eurotrash dance musique I can't identify booms through the black cavern, and flashing colored lights make it seem like Shangri-La is right here at Zamboni.

Near the entrance is a giant fish tank. A beautiful mermaid with long blond curly hair and a fishtail cavorts and water-plays inside, surfacing periodically with a happy smile on her wet face.

The mermaid takes my breath away. I wonder if she's always wanted to be a mermaid and this is her dream job. Or is she working this gig till she gets her big break and lands a role in *Cats*, the Broadway musical, now and forever? I have a vision of diving in and swimming with her, becoming her hot merman lover, and having lots of little minnow babies.

Johnny tugs me into the main room and we hit the dance floor hard. It's jammed with freaky-haired trendazoids writhing and posing: everybody seems to be dancing with everybody. Johnny and Arnolpho do a bump hump hustle grind that's pure arty filthy funk. It's so great to shake it and bake it, dance like the wind, swallowed in the warmth of the undulating crowd, cavorting in the sea of beautiful people.

When it's time for liquids we head to the VIP lounge. The huge bouncer dude recognizes Prince Charming and waves him in. Betsy, Arnolpho, Buddy, and Johnny follow. The huge bouncer dude stops me: clearly I'm not VIP material. But how does he know? Do I exude an unimportant air? Luckily Johnny fetches and hauls me in.

The air really is sweeter in the VIP lounge. People really are prettier. Even I am almost handsome in here. Scattered among the Very Important People sits a vampire with devil rings around his eyes, hell-black hair, death-white skin, and slash-red lips. Vampirellas sit on either side in Madonna-style bullet-bra'd bustiers. The vampirellas kiss the vampire quite violently, biting and sucking hard on lips and tongue with teeth.

Oh my God, there's Andy Warhol! He's standing in the corner, surrounded by a buncha pasty-faced wasters. No, wait a minute. That's not Andy Warhol. It's some guy dressed up like Andy Warhol. Well, I guess if you make art out of a soup can, your look is fair game. And the faux Warhol seems to be doing very well with it. His posse of art wankers are young and nubile in their own emaciated thinking-man's-white-trash way.

A tremendously old wrinkled geezer in a blazer with a nasty comb-over is being propped up by a fabulously handsome fellow in a big flat-brimmed Boy George hat with a tiny T-shirt that says, 'SUPERSTAR.' A thick pug-ugly mope stands behind them in a large square suit. He looks like he could pull out your heart and make you watch it stop beating. They're all facing a pair of Barbie-looking chicks in very short identical silver dresses with straight blonde hair in ponytails coming out of the sides of their heads. One left, one right. Hard to avert my eyes from the four Barbie breasts blazing out from under all that silver. Barbies are telling an animated story. The beautiful Boy George boy is responding with gay animation. Pug-Ugly's face never moves. Wrinkled Geezer's eyes flutter like his pacemaker's giving out.

A white man with a bad haircut in khakis and a tan button-down shirt is playing pocket pool. Kind of a high-strung Subway Vigilante-looking loner. Wouldn't wanna spill a drink on that guy.

In the center of a circle of spectacular, freakish, stork-legged supermodel types stands a leather-clad bleached-white spiky-haired dude who looks like hard-rocking pop star Billy Idol. How fucking perfect is that? Two losers dressed up like celebrities in the same VIP room. Get a look of your own, mother-fucker!

Wait a minute, upon closer inspection, it *is* Billy Idol. 'Rebel Yell.' 'White Wedding.' He's got that Billy Idol fuck-you sneer smeared across his thick rich Brit lips. He's a big fat star. A Very *Very* Important Person. Wait a minute, *is it* Billy Idol? I wanna ask Johnny if she thinks that's really him, but I don't want to seem like a dweeb, so I don't.

Arnolpho materializes, holding six long flutes of lip-tickling ain't-life-a-gas champagne, and says with a little grin:

'I'd like to propose a toast.'

We all murmur in wicked anticipation.

'To cocks that accident'lly pop out.'

We laugh as we toast:

'To cocks that accidentally pop out.'

It's fun watching people check out Prince Charming, his exquisite cheekbones, and his blondy lion mane. Andy Warhol Wannabe sees him, scans past, then snaps his head back to stare at Prince Charming with a combination of puppy love and doggy lust. One of the Barbies whispers into the ear of the other Barbie, then they swing their identical heads in beautiful unison and stare right at Prince Charming. No bones about it. They nod at the same speed in undisguised admiration.

And yet Prince Charming doesn't even seem aware of it. How can he be so unstuckup? His arm drapes naturally around Betsy's shoulder, and she leans in gently on his big broad chest. It must be hard to be the girlfriend of Prince Charming, a dude so beautiful that everybody wants to have sex with him. But Betsy seems so nice and sweet and easy with it. They look perfect together.

Somewhere in the depth of the evening we adjourn to 69 Fifth Avenue, where Arnolopho lives with Buddy in his spectacular postmodern skyscraper pad. The night is a blur of fairy dust and champagne, chocolate-covered strawberries, Cole Porter, Chaka Khan, Astrud Gilberto, and some fine, hard laughs. And suddenly the sun's first pink peeks its cheek across the skyline.

Lounging on the terrace, looking out at Manhattan in the dawn's early light, Arnolpho chops out six long white cocaine rails, and as we greet the day, all is right with the world.

CHAPTER 18
PRETTY PETER ENVY

As many times as I come and go through Times Square I never get tired of the wonderful juxtaposition of cultures in the Deuce: the electronic shops and mom'n'pop cobblers that have been there since the forties, the T-shirt emporiums and the billboards of the stars under the screaming neon marquees, *La Cage aux Folles* meets *Rambo* meets *Rambone*, the society dames rubbing whatevers with the seedy junk-blow-weed-whatever-ya-need dealers, while the glorious whores on Seventh Avenue stroll past the sightseer families huddling together in their I♥NY T-shirts trying not to get mugged while they figure out how to get tickets for *Cats*, now and forever. In 1985, as far as I'm concerned, there was nowhere more American, and I loved every square inch of Times Square. It's different now that they've Disneyfied and Starbucked it up. But back in the day, there was still grit and funk in the beating heart of the city that never sleeps.

I walk past Show World, the Carnegie Hall of adult film and performance. I'm happily headed to a callback for an audition where I could make excellent $ acting in a telephone commercial. No, it's not gonna make me into a star, but at least I'm a professional actor guy.

Suddenly, as I turn onto Broadway, everything changes. There, staring at me mockingly, is a fifty-foot-tall

PRETTY PETER

He's smoldering on a huge billboard in a crème de la crème hotter-than-hot Levi's ad. My jaw drops unconsciously as I'm struck dumb by the enormity of the King Kong-sized Pretty Peter. It's like we're in ancient Greece and he's become an Olympian god, so big it's easy for us mortals to worship at the altar of his beauty.

I simply cannot believe it. Pretty Fucking Peter. The guy whose penis is larger than his IQ, who can't even walk and clap at the same time. This guy is a star? Next thing you know, they'll team him up in an action buddy movie with Eddie Murphy, and he'll be on the cover of *People* magazine, banging Cher.

And I'm going to a callback for a telephone commercial?! Screaming, 'Whatya wannnnnnn-em to do?' to a bunch of drunken Ladies. Getting ignored by Brooke Shields and her people. Getting screamed at by her mom. Not having sex.

I can't stand looking at the fifty-foot-tall Pretty Peter. I can't stop looking at the fifty-foot-tall Pretty Peter.

I am in hell on earth.

The telephone callback evolves into a two-man competition between me and an actor who's on Broadway. To my great amazement I beat him out for the job. He will soon be cast in a TV pilot about four Manhattan ne'er-do-wells. That pilot will become *Seinfeld*, which will become one of the most beloved and lucrative TV shows in the history of the world. It will result in the actor becoming internationally famous and wealthy beyond his wildest dreams.

That actor is Jason Alexander.

But I beat him out for the AT&T commercial.

CHAPTER 19

CALVIN KLEIN IS MUCH HOTTER THAN THE POPE

'Pretty Peter! Bodacious billboard, baby!' Tom Cat congratulates, while Large Mark chimes in:

'Pretty Muthuhfuckin' Peter!'

Pretty Peter struts with the air of a ridiculously handsome man who's just won the lottery. I hate to admit it, but now that he's fifty feet tall on a billboard in Times Square, he looks even hotter. I flash on the fellatio I watched him get in the bathroom. Is there no justice?

It's TGIF night and Chippendales is hophophopping. The Men are in Friday night mode, hustling love and money.

I'm so hoping Nick de Noia's not in the house tonight: I definitely do not need the aggravation.

Speak of the devil. I hear furious angry shouting from the office upstairs. Nick de Noia's voice is prominent.

The door upstairs slams. Everyone in the too-too-crowded dressing room shrinks.

The Snowman heads for the door. Technically he's not supposed to be in the dressing room thirty minutes before or after the show, because it's so ridiculously small in here. But no one ever busts the Snowman, 'cuz he's the man among the Men of Chippendales. But this is just the sort of thing that Nick loves: reaming somebody when he's steamed.

The shitty rickety spiral staircase shakes as Nick pounds down it. When he sees the Snowman, he bellows and screeches, digging in his claws and fangs:

'Helloooooooo?! What the fuck are you doing in here before the show?'

'Uh . . . well, I was just . . . ,' the Snowman whimpers in full apology mode.

'I asked you.' Nick's voice sounds like a tightening noose. 'What the fuck you're doing in here before the show?'

'Sorry, Nick . . .' Strange to see the Snowman all contrite and submissive. Strange, but really fun.

'Do you want to get fired?' Nick demands, looking for a fight. 'Are you asking me to fire you?'

'No. Sorry, Nick, it'll never happen again.'

Nick shoots death daggers at the Snowman, who tries to hide behind his mustache.

'Get the hell outta my sight,' Nick spits.

The Snowman breathes relief and leaves.

'This is a very important night,' Nick de Noia continues holding court. 'Several good friends have decided to join us this evening. The first is one of the most powerful men in the business, Robert Wayne. He's a faaaaaaabulous agent, he has a wonderful eye for talent, and he can make a career. The second friend needs no introduction, but in case you want one, Calvin Klein is here tonight, in the flesh!' Nick de Noia is star-fuckingly tickled pink as an overexcited murmur circulates among the Men.

'Needless to say,' Nick continues, 'I expect perfection. I want these Ladies to go crazy tonight. Crazy! I want champagne kisses and hot buttered buns. Helloooooooooooo?!'

Nick makes a big crazy face as a tension-packed laugh follows his last syllable.

And suddenly Nick de Noia is gone.

I duck into the costume room and throw Johnny a silent hello. She shakes her curls and shrugs like Alice after she's lived in Wonderland too long:

'Calvin Fuckin' Klein.'

I chuckle:

'Pretty Fuckin' Peter.'

'Didjoo see it?' she asks.

'I almost lost my lunch,' I reply.

'Shit is fucked up,' Johnny shrugs as she goes back to work.

'Shit is fucked up,' I agree as I go about shedding my street clothes and slipping on my tux and wheels.

Robert Wayne and Calvin Klein are here tonight. Robert Wayne is a career maker. And Calvin Klein is only slightly less famous than the pope. No, actually, the pope's had a bad year; Calvin Klein is much hotter than the pope. This is my moment. I'm gonna go out there and make all those rich bitches understand that David Henry Scary is the master Master of Ceremonies. I will force them to make me a star.

CHAPTER 20

THE GRAND, EXALTED, GLORIOUS, MAGNIFICENT, HIGH EMPEROR

There are times when it seems a man can do no wrong. Tonight is that for me. Everything's moving in slow motion and I'm one step ahead. Chippendales is jammed, the crowd is bitch-in-heat hot, and I am having the show of my life.

When I introduce the Construction Guy as Chippendales's answer to Don Johnson, it gets a medium jolt outta the Ladies, but nothing to write home about. I only used the Don Johnson reference because the Construction Guy assured me that he'd cleared it with Nick and insisted that it was crucial to the success of his act, especially with the low-quality rose he waved under my nose with much disgust.

Miraculously, Slick Rick's prick does not make a great escape from its G-stringed confines tonight. As far as I know, there was no fallout from his 'accidental' phallus flashing episode – which only fuels the Slick-Rick-as-Nick's-butt-boy fire.

I do all my new improv bits, culminating with Large Mark and Tom Cat pretending to work me over, then dragging me all over the red floor of the Pit.

When I look up at Crazy Eddie, he flashes a redheaded, freckled, party-hearty thumbs-up. Me and Crazy Eddie are having a blast. It's INSAAAAAAAAANE!

At the end of the show, when Nick de Noia stands in the crow's nest like the Grand, Exalted, Glorious, Magnificent, High Emperor of Chippendales and I trumpet his genius, he beams down at me from on high and gives me a nod that I'm sure means he's convinced Robert Wayne to pluck me up from the Pit and make me into a big shining star.

The dressing room is wet and wild, as a jocular joie de vivre sweeps through the Men. Prince Charming's ribs bleed red from where some bachelorette clawed him, but that doesn't stop him from stacking and counting his $.

The dressing room door opens, and 'Thriller' gets louder. The door shuts, and 'Thriller' gets quiet again. An icy chill freezes my bones, blood, and balls, as the sound of scared silence falls with a pall. Yes, Hurricane Nick has landed, with winds up to 100 miles an hour and tidal waves 30 feet high. Looking for a shelter in the storm I slip-slide right through into the costume room, where Johnny sorts soggy sloppy G-strings.

Footsteps head this way, as panic rises inside: nowhere to run or hide. Johnny and I brace for the deluge.

Nick enters the costume room in a fabulous mauve suit with rage firing wild in his eyes.

Johnny is really going to catch some heavy heavy shit tonight. I feel so bad for her, but there's nothing I can do.

'What the hell is going on here?' Nick de Noia demands, fixing me with his fury.

Wait a minute: me? That can't be right. I'm not sure if I should answer this question. So I don't.

'Who the hell told you to call the Construction Guy Don Johnson?' he asks, as an angry vein pops up on his tan neck.

I'm so paralyzed by his fury that my mind freezes on this thought: This is one angry dude.

'Helloooooooo?! Who told you to call the Construction Guy Don Johnson?' Nick is at maximum exasperation. Enter at your own risk.

This time I'm able to focus on Nick's question, and I breathe a sigh of most intense relief. I have a get-out-of-jail-free card. The Construction Guy signed off on the Don Johnson thing. Right here in this very room. And I have a witness: Johnny, the lovely and talented costume mistress herself.

'I'm sorry, Nick,' I say, though I'm not really sorry at all. 'He said he cleared that with you.'

'He **what?!**' Nick de Noia explodes.

'Yeah, that's right,' Johnny, God love her, corroborates my claim. 'I heard him. David even asked him if he was sure you knew, and he said you did.'

'Don Johnson? Helloooooooo?! He looks as much like Don Fucking Johnson as my mother.' Nick seethes. 'It's an embarrassment. There's nothing Folies Bergère about Don Fucking Johnson.' Nick de Noia shakes his head at the sheer magnitude of the violation.

A deep sigh, and Nick instantly morphs into a sane, sensible, handsome, well-put-together fellow. Then he says:

'I loved the improv you did tonight David. It's *really* fun.' When Nick flashes me that jolt of charming smile, I emotionally salivate, dog to his Pavlov, and sigh like his love puppy:

'Thanks, Nick.'

Behind him, Johnny lampoons my toadyism with a smarmy face.

'Why don't you come up to the VIP when you've changed and I'll introduce you to Robert Wayne.' Nick de Noia puts his hand on my arm like I'm family. At that moment I would follow this man through the gates of hell.

'Thanks, I will,' I beam.

Then Nick de Noia is gone.

Johnny mocks me as she mimics:

'Thanks, I will.'

'Am I *that* pitiful?' I ask.

'Yes, you are *that* pitiful,' she answers with good-natured sweetness. 'But consider the source: Little Miss Pitiful herself.' Johnny does a funny little curtsy, which is interrupted by an eruption from the dressing room.

'Don **FUCKING** Johnson?!' I hear Nick scream, 'Helloooooooooo?! Who the hell told you to say that? What the hell is wrong with you?'

The Construction Guy does not reply. What do you say to that?

'Who the hell do you think you are, fucking with my show?' Nick bellows.

The Construction Guy mumbles.

'No, no, no. Don't give me that shit. David said you told him you cleared it with me, so don't try to weasel your way out of this. I want an explanation, and I want one now!'

The Construction Guy mutters.

'And your ass is fat, mister. I told you to do something about that bubble butt, didn't I? Well, didn't I?'

The Construction Guy whines.

'Well, you're FIRED!' Nick says loud, cold, and hard. 'That's right. You're FIRED. I never wanna see that fat ass in my club again.'

Silence.

The door opens and music enters. Door closes and music stops.

And thus Nick de Noia chews up and spits out another Man.

CHAPTER 21

GIRAFFE, KABUKI, AND PINK PUG

The VIP lounge is awash with $ and tits and drugs and asses. Pretty Peter emerges from the bathroom looking well fucked. He's spectacular in his civvies. Unlike Prince Charming, he seems constantly and intensely aware of his own beauty. A tiny Asian spinner follows him out of the bathroom with cat-black bangs in the middle of a round brown face, a ho-red minidress and majestically long spike heels. No expression is on her Kabuki face. She's followed by a giraffe of a chick with hair piled high on her head and legs up to her neck. I have a vision of Giraffe and Kabuki doing some stand-up sixty-nine. What a sight that would be! Then you put Pretty Peter into the mix, well, the mind boggles. He does a victory lap with his mini and maxi babes, getting much love and looking like a man god in his Levi's.

Slick Rick is being madly chatted up by a very Lawng G'Islandy couple with leathery tans and hard hair, wearing a ton and a half of gold. The wife's titties are blasting out of the gold blouse she's stuffed into. The husband looks like he swallowed a bowling ball. Are they trying to have a three-way with Slick Rick?

Wait a minute, there's Nick, flirting and flitting through the crowd of Very Important People. His pink lips land in Slick Rick's black ear and whisper in it while his hand lands over Slick's heart. Slick Rick's mouth pops open, like he can't believe how exciting this news is.

The Leathery Tans are excited by all this excitement, even though they have no idea why.

Slick Rick apologizes to them politely then hightails it after Nick de Noia. The Leathery Tans drink in Slick Rick's fantabulous ass with sexual envy, look at each other and nod salaciously: Man, I'd like me some of that.

Slick Rick heads hard for the door and exits solo. Clearly, Nick has sent him on some terribly important mission.

I follow Nick, who joins an impeccably dressed, immaculately groomed, plump pink pug of a man. They whisper excitedly as they touch each other. Pink Pug makes a crazy face of surprise and saucy naughtiness. He looks familiar, but I can't quite place him. He and Nick chitchat for some time, like aristocrats gossiping wickedly in the royal court about what time the peasant will be getting his head cut off tomorrow.

Hold the phone: That's Robert Wayne! Those little pink lips and beady canine eyes, the twitchy little manicured paws, the big hanging jowls. Robert Fucking Wayne: the man, the myth, the legend. Thick as thieves with Nick de Noia.

Pause in the conversation. Wayne points his white pug paw while he nods his head, desire radiating out of him.

I follow his eyes as Nick de Noia discreetly points to confirm the object of Robert Wayne's desire:

Large Mark, truly huge in baggy white tank top and thin black stretch pants with piping down the side of either leg. His hair is a puffed-up wave. How he gets it to stay there, like it's perpetually about to break, I'll never know. He's in a very animated conversation with Tom Cat. They're entertaining two stacked-to-the-max Brooklyny babes in pink puffy numbers that look like they were bridesmaid's dresses at the wedding from hell. How gigantic their hair is! How huge their breasts! The thought of bagging Large Mark and Tom Cat, these gorgeous specimens of Chippendales manhood, seems to have them positively giddy.

I sidle over slyly and park myself behind two fat guys in Hawaiian shirts, so I can watch the festivities unfold and present myself to Robert Wayne at exactly the right moment.

Nick cruises over to Large Mark and exchanges a fanciful greeting. Large disentangles himself from Cat and the Puffy Pink sisters and Nick leads him like a large pet at the heels of his master.

When they arrive back at Robert Wayne, Nick de Noia introduces Large Mark with a jaunty nod and a genteel gesture:

'May I present the one and only Robert Wayne. Robert, this is Mark.'

Large Mark towers over Wayne, twice as tall and dense. Looks like he could pick Wayne up with one huge hand and snap him in half. Wayne's pug shoulders slouch under a tailored gold-buttoned blue jacket that appears very expensive. Large Mark's prehistoric shoulders are displayed under a white wife-beater tank top that looks very cheap.

Robert Wayne looks Large Mark up and down like a giant rump roast he'd love to feast on, all-you-can-eat-style.

It looks like being made into an object of lust by this man makes Large Mark very very uncomfortable.

Robert Wayne takes a small mincing step toward Large Mark, who frowns and holds his ground. Wayne takes his delicate well-manicured hand and places it on Large Mark's mammoth arm, with unmistakable sexual intent.

Quick as a crocodile snaring an old slow yak, Large Mark snatches Wayne's limp little wrist, and it disappears in his massive mitt. Large Mark twists and squeezes, and Wayne goes limp. Looks like if Large lets go, Wayne would crumble to the floor.

'Don't fuckin' touch me!' Large Mark barks, eyes full of 'roidful venom and homo-hating rage.

Robert Wayne wears a face that's a queer mixture of pain, submission, shock, fear, lust, and schoolgirl crush.

Nick looks, for once, like he doesn't know what the hell to say.

Large Mark gives Robert Wayne's thin wrist one final twist, which makes this painful sound escape:

'Oooomph!'

'Fuckin' faggot!' Large Mark hisses hatefully. Then he drops Robert Wayne's wrist and storms off.

Wayne looks like he doesn't know whether to piss himself, scream bloody murder, or cum.

Large Mark walks back to Tom Cat and, leaning in, says a few sharp words. They grab the Puffy Pink sisters and bomb out of the VIP lounge.

Robert Wayne pulls himself together and whispers something that seems disparaging to Nick de Noia, who looks pissed off.

Somehow I feel this is not the best time to make my move. But if not now, when? Fuck it, I'm going in. I don't care. All I've got to lose is my dignity, and that's long gone.

Just as I'm sliding by the two fat Hawaiian shirts, Robert Wayne shakes his head, leans in to Nick de Noia, and together they exit, leaving a trail of Very Important People in their wake.

I follow Nick de Noia and Robert Wayne all the way through Chippendales like I'm a detective in a thriller. But when they blast right out the front door, I lose them, and they're gone, taking my shot at stardom with them.

I really want some blow.

CHAPTER 22

A FAG'S FAG

Back in the dressing room, Large Mark and Tom Cat are hanging with the Puffy Pink sisters. It's strictly against the rules to have Ladies in the dressing room. I wonder if Nick de Noia would fire them if he caught them. I wonder what the fallout will be for Large Mark hate-criming Robert Wayne.

For several weeks I will investigate the consequences of this incident, but as far as I know, Large Mark was never punished for his violent homophobic outburst in response to Robert Wayne's sexual harassment. But then, punishment often seemed so random and arbitrary at Chippendales.

Large Mark and Tom Cat do not acknowledge my presence. Nor do the Puffy Pink sisters. Apparently my cloak of invisibility has lowered again. I check in the cramped bathroom to see if the Snowman is getting fellatio from at least one raving beauty, if not a bevy.

I peek my head in, but there's no head going on in the head.

I poke my nose into the costume room, but Johnny has flown the coop.

'So, ya know who's upstai's?' Large Mark asks.

'No,' the Puffy Pink sisters say, extra excited to be here, with Large Mark and Tom Cat, in the inner sanctum of Chippendales. They speak in one thick nasally Brooklyny voice, apparently sharing one brain. 'Who?'

'Slick Rick, the Waiter Guy from the show,' says Tom Cat, 'and Calvin Klein.'

'No shit!' the sisters pinkly scream.

'No shit!' Tom Cat and Large Mark say at exactly the same time, as if they've rehearsed it many times.

Is that really true? Or is this just Large and Cat playing more badboy mindfuck games?

'Calvin's a majuh fag, ya know,' says Large Mark.

'And you know who else is up there, behind closed doors, with Slick Rick the dick licker, and Calvin Klein, the major fag?' asks Tom Cat.

The Puffy Pink sisters say with wide eyes:

'No.'

'No. Body.' Large Mark fills the words with loads of homosexual undertone.

'Nobody,' confirms Tom Cat. 'And you know what that means?'

Large and Cat mime holding erect penises near their own open mouths and pretend to move the imaginary dicks in and out, while thrusting their tongues into their cheeks in time with the fake phallic thrusts, creating a wonderfully lifelike illusion of fellatio.

The Puffy Pink sisters giggle like this is the very height of comedy. Then they say:

'Is Calvin Klein really . . . a fag?'

'Majuh fag,' says Large Mark.

'Huge fag,' finishes Tom Cat. 'The man's a fag's fag.'

I have no idea whether Calvin is gay or straight or whatever. Unless he wants to have sex with me, I don't see how it's any of my business. This is just what I heard. What these Men said.

Just then, Slick Rick walks out of the upstairs office and descends the spiral staircase. All eyes are upon him, as he lands on the dressing room floor, looking troubled.

'I hope you got it in writing,' Tom Cat wisecracks.

Slick Rick stops and stares, disoriented. Then he combatively demands, like he's ready to rumble:

'What the fuck are you talkin' about?'

'When Calvin promised to put you in one of his ads, I hope you got it in writing before you let him bend you over the desk and play hide the salami.' Tom Cat goads hard, clearly going for Slick Rick's jugular.

'What the FUCK are you talking about?' Slick Rick's whole body flexes and tenses. Seems like he knows exactly what they're talking about. And it's really pissing him off.

'We're just hopin', for your sake, that you got some kind of written guarantee before you let him blow his load down your throat.' Tom Cat addresses Slick Rick like he's deeply concerned. No, actually, he's more like a person making a mockery of someone who's deeply concerned.

'An' we wuh curious if ya swallowed,' Large Mark says matter-of-factly, like he's wondering whether a cup of coffee is decaf or regular.

The Puffy Pink sisters are beside themselves, desperately

trying not to laugh and looking extremely excited by all the testosterone bombing around the dressing room.

'Fuck you,' spits Slick Rick. 'Nothing happened.'

He looks totally convincing. And I have no evidence, or reason to believe that Mr Klein and Slick had sex, or that Mr K ever exchanged sex for favors. It just seemed like Large and Cat trying to get Slick's goat.

'Cocksuckin', buttbangin', assmunchin', that doesn't sound like nothing to me,' Tom Cat says to Large Mark and the pink girls. 'Does that sound like nothing to you?'

They all shake their huge-haired heads while answering variations of:

'Nope.'

'No way.'

'Don't sound like nuthin' to me.'

Slick Rick looks like he'd love nothing more than to shove his fist right down Large Mark's big bloated neck and put his trendy-booted foot right up Tom Cat's hot tight ass. But it's controlled fury. He sees what they're doing, pressing on his exposed nerve, trying to get him to make the first move so they can defend themselves and kick his ass all over the dressing room, out onto First Avenue and into the East River. The anger looks like it's choking Slick Rick's black throat, where veins flood with blood. He's dark and dangerous, like he's about to either ex or im plode. He takes a deep breath, steels himself, and in a low, dangerous voice says:

'Nothing happened up there. Now get the fuck outta my way.'

Large Mark makes no move to get the fuck outta Slick Rick's way.

The air, already dank with locker room stink, is so thick it's hard to breathe. As the boiling point is reached, and trouble bubbles to the top of the pot, in struts the Snowman, sapphire eyes shining, all attitude all the time. Immediately he senses tension and says:

'What are you girls up to?'

It's funny how he addresses the question to Large, Cat, and Slick, and not the Puffy Pink girls, who are the only people in the room with vaginas.

'Well,' says Tom Cat, 'we were just asking Slick Rick about his suckfuck fest with Calvin Klein upstairs.'

The Snowman nods, totally up for torturing Slick Rick.

'Did he swallow?' the Snowman asks very serious, like he's a reporter trying to set the record straight.

'Fuck you,' Slick Rick says violently. 'Fuck all of you.'

Suddenly I'm glad I'm invisible.

Slick Rick picks up a small vase full of flowers and throws it as hard as he can toward Large Mark's head. Large doesn't even move, as the vase shatters right above his head, red flowers flying, blue glass shattering, and water splattering.

One Puffy Pink sister screams:

'Ahhhhhhhhhhhh!!!'

This makes the other shriek:

'Ahhhhhhhhhhhh!!!'

Large, Cat, and the Snowman go from stunned astonishment to staring at the Puffy Pink sisters, who stop screaming and shrieking at the same time.

The Barbarian opens the door with surprised eyes:

'What the fuck's goin' on in here?'

Slick Rick takes this opportunity to crash past everyone, and he blows through the door, slamming it shut so hard that the shitty spiral staircase rattles.

'Nuthin' . . .'

'It's cool . . .'

'Just a little flower accident.'

The Barbarian shrugs, grunts, and leaves.

Large Mark brushes a flower from his hair and steps away from the shattered glass. The Puffy Pink sisters look embarrassed by their outburst. Everyone seems to want to carry on like nothing weird just happened. Fine with me, I've been doing that for years.

Tom Cat addresses the Snowman:

'Hear you got reamed real good by our fearless leader tonight.'

The Snowman shakes his pornstar mustache ruefully:

'One of these days I'm gonna rip that cocksucker's head off and shit right down his neck.'

The Snowman gets a big laugh outta the group, and the pink girls turn pinker.

This is the second time I've heard someone indicate they'd like to kill Nick de Noia.

'I'm so fuckin' pissed at dat assmunch.' Large Mark's fist clenches. 'Up in the VIP jus' now, 'e tried ta pimp me out ta one of 'is faggot-fuckin' butt buddies. I sweah ta God, I'm gonna pull 'is eyebawlls out an' skullfuck da bitch.'

More laughter.

This is the third time I've heard someone indicate they'd like to kill Nick de Noia. It's the first time necrophilia has been involved.

'Hey, we could have a skullfuck gangbang!' Tom Cat looks pleased with the big laugh he gets.

This is the fourth time I've heard someone indicate they'd like to kill Nick de Noia.

And the second time I've heard necrophilia suggested.

CHAPTER 23

THOSE FAKE TITS LOOK PAINFUL

After the laughter dies I can't take it anymore, so I slither outta the dressing room unnoticed. Only one place to go now:

Crazy Eddie's.

Strolling through the packed masses, I'm puzzled by Janet Jackson. There she is, on the video screen, twenty feet tall, grabbing her vagina and singing about how nasty she is. I wonder if she's *really* nasty or if she just wants to be nasty because it's the only way she could get some attention in the Jackson household. She kinda looks like she's only *pretending* to be nasty on the video. She hasn't yet had her breast exposed during the Super Bowl, but she will.

Suddenly I'm climbing the steps leading up to the DJ booth, desperate for a jolt of Crazy Eddie's redheaded devilmay-careness.

In Crazy Eddieville, Prince Charming and Betsy are hanging

with an unidentified woman with an excess of flesh stuffed into a sleeveless black-and-white-striped dress. Tits, jowls, throat wattle, and chubby cheek flesh flap everywhere as she wiggles and jiggles to Madonna's 'Material Girl.'

When I finally tear my eyes away from this fleshy spectacle, I take in the Charmings. Wait a second, something's different about Betsy. What is it? I scan up, scan down. There it is: Her breasts are much bigger than they were the last time I saw them. Can that be right? I try to study them without staring, which is just as hard as it sounds. No, they're definitely bigger. Like twice as big. They look weird, hard, and mannequinish, like you could chip a tooth on them. I wonder if they would look weird if I didn't know they were fake. Hard to say. But they sure look weird now. I just can't wrap my mind around why she would want to have silicone sacks surgically inserted in her breasts. It's not like there was anything wrong with them to begin with. I never saw them disrobed, but in her clothes they seemed extremely nice.

I flash back to the troll agent telling me I hadda get cosmetic surgery. Where was Barbra Streisand when Betsy needed her? Jeez, this whole fake-tit thing is really fucking with me.

'Hey, it's the mouth that roars!' Crazy Eddie shouts in his filthy-cigarette-butt-filled-ashtray voice. With all that red in his hair, face, eyes, and freckles, the man is a vision in crimson.

'Hey dude, what's goin' on?' I ask.

'Partyallthetime motherfucker! Par-tay!' he salutes me with his glass full of alcohol, which he merrily chug-a-lugs.

I smile at Prince Charming and Betsy:

'Hey you guys, how's your night?'

'Excellent,' Prince Charming answers with a nod of his gorgeous head.

'Good,' Betsy says with a sweet smile. 'I loved what you did in the show tonight. That whole smoke thing was so cool. Did you just ad-lib that?'

Wow, I like Betsy even more now that's she's complimenting me. I feel bad that she got implants. She seems like such a nice person.

I wait for someone to introduce me to Material Girl, who seems to be in her own little Material World.

No one does.

'Hey man,' Crazy Eddie shouts like a rusty hinge, 'didja hear Slick Rick let Calvin Klein blow him tonight?'

I don't know how to respond to that. I don't think they actually did have sex, and I wanna defend Slick Rick because I hate how all the vicious gossipmongers pick on him. However, I don't want to embarrass Crazy Eddie, because I like him so much and he makes me so happy.

So I say nothing.

Material Girl's fat face beams and her flesh wobbles as she expresses her excitement:

'That is so awesome. Calvin Klein giving somebody a blowjob right here in the club. That is totally totally awesome.' She takes a step toward Prince Charming and makes a flirty face while pointing her mammoth tits at him. 'I mean, Calvin Klein, don't you think it's awesome?'

Prince Charming doesn't react in any way to all this sexual energy flooding at him. He just smiles benignly and blondly, like the Jedi knight of male strippers.

But Betsy is not so calm. Her jaw sets, she shoots Material Girl a withering look with a proprietary blast of get-the-fuck-away-from-my-man. It's completely lost on Material Girl. Betsy presses into Prince Charming, need and pleading written in the language of her body. Those new fake tits look painful.

Material Girl backs off and retracts her gunboats.

Betsy's implants suddenly make a lot more sense.

Crazy Eddie performs his magical sleight of hand and suddenly the bratty ratty Beastie Boys boom about fighting for your right to party.

A burst of collectively unconscious madness is released from the crowd on the dance floor and bursts into the universe, as Crazy Eddie, artist-alchemist, turns the crowd into a golden mass of happy partiers.

'CALVIN FUCKING KLEIN!' Crazy Eddie shouts loud. 'Can't you just see that billionaire gagging on Slick Rick's big black cock?' Crazy rasps a loud and hearty Falstaff laugh that rattles around the DJ booth and makes you glad to be alive. 'Hey, what the fuck, why not? I'd let somebody gobble my knob to get rich and famous. I say, more power to him, the slick fucker.'

Why the fuck not, indeed?

CHAPTER 24

MELANCHOLY'S MOUTH

Loaded, I walk by the back bar. A polyester blue woman stops me. She's maybe twenty-five, with a flippy outtadate do. I smell alcohol, but she doesn't seem too drunk. Just drunk enough. She's pudgy but not fat. Her dress is short – too short, judging by the way she keeps tugging it down. Makeup sits like layers of pound cake on her face. She seems to have remarkably small breasts for someone so large. A sweet melancholy hangs about her and softens my heart before she's even said a word.

'Uh . . .' she starts, then seems to lose her nerve. She exudes a vulnerable shy insecurity. Even though I'm not remotely attracted to her, I think I can maybe convince her to have some intercourse with me.

'What's up?' I ask, with what I hope is a sweet smile.

'Well, uhm, you're the emcee guy, right? On the roller skates?' Melancholy is so tentative and adorable.

Could this be the groupie I've been waiting for since I started working at Chippendales Male Strip Club? My heart pumps blood faster.

'Yes,' I say, 'I'm the master of ceremonies.'

'Well, uhm . . . ,' she hesitates again, like this is really hard for her.

Yes, of course you can have sex with me, I think, as I look into her watery eyes with sensitive thoughtfulness and say:

'What can I do for ya?'

'Well . . . ,' she says.

'Yes,' I say. Yes, you can have me. Yes, we can go to my place, or your place, or to one of the bathrooms, if you like; they're very popular places to have sex here at Chippendales, yes I say, yesyesyes.

Finally Melancholy continues:

'I'd really like to meet that guy who's on the billboard, you know, in Times Square. He's so . . . and I'd really like to meet him. And, uh . . . I thought maybe you could introduce me. I mean, I don't . . . well, it's not like . . . I'm sorry, I'm a little nervous, but I'd be willing to give you, uh . . . a blowjob, if you'd introduce me to him. I don't want you to get the wrong idea about me, I've never done anything like this before. But I just think he's so cute, and I'm too . . . I mean I think he looks really sweet and I'd really love to meet him . . . See, I'm kinda shy, and my friends keep telling me that if you want something, you should just go for it. So . . . I'm just going for it.'

My mind reels. A blowjob to meet Pretty Peter? Just when you think you've seen everything there is to see at Chippendales, BOOM! it knocks you flat on yer ass.

Actually I *would* like a blowjob. I enjoy blowjobs very much.

But my God! Pretty Peter looks *sweet*? Handsome, hot, hunky? Sure. But *sweet*? What happened to this poor girl? I wanna tell her I don't think offering a blowjob to a man you've never met so you can get introduced to a gorgeous brain-dead asshole is what your friends had in mind when they told you to 'go for it.' And if it is, you need some new friends, girl. And why me? What is it about me that screams: here's a man who'd happily exchange a blowjob for an introduction to a hot model who can't chew gum and think at the same time?

After all that, here's what I say to Melancholy:

'Sure, that sounds cool . . .'

It's all quiet in the dressing room, so I slide Melancholy right on in. As I walk to the bathroom door, I think, Wouldn't it be funny if Pretty Peter were already in there getting head? Would she still blow me so she could then blow him? Has oral sex always been this popular? Have blowjobs become a new form of currency in the 80s? I'll trade you two blowjobs for an oil change and a 'Frankie Says Relax' T-shirt.

I knock on the bathroom door. No reply. I crack it as my heart bangs like it's gonna bust right outta my chest. The bathroom is small and empty. We enter, and I shut us in.

In defiance of Chippendales custom, I lock the door. I guide her so she's sitting down. I unzip and extract myself, already stiffening in anticipation. I close my eyes and a hardness fills me as I hear a sleazeball baritone Loverstudguy voice in my head:

Oh yeah, baby, you love it, don't you, baby? Come on, baby, give it to me. Oh yeah, baby, you love it, don't you?

Melancholy tentatively sucks, like a baby getting used to a bottle.

OHHHHHHHHH!!! my pleasure center moans. I forgot how great blowjobs are. I've *gotta* do this more often.

My pelvis, acting without authorization, now pumps hard toward the back of Melancholy's head. I don't think: Now, I'm going to pump hard. My pelvis just goes all Elvis. Melancholy's not ready for it, so I slide all the way to the back of her mouth and several inches down her throat. This has two immediate consequences:

(1)   Her gag reflex is activated.
(2)   Her teeth scrape painfully upon my penis.

OWWWWWWWW!!! my poor dick yowls, as it deflates, blood draining away at an alarming rate, while my eyes slam open.

Melancholy retches. Oh my God, she's gonna puke on my penis. She coughs a few times, tries to clear her throat miserably, then starts crying.

BAM! I flash back with a sickening thud to ten years earlier, as an unholy self-loathing spreads from the inside out, and I see the bony face of a damned woman, who'd been battered in some unspeakable way. She wants me to help her, but I can't, I'm limp, and dread fills me past capacity.

BAM! I'm back in the bathroom at Chippendales, shaking, can't breathe, I think I may fall over, it's too hot in here, no air. I bend at the waist, hands on knees, trying desperately to do the most basic thing a human needs to survive:

BREATHE.

I find Melancholy's face. Her sad swollen eyes stream tears mixed with mascara, a black river of sorrow rolling down her round face. Saliva, snot, and cock juice dribble on her lips, as snooge runs from her nose.

This gives my brain something to focus on besides how I'm flooding myself with horror. Ah, there it is: air, glorious air! What a blessed relief. My first thought: Man, we really take this whole breathing thing for granted, don't we? I do a quick inventory. My penis is red and angry, looking exhausted and worn out, but no skin is broken. I impotently put it away.

I refocus on Melancholy. Her face is splotched and mottled with sad, shameful regret. I look into her raccoon eyes, but she looks away, buries her face in the cradle of her hands, and sobs, shaking with ache that emanates from some fountain of sorrow all the way inside.

I wish I could be one of these guys who doesn't give a shit. I wish I could tell her to shut the fuck up and suck it, a deal's a deal, can the malarkey and do the deed. But I can't.

I zip up and squat down on my haunches so Melancholy and I are eye to eye. I lightly touch her hand, which is covering her crying eyes. She jumps a little, not expecting the contact. She pulls back and looks at me like a baby bird who's fallen from the nest, can't find its mother, and sees danger everywhere.

Damn. What happened to her?

'I'm sorry,' I say. 'I didn't mean to . . .' I don't quite know how to finish that sentence, but I try to reassure her with a nice smile.

Her face changes from frightened to sad to relieved to eased. Her crying stops, she sniffs in some snot, and says:

'No, I'm sorry, I don't know what I was . . .'

Quite a pair we are: Inarticulate and Incoherent.

'If you still want me to introduce you, I will,' I say, 'but I should tell you, he's not a very nice person.'

'Really?' she asks skeptically.

'Really. He's as dumb as a sack of axes, and he's always having sex with women and then walking away like he owes them money, which he usually does.'

'Really?' she asks, not convinced but listening.

'Really.' I answer like there's no room for doubt. 'Look, I know he's hot and he's pretty and he's on billboards everywhere, but he's not a basket you wanna be putting your eggs into.'

Melancholy sighs, and I can hear the wheels grinding inside her head. Finally, as some kind of resolution seems to settle in her, she nods, and says:

'OK . . . Do you want me to finish the blowjob? 'Cuz . . .'

Melancholy really seems like a sweet person. Or a self-punishing idiot. Or both.

Either way, my sexual appetite has completely disappeared.

'No,' I say, 'That's OK. Are you all right?'

'Yeah.' Melancholy smiles sadly. 'Thanks.'

I hand her a wad of tissue. She blows a big ol' load of snot into it, stands, and flushes it down.

'I think I'm just gonna go home,' she says.

'OK,' I say.

'Sorry,' she says.

'Me, too,' I reply.

We walk out of the bathroom of the dressing room of Chippendales Male Strip Club and into the rest of our lives, never to lay eyes upon each other again.

CHAPTER 25

NO, *YOU* GET THE FUCK OUTTA HERE

I walk Johnny home many a night. At her crib, we listen to Bessie Smith and Blondie and P-Funk while MTV's on with the sound turned down. We talk about everything. Except having sex with each other. I've got it in my head that I'm gonna wait for her to make the first move, and that is proving to be a very effective method of birth control.

About 2:30 one Friday night/Saturday morning, we somehow manage to get onto the subject of birthdays.

'What month are you?' Johnny asks.

'June,' I say.

'Me, too,' she says.

'When?' I ask.

'June two,' she says. 'And you?'

'Get the fuck outta here.' I'm incredulous.

'What?' Johnny asks.

'When were you born? Seriously,' I ask.

'June second,' she says, like, so what?

'That's *my* birthday,' I say.

'June second?'

'June second.'

'Get the fuck outta here,' says Johnny.

'No, *you* get the fuck outta here,' I reply as I extract my driver's license from my wallet. It's not a bad picture. I look like a cross between a poet and a gunrunner. Date of birth: 6–2–57. Right there in black and white. I hand it to Johnny, and amazement widens her eyes.

Johnny extracts her driver's license and hands it to me. It's a great picture. She looks like a cross between a rock star and a porn star. Date of birth: 6–2–65. Right there in black and white.

'Unfuckingbelievable,' I say.

'Unfuckingbelievable,' she says.

'Gemini,' I say.

'Gemini,' she says.

'The twins,' I say.

'The twins,' she says.

'Unfuckingbelievable,' we say together.

It may seem slightly ridiculous to take this admittedly unlikely coincidence as a sign from the universe that we belong together. And yet, at the time, I am profoundly certain that this is the case.

I know it like I know my birthday, 6–2–57.

When Johnny smiles at me, the same thing seems to beam out of her.

Or maybe I just want it to.

CHAPTER 26

PLUNGING THE NEEDLE INTO THE TENDER CHEEK

I fall in love every night at Chippendales. This evening it's a twenty-fivish Caucasian Diana Ross. Her skin is so white, her eyes so black. She's in a harlot-scarlet Japanese jacket over a tight black skirt out of which slender elegant legs descend. If she were a song she'd be 'My Cherie Amour.' She's so classy, sipping champagne, whispering with her friend, a glam femme fatale. They don't buy one single kiss the whole night. I love her bemused detachment. I want to know where she lives and works and eats. I want to be best friends with her, laugh at this mad spectacle with her. I fall madly in love with My Cherie Amour, and I never say one word to her.

Tonight I have a problem. My sock's got a big ol' hole in it, and I'm getting a bastard of a blister. So I decide to make a quick trip to the dressing room during my break. I'm gonna try to find a bandage and a new sock, urinate and rehydrate, all in nine minutes. So I rush through the Ladies to the dressing room, whip in, and pop my head into the costume room, where Johnny is prepping Prince Charming's number.

'What are you—'

I cut off the surprised Johnny urgently:

'Sock and Band-Aid!'

I love that she doesn't ask me a lot of fool questions, just drops everything and starts searching in bags. While I rip off my skate and the offending sock, she rummages intensely, then presents me with one sock and one Band-Aid. She whips it onto the blister, slides on the new sock, and I slip back into the skate, like a pit crew at the Indy 500 changing a tire.

'Thanks, gotta run.' I knock her a quick airkiss.

'Anytime, big boy,' Johnny smiles and airkisses back.

And off I go, digging her all the more.

Next stop: dressing room bathroom. As I throw open the door, my eyes and mouth pop out and open when I see:

Large Mark, bent over, his black spandex pants at his ankles, bare-naked ass-mooning Tom Cat, who stands behind him with a syringe full of what must be steroids, plunging the needle into the tender cheek of Large's ass.

They turn startled and stare at me.

I stare, startled, back.

'Shut the fuckin' door, man!' Large Mark barks.

'Get the fuck outta here!' Tom Cat hisses.

I'm flabbergasted. I can't take my eyes off Large Mark's ass, exposed and waiting, and Tom Cat, plunging in the spike like a tiny sharp metal cock. I smile as this accidentally comes out of my mouth:

'You guys should just fuck each other and get it over with.'

Red 'roid rage flares as Cat yanks out the spike. Large pulls up his pants and shouts:

'Who you cawlin' a faggot, ya faggot?'

Faced with this violent homo-crazed reaction, I beat a meaty retreat. Cat literally chases me out of the dressing room shouting:

'I'm gonna kick yer faggot ass!'

Luckily I'm quick on my wheels, and I disappear into the big-haired jungle of Chippendales. I shake my amazed head: curiouser and curiouser it gets at Chippendales.

CHAPTER 27

THE SCREAM, AN ANGEL, AND
THE MOOK TRIPLETS

June 2. You say it's your birthday, it's my birthday, too, yeah.
As I walk up to Johnny's marijuana distribution center apartment I can't help but think again that the coincidence of our
having been born on the same day is proof that we are meant
for each other. Or at the very least that we should have some
hot yet sweet birthday sex at some point today.

I knock on her door. No answer. Knock again. Nothing.
I try the knob, and it opens, so I step in. It's shockingly tidy
for being such a stained-carpeted, shoddy-fixtured, peeling-
paint pad. TV's on, with the sound muted. Suddenly I
imagine I'm in a horror movie. Johnny's disemboweled body
is in the bathroom. A mentally ill serial killer in a hockey
mask with a dark secret is waiting for me with a very sharp
sling blade.

'Hello,' I call out.

No answer.

'Helloooooooooo!' I say it just like Nick de Noia: annoyed, excited, and expectant all at the same time.

No answer.

I hear the sound of water coming from the bathroom. Johnny must be in the shower.

Now I'm in another horror movie. Only this time I'm the mentally ill serial killer with the dark secret who preys on babes in showers.

Sensing an opportunity for mischief, I silently slither into the bathroom. Through the shitty opaque plastic shower door I can see the outline of Johnny's naked body soaping up and washing off. My heart pings and skips the occasional beat, and I have to work hard to control my racing breath. I'm so alive and high, and I'm not on any drugs whatsoever.

I inch very close to the shower door, so that when she opens it, I'm gonna be standing right there, staring at her with big crazy eyes.

I can't wait for the moment when she sees me and screams, and the hairs on the back of my neck stand straight up, while a thrill shivers me.

I want the moment to never come. I want to live forever in this delicious anticipation.

The shower sprays: hissing, spitting, hitting Johnny's naked-ness, flowing over it, then down and out the drain.

Johnny turns off the water and wrings the water out of her wet curls. Because I can only see her outline, it's like nude Balinese puppet theater. That makes it even more exciting.

Slooooooooooowly Johnny opens the shitty plastic door. She feels me standing there, and her whole body flinches, then freezes solid.

The scream reflex kicks in, and Johnny lets loose a hair-tightening, toe-curling, corpuscle-curdling cry that comes out of her like a terrified opera singer hitting the high note and holding it.

The actual raising of the hairs on the back of my neck is even more wild and exciting than the fantasy of it was, and I'm delighted by how alive I am.

The instant Johnny stops screaming bloody murder, her face twists from scared-beyond-death, to confused, to what-the-fuck-is-wrong-with-you? Suddenly I know I've done a badbad thing. Suddenly I realize that I should have considered the consequences of my actions before I decided to scare the bejesus outta Johnny like some sick, twisted, psychokiller.

This is confirmed by the furious glare Johnny shoots me while covering her nudity with a towel.

'Oh shit, I'm sorry.' I hope I look like a nice guy feeling deep regret for having played a good-natured though ill-conceived practical joke – as opposed to a sadistic lunatic who might stick a firecracker up your cat's ass, light it, and watch in glee as your kitty explodes in a puff of cat guts and flying fur.

'What the fuck are you doing?' Johnny snaps. I can't tell if she's I'll-forgive-you-soon annoyed or you've-blown-any-chance-you-ever-had-with-me furious.

'I'm really sorry . . . I didn't mean to . . .' I leave the bathroom as fast as I can, and Johnny slams the door behind me. The last I see of her wet face is an exasperated anger that my mind amplifies to staggering proportions. Or maybe there's no exaggeration. I can't tell. My brain just won't stop playing tricks on me.

All of a sudden I'm not having a very good birthday.

Johnny emerges from the bathroom with wet curls, wearing a pair of tight jeans, cuffs at the bottom folded inside out. A big thick studded belt hangs on her swively hips. A Yankees shirt with the collar and bottom ripped off exposes her flat firm belly flesh from below the ribs to the top of her pubic bone. Her lips have an annoyed pissed curl to them.

'Hey,' I say, 'I am really really sorry. You know how sometimes you get an idea that *seems* like a good idea, but then when you do it, it turns out be a really *bad* idea, and you're really sorry for doing it, 'cuz it doesn't reflect your true character, and you swear you'll never do it again? Well, that's the . . . situation here. And, to make up for it, I wanna take you shopping, wherever you want, on your birthday. Furthermore, I'd like to point out that to fuck up is human and to forgive is divine. So really, I've presented you with an opportunity to be divine. And in conclusion, like I said, I'm so so sooooo sorry.'

Johnny shakes her dripping locks while a half smirk works its way onto her face. Her hands plant with sass on her Latin hips and she sighs:

'You're an asshole.'

'I will not deny it, I am an asshole. But I'm an asshole who's saying he's sorry and offering to take you shopping on your birthday, *our* birthday, wherever you want, no questions asked, to make up for being the asshole I am.' I shrug with palms up.

'Anywhere?' Johnny asks.

'Anywhere,' I answer.

Johnny studies me for some time:

Risk. Reward.

Then she shakes her curls, uncurls her lips, half-sneers, half-smiles, sighs, and says:

'OK.'

And suddenly our birthday is back on track.

Imagine my delight, as an American man raised to worship at the cathedral of Yankee Stadium, when Johnny, unprompted, says that she'd love to go see the Yankees play on our birthday.

Pulling up on the 1 train, packed in with all those Yankee-cap-wearing palookas, the sight of the stadium stirs my heart. Kinda the way I imagine an Islamic fellow might feel approaching Mecca, a Catholic the Vatican, a Jew Jerusalem.

'You up for trying to scalp?' I mutter out of my mouth corner like a bootlegging gunrunner.

'Definitely,' Johnny says with an of-course-I-am shrug. A woman after my own heart.

Just as we're about to start the process of illegally purchasing tickets, a man with no distinguishing features materializes in front of us.

'You guys looking for some tickets?' he asks in a voice you could never pick out of a lineup.

His very ordinariness makes me leery. He seems more like an undercover cop than a scalper.

'Uh,' I answer wary, 'possibly.'

'Well.' His run-of-the-mill eyes find mine. 'I have a couple of tickets and my friends can't make it. They're right behind the dugout. Are you interested?'

This guy might as well have 'COP' stenciled across his bland forehead.

'Well,' I say, hedging my bet, 'maybe, but we're not, uh . . .'

'Engaging in any illegal activities,' Johnny chimes in behind me with impeccable timing.

'Oh no,' Mr Generic chuckles blandly. 'I'd like you to be my guests.'

Johnny and I exchange a glance and a shrug.

'Sure, that'd be great,' I say.

'Thanks so much.' Johnny smiles sweet.

I like a person who knows how to say thank you.

Yankee Stadium. June 2. It's a beautiful day for a birthday ballgame! I don't know how it's possible, but the sky is bluer, the grass is greener, and the air is sweeter in Yankee Stadium. Smells like victory. For the uninitiated, sitting behind the dugout is like being front-row center at the opera. You're so close you can actually smell the ballplayers.

Mr Generic buys us popcorn, and we chat amicably.

As we rise for the seventh-inning stretch, Johnny and I look over to thank our kindly birthday benefactor.

Only he's gone.

Poof!

Johnny and I look at each other with amazed faces.

Our birthday angel has vanished.

One of the things I love about New York, New York, is that the weather is as crazy as the city. After a perfect blue-sky birthday, as dusk sinks in, a storm races in like a fire truck blasting up Fifth Avenue.

After a mahvelous meal and a deelish cannoli in the old East Village, we proceed on a shopping spree. Cool shoes, a Talking Heads CD, and a leather jacket are bought by yours truly for Johnny. A vintage Japanese baseball shirt for me. We barely make it back to her pad before the skies open and a rain of biblical proportion washes the mean streets clean. Johnny and I settle in, as the Heads burn down the house.

Johnny regales me with war stories about growing up brown in the Deep South. Not fitting in with the white people, not fitting in with the black people. I want to tell her about me. The words are in my mouth, aching to come out. It's almost crippling, like when you need to pee so bad it makes you dance spastically. But I don't. I can't. No matter how hard I push, my mouth will not let the words out.

Next thing I know, Johnny is kissing me as the rain pours down, smacking wet off the sidewalk outside the window. Her tongue is soft and moist the air damp our clothes floating off she's warm butterscotch curving flesh muscles and ripples nipples swallowing me happily my sweet Lord she's as talented as she is soulful and so nice to look into her eyes as she pulls me on top of her and the storm whips hard rain falling splattering violently wet drops fly through the open window and sizzle on our skin then like we're in some cheese-filled romance novel KABLAAAAM! lightning claps a big bang through the heavens as if the gods are applauding me and Johnny a perfect fit sliding open with no resistance surrounding enveloping a happy grabbing grasping gasping clasping filling full pounding the rain flooding the kiss of wet pouring heat fat drops of rain slamming the asphalt the smack of skin on skin hands clutching—

'Yo, what de FUCK!' a loud voice from the stoop booms into the room.

'Whaddaya mean, what da FUCK?' another louder voice answers.

'He means what da FUCK, dat's what da FUCK he means!' a third shrill voice chimes in.

It's distracting, frankly. Johnny and I stop making love and listen to the Mook Triplets.

'FUCK you!'

'Fuck YOU!'

'FUCK da BOT' of youze!'

Johnny and I laugh eye to eye, lip to lip, hip to hip, breathing each other's breath. It's so good to be laughing inside Johnny on my birthday.

Our birthday.

'Now ya PISSING me awf!'

'I'm pissing YOU awff? You're pissing ME awf!'

'Hey, don't look at me, youze are BOT' pissing ME awff!'

I pull out with a pop, stand fully extended next to the open window, and shout out:

'You guys wanna keep it down, we're trying to fuck in here!'

The Mook Triplets shut up. We hear chuckling, then:

'Sorry.'

Johnny howls in spectacular naked laughter. I jump back onto the fold-out bed and into Johnny, where I remain, in various permutations, until dawn's pink fingers prick us, and it's not our birthday anymore.

CHAPTER 28
STUD OR HOUSEBOY?

On the day after our birthday there's a twinkle in my step
and a spring in my eye. Suddenly the world is a kinder
gentler place. I buy Johnny roses on my way to work. I
wonder if the now-exiled Construction Guy would approve
of any of them. Won't have to worry about that, seeing's how
he's now an ex-Chippendales dancer. He's been replaced by
Tiny Tim, nicknamed in that time-honored tradition that's
made fat men into Slims and bald men into Curlys. Tiny Tim
is barely a six-footer, but *mon Dieu* the man is vast: chest,
neck, and head inhumanly gigantic, torso tapering to a tiny
waist with small cupcake ass cheeks. Tiny Tim is so 'roid-
bloated and massive-muscled he can barely walk. He's like
an action figure whose arms and legs you have to reposition
if you want him to move. And he's not even really handsome. His skin is splotchy, his jaw juts, and his nose and eyes

are too small, like they're the only things not on steroids. I can't wait to see this big lunkhead try to dance. Wouldn't it be funny if he busted a move and his hamhock of an arm broke off 'cuz it was so stiff and brittle?

I slide into the costume room, and there she is, knee-deep in monkey masks: Johnny, the curly stunner I spent so many happy hours inside during the wee wee hours of our birthday. She feels me enter, turns, and smiles like a freshly and well-loved woman.

Sex changes everything. Whereas pre-sex there was an easy comfort betwixt me and Johnny, post-sex I don't know whether to treat her like my girlfriend and give her a deep french kiss or act like we're still just co-employees trying to help each other maintain our sanity amid the madness.

I hand her the roses while I say:

'Hey, how's it going?'

Johnny doesn't blush exactly, but she does go kinda shy and girly, which, in a sarcastic tough chick, is unbelievably endearing.

'Oh uh, good, thanks.' A half grin blooms on her face as she takes the roses.

We do not kiss. We do not make plans for the rest of our lives. We do not make plans for later that night.

Arnolpho whisks into the room with a swish in a crisp new blue jacket, looking for fun as only a randy Brazilian can. He stops dramatically and cocks his head like an animal checking out the room.

'Did Miss Thing get some birthday love from Mr Thing?'

We smile like high school kids reveling in getting caught at something fun and naughty. Arnolpho lights up, practically tasting the deliciousness of this juicy morsel. He pauses dramatically, directs his dancer body and gorgeous gadfly face at Johnny, and asks:

'Well? Stud or houseboy?'

The way he says it, you half-expect Oscar Wilde and Dorothy Parker to pop into the costume room and dish out a witty bon mot.

'Definitely a stud.' Johnny nods her curls nonchalantly.

I can't stop a smile from appearing.

'Excellent.' Arnolpho nods. 'I would 'spect nothing less.' He pauses now to take us both in. 'Well, isn't this jus' mah-velous. I feel like Tony Randall in a Rock Hhhudson-Doris Day movie!'

'Yeah, but which one of us is Rock Hudson and which one is Doris Day?' I ask.

'Thas' for you to know an' me to fin' out.' Arnolpho waggles his head suggestively, points to Johnny, and says, 'We hhhave to talk, girlfrien', I want all the filthy details.'

'Only if you're a good girl,' Johnny teases.

''Cuz inquirin' minds . . .' Arnolpho pauses, and Johnny joins him in perfect unison, complete with finger snapping and head wagging:

'Wanna know.'

And with that Arnolpho airkisses us and sashays away.

Johnny and I share a chuckle:

Oh that nutty Auntie Arnolpho!

I now have to tux up. But when I take off my pants I feel oddly shy. And believe me, I'm not the shy type, naked-wise. I've taken off my pants in front of Johnny, in this room, dozens of times, never feeling an inkling of self-consciousness. But now I do.

Sex changes everything.

CHAPTER 29

WITHOUT FEAR OF MOCKING HUMILIGRATION

Highlight of tonight's show: Tiny Tim. It's important to understand that the Construction Guy number is choreographed so that a trained moose can do it. In fact to call it choreography is to insult choreographers everywhere. It basically consists of the following:

Trudge to point A. Pose.

Trudge to point B. Pose.

Trudge to point C. Pose.

But here's where it gets tricky: You have to do all that trudging and posing while removing clothes until you're nearly nude, while lip-synching to 'Hello' with Lionel Richie to a rose. Then you have to throw the rose, bring a big beautiful babe into the Pit, get on one knee, look into her eyes, and woo her until she swoons.

Tiny Tim immediately gets lost. After doing hand-to-hand

combat with his blue jeans for quite some time, he barely manages to beat them into submission before tossing them off. But he's so shackled by the manacles of his steroid-jacked muscles that he can barely throw the rose, and his lame toss doesn't even make it to the Ladies. And he doesn't have the wherewithal to retrieve the fallen flower and walk it over to a big beautiful babe. So it just lies there, a crushed red testament to his stupidity and incompetence. When he brings a babe into the Pit his muscle mass makes it nearly impossible for him to get down on one knee. Then he gets lost in the song, so he's lip-synching different words than Lionel's crooning. And it's not like it's that difficult a song. *Hello*. I mean, come on. Watching his lips move out of time with the words on the sound track, it looks like he's in a badly dubbed foreign film about a bucket-headed mutant from a land of gigantic brain-dead strippers. The big beautiful babe wears a what-the-fuck's-wrong-with-you? look on her face. Definitely not the desired effect.

I look up at Crazy Eddie in the DJ booth and do a tiny Tiny Tim impersonation. Eddie throws back his freckles and laughs his ass off.

After the show, when I trudge into the womb of the costume room, Johnny is packing up her stuff instead of sorting sodden disgusting-smelling costumes as she mumbles and mutters:

'Motherfuckin', scumfuckin' bitch!'

Even though we've had super hot birthday sex and we're rapidly becoming best friends, I don't know what to do. Back off? Comfort? Cajole? Sympathize? Humor? Shit!

When Johnny feels someone in the room she wheels around with flashing angry eyes. When she sees it's me she unclenches and heaves a deep cheek-puffing sigh, accompanied by a sarcastic roll of her oak eyes.

'Should I ask?' I ask.

'I got fired.' Johnny says flatly.

I think she said she got fired. But that seems so wrong. So I ask:

'You *what?*'

'I got fired.'

'Fired?'

'Yup.'

'Why?'

'Bullshit, politics, cockbitin' morons. Take your pick.'

'But what did they say?' I sink with the news.

'Some dry-cleaning bullshit. It's 'cuz they squeezed Nick outta New York and they wanna save money, greedy fucknuts.' Loathing pours out of Johnny. Oddly, it makes her even sexier.

Oh yeah, come to think of it, I haven't seen Nick de Noia in a while. I didn't know he got squeezed out. So I ask:

'Where *is* Nick?'

'I don't know. Him and Banerjee and the Edwards Brothers had some huge blowout, they're filin' lawsuits and temporary restraining orders, it's sick. I mean, there's so much fucking money around here, and the second Nick is gone, they come after me for twenty-three dollars in dry cleaning. Well, they can all suck my dick.'

All I can think to say is:

'Damn.'

'I gotta get the fuck outta here anyway. I didn't come to New York City to wet-nurse a buncha pretty boys. Fuckit. Good riddance!' She ends with triumphant defiance.

And I fall in love with Johnny a little more.

Is Nick's reign as the king of Chippendales over? Is the show gonna suck eggs now that he's not riding herd and cracking whip? Is it gonna be every-man-for-himself mayhem when the lunatics take over the asylum? Will Slick Rick survive Nick's exile? But more important, who will the puffy white Marshmallow Man expose his sad fat ass to without fear of mocking humiligration? Who will share my disdain for the vainglorious egomaniacs? Who will mock with me the surreal absurdity of this topsy-turvy universe? But most important, now that Nick de Noia is gone, how the hell am I gonna get to be a star at Chippendales Male Strip Club?

PART III

THE HOUSE OF DEATH

CHAPTER 1

TOO YOUNG TO BE IN LOVE

Roooooooooooooooooad triiiiiiiiiiiiiip!

I board the van with Johnny, Prince Charming, his suddenly big-breasted girlfriend, Betsy, and the hairy Barbarian, along with Arnolpho and the beautiful boy Ensemble Dancers. Plus the one and only Slick Rick, who hunkers down in the back of the van, alone on Slick Rick Island. The air is stale yet jovial, and a giddy anticipation bubbles among us. We're off to Philadelphia!

Apparently, Nick de Noia's blowout with the Edwards Brothers and Banerjee has resulted in him becoming persona non grata at the Sixty-first and First Chippendales. This is pure scuttlebut, but I heard Nick blackmailed Banerjee into giving up the touring rights to Chippendales by threatening to expose some arson job Banerjee had allegedly paid for. According to my sources, Nick's not legally allowed to mount the show within a fifty-mile radius of Manhattan. So he's assembled a touring show and convinced a club in Philly that he can pack and rock their joint every Monday and Tuesday night. Of course, Nick doesn't say word one about this to any of us peons, but the rumor mills are working overtime.

Nick's bringing the special essentials down from New York, then filling the Philly show with locals. I made a sweet deal for myself. Nick offered $200 a show, I got him up to $250, and that's in addition to the week's worth of shows Wednesday to Saturday at Sixty-first and First. So I feel special and essential as I snuggle into my seat with Johnny, who's traveling as my civilian companion.

'Y'awright?' I ask her soft.

'Yeah,' she answers back. 'I'm just so glad I don't work for these scumbags anymore.'

I don't feel that way. I'm glad I still work for these scumbags. But I don't tell her that. I kiss her lips, she kisses mine, and we lovingly canoodle.

When the hairy Barbarian glances back at us, disgust registers on his face:

'Jesus Fucking Christ, will ya knock it off? Yer makin' me sick, here.'

This is a man who makes his living stripping for women and kissing them while taking their $. And he's grossed out by two humans exchanging sweet love and affection? Is this what it means to be a man at Chippendales?

Arnolpho pops his head up like an impish gay Brazilian prairie dog looking for fun or trouble or both. Smiling brightly he says:

'But can' you see how in love the young lovers are? Don' you think young love is beauuuuuuuutiful?'

If he weren't so sweet, the teasing might seem mean. But the way he says it, Arnolpho comes off as affectionately joie-de-vivre-ful.

Suddenly he breaks into song, an old standard, 'Too Young to Love.' Arnolpho wraps his luscious pipes around the sweeping, timeless tune, crooning about how everyone says these two lovers are too young to love.

The beautiful boy Ensemble Dancers join in, and being ex-Broadway chorus gypsies, they have exquisite, powerful, and highly trained voices, so they sing in glorious, soaring three-part harmony.

By the end of the song, even the Barbarian, well-schooled in the Sinatra canon, has joined in, full-throated and on-key. The van is filled to the brim with this beautiful goofy rendering of this exquisite melody.

Johnny and I laugh, as the climax reveals that the two lovers were not too young at all.

Whoops and hollers follow as the van full of studs and lovers roars towards Philly. After we've settled, my eyes fall on Betsy, sitting with Prince Charming. She looks even more different. It's not the new huge hair, which is a big puffy permed streaked *New Wave Hookers* meets B-52s do. Or the new huge tits. I realize I haven't seen her in a while, but I swear her nose looks smaller and perkier. Her lips seem bigger and thicker. And her eyes are kinda pulled back tight. I lean in to Johnny and whisper:

'Is it just me, or does Betsy look like she's totally had work done?'

Johnny nods knowingly and whispers back:

'She had a nose job and an eye tuck. But don't tell anybody.'

'Don't tell anybody?!' I whisper incredulous. 'Does she really think nobody's gonna notice that she has a new nose in the middle of her face?'

Johnny shrugs with a beats-me look.

'What about the lips?' I whisper.

'Collagen or monkey glands or some fuckin' thing,' she whispers back. 'But you didn't hear it from me.'

Arnolpho thrusts his gorgeous head into the conversation: 'What are we whisperin' 'bout?'

'Miss Betsy's magical makeover,' Johnny whispers.

'Li'l Miss Scary Drag Queen, you mean?' Arnolpho meows back.

I stare back at Betsy. She does look kinda like a drag queen. Seeing what this natural beauty has done to herself makes my heart sink like a sad stone.

'But why would she do all that?' I ask. 'She was so pretty already. She looks kinda . . . inhuman now.'

'You try fuckin' Prince Charming,' Johnny whispers back sarcastically.

'You should know, Miss Thing,' Arnolpho hisses.

'Did you fuck Prince Charming?' My eyes bug in surprise.

'Kinda,' she shrugs with indifference.

'How do you *kinda* fuck somebody?' I ask. I'm not mad or upset. With my track record, how could I be? I'm just curious.

'Well, you know, you just kinda fuck 'em,' Johnny answers matter-of-factly.

'Uh oh, are the young lovers hhhavin' their first spat?' Arnolpho asks a little too gleefully.

Johnny and I answer at exactly the same time:

'No.'

'But I do have one question,' I say.

'Fire away,' says Johnny.

'How was he?' I pause for a moment. ''Cuz inquiring minds . . .'
I glance at Arnolpho, and together we say:

'Wanna know.'

'Well, it was cool being with somebody so . . . uh . . . perfect,
I guess. But at the end of the day, there wasn't much there.'
Johnny sounds like she's reviewing a meal at a mediocre restaur-
ant.

'Pretty potatoes but no meat?' Arnolpho asks.

Johnny thinks, then answers carefully:

'No, it was more like fucking the Wizard of Oz. Very impressive to look at, but when all's said and done, it's just a little
man behind a curtain, and you never get to Kansas.'

'An' baby,' Arnolpho agrees, 'there's no place like home.'

I look over at Prince Charming, sitting serenely, staring
ahead, utterly untroubled. I wonder what he would think if
he knew we were deconstructing his lovemaking skills. Looks
like he could care less. Wonder what the highly-surgicalized
Betsy would think if she knew Johnny fucked her man? I sense
she would not be as unperturbed.

At this point, if I knew with absolute certainty that it would
make me a star, would I have the cosmetic surgery?

Absolutely.

CHAPTER 2

UGLY RUNT AND ALMOST HANDSOME

It looks like a gigantic spaceship has landed in the middle of a cow pasture. Don't look like Philly. 'Cuz we ain't in Philly. We're in Media, Pennsylvania, miles outside Philadelphia. Media? Damn!

When I stride into the gigantor state-of-the-art megaclub with Prince Charming, Slick Rick, Arnolpho, Betsy, and Johnny, it feels like we're starring in our own rock video, walking in slow motion as hungry heads turn our way, and hot whispers flow from flapping lips into admiring ears. I have never felt cooler in my life. I hope someday, somehow, that I can be this cool all by myself. But I don't see it happening.

This club is vast. Vaster than vast. You could fit three or four of the New York Chippendales inside this place. It's squeaky clean and smells like air freshener.

Nick de Noia is auditioning local talent to be Hosts and

Waiters. He has them stripped down to their nay-nays. Yes, they're pretty, they're buff, they're cut. But they're not *as* pretty, *as* cut, or *as* buff as their New York City counterparts. Nick's putting them through their paces: slapping their almost-faaaaaaabulous asses, pinching their nearly perfect abs, inspecting their teeth and gums like they're racehorses.

'Helloooooooo?' Nick bellows, butch yet nelly. 'This is not rocket science, fellas. Step, turn, clap.' Nick demonstrates. Step, turn, clap. It's astonishing how much style and grace he manages to put into this rudimentary movement.

'One, two, three . . . and . . . step, turn, clap.'

Half the Media Men step, clap, turn. The other half turn, step, clap.

The ugly runt of the Media wannabes does a step, turn, stumble.

Nick erupts at Ugly Runt:

'What the HELL was that?'

'Well, I was just trying—'

'Trying?' Nick cries. 'That's not trying, that's failing, and I—' Ugly Runt interrupts Nick:

'I don't think—'

'Helllooooooooooo??' Nick cuts him off. 'Did I ask you to think?'

No reply.

'Get out.' Nick points dramatically toward the exit.

'I don't understand—' Ugly Runt looks confused and hurt; humiliation and shame turning his face into a painting of misery.

Jesus, I feel bad for the guy.

'What don't you understand? *Get*? Or *Out*?' Nick looks like he's waiting for a reply. But Ugly Runt seems gun-shy, so silence sits in that vast cavern of a club, interrupted only by the sound of a technician hammering offstage left.

'Will you PLEASE stop that racket? I can't even hear myself think!' Everyone turns to Hammering Technician, who immediately stops hammering, then looks like he'd rather be facing a firing squad than staring down the gun barrel of Nick's anger.

'Thank you.' Nick manages to put more fuck-you than thanks into his thank-you. 'Now. You.' He points to Ugly Runt. 'Out. Go. Good-bye!'

Ugly Runt turns and leaves, looking like a little kid about to cry.

Nick seems to have gotten a big ol' boner from the whole thing. He waits until Ugly Runt (who, by the way, is actually quite attractive by normal human standards) has vacated the room. Then he turns gracefully to the wannabe Media Men and very calmly, very sweetly asks:

'Does anyone else have anything else they'd like to share with the group?'

Naturally no one has anything else they'd like to share with the group.

I glance at Hammering Technician. His look of trepidation and anxiety has turned to pissed-off disgust. I wonder if he wants to kill Nick de Noia right about now.

I now believe that every time you abuse somebody, you're buying a lottery ticket. And when you win, somebody you abused comes and kills you.

Nick glides over to the hottest wannabe Media Man, who's tall, blond, nearly nude, and almost handsome. Nick stands behind him, puts one hand around the man's naked waist and the other on his barely covered ass. Nick takes one step forward, guiding Almost Handsome to take one step forward, while addressing him like he's a dim child:

'Step.'

Nick spins Almost Handsome all the way around while he says:

'Turn.'

Nick puts both arms around him, grabs his arms and claps his hands together while saying:

'Clap.'

Nick's so close to Almost Handsome, he's practically rubbing his trousered dong against the man's ass, manhandling him like he's a large, beautiful, dim child.

'Got it?' Nick asks.

'Got it,' Almost Handsome answers.

Nick slaps him on the ass: WHAP! The loud smack of hand on flesh echoes through the quiet of the club.

Nick says slowly like he's the host of a kiddie show:

'OK, here we go . . . one, two, three . . . and . . . step . . . turn . . . clap . . .'

Almost Handsome nails it, with a little style even.

Glee shoots out of Nick when the guy succeeds:

'Wonderful! Absolutely faaaabulous. OK, now we're getting somewhere.'

Intense pleasure fills Almost Handsome's face, and you can see it flow through him.

'OK,' Nick smiles so pretty and nice. 'You're in. Go downstairs and get fitted.'

Almost Handsome practically skips out of the room. I have a vision of him calling his buds with the good news:

'Dude, I'm a Chippendale.'

Nick de Noia can really make you feel like a star.

But I wonder if Hammering Technician is now lamenting the new asshole Nick tore him, and contemplating burying his hammer in Nick's thick skull.

CHAPTER 3

I DON'T WANNA BE A PAIN IN THE ASS

The dressing room is in the basement in Media and it's about a billion times bigger and smells a billion times better than its counterpoint in New York. The air crackles as dancers, lackeys, newbies, wannabes, stars, and one Master of Ceremonies prep for the grand opening of Chippendales, Media-style. I'm stoked at having the chance to be a virgin with this show again. And this time I can enjoy it, 'cuz now I actually know what the hell I'm doing. Plus, I went to elaborate lengths to get Johnny a ringside seat. I plan to hang with her in my minibreak, and I'm looking forward to goofing with her throughout the show.

About half an hour before kickoff, a buttoned-down lackey sidles up to me, and milquetoastishly says:

'Hello, Mr Skerry. I just wanted to let you know that we're not gonna be able to seat your girlfriend ringside. I hope you understand, those seats are just too valuable to give away. But we've got her an excellent seat, and, of course, all her drinks will be comped. Thanks so much for your cooperation and understanding.'

He's like a living breathing version of a tape recording you hear when you call up and complain to a utility company. I have to work hard to resist the urge to punch him in his bland, smug, smiling face. Feels like disrespect, confirmation that I don't matter, a symbol of how I've spent my whole adult life sucking on the short end of the fuzzy lollipop. It's like the universe is screaming at me: You're not now, nor will you ever be, a star.

Only this time I'm sick and tired, and I'm not gonna take it anymore. 'Cuz now I'm the Man, I'm the Guy, I'm the Master of Ceremonies.

'Hey, look, I don't wanna be a pain in the ass,' I say as I commence being a pain in the ass, 'but this is just not right. I cleared this with the GM *and* the floor manager. I know you gotta make yer money, but this just isn't right.' I feel I'm being firm but not abusive.

'I don't think you understand—' Lackey is cut off by me, the angry MC.

'No, I don't think *you* understand. Your boss promised me a ringside seat for my girlfriend. And if she doesn't get one, I don't go on. And you don't have a show. Do you understand *that*?' Feels good to lay some smackdown on this shameless puppet of the imperialist corporate machine.

Lackey inches away from me. He looks like he suddenly hates his job. I am the rock, his boss is the hard place, and he is caught painfully between us. He sighs and starts to say something. Stops himself and sighs again.

'All right, I'll see what I can do.'

I'm deeply satisfied that I've managed to wipe that smug smarmy smile off his face.

Twenty minutes later Lackey is back, looking much the worse for wear. Barely disguised desperation floods out of him:

'I'm sorry, but we just can't give up that seat. They're going for a lot of money. You know, being opening night and all. I hope you understand.'

I'm getting a little too much enjoyment out of making him sweat.

'No, I *don't* understand,' I say as my eyes squint. 'I don't understand at all. But you better understand this: I'm not going on unless she gets a seat ringside. Which is what *your GM* already agreed to. And if I don't go on, you're gonna have a thousand very angry females on your hands. Unless *you* wanna go on. Do *you* wanna go on? 'Cuz if you do, help yourself. Otherwise you got no show.'

It's so intoxicating grinding this man under my heel. Retribution for all the heels I've been ground under.

Lackey doesn't even argue. It's five minutes till showtime, and he knows as well as I do that there really *are* a thousand screaming, naked-craving, male-stripper-hungry Ladies who will go apeshit if their desire is denied. He just shakes his head, tuts, and bustles away.

Four minutes later, Lackey's back again, looking more unraveled than buttoned-down. He's sweating, his eyes are tight and wired, and he appears on the verge of nervous exhaustion.

I, on the other hand, have never felt so calm and powerful.

'All right,' Lackey sighs like he's finishing the Paris Peace Talks, 'your girlfriend can sit ringside. Now we've gotta get you on, because the show is scheduled to start,' he looks at his watch, 'now.'

'All right,' I say, as a highly satisfied smile slides onto my face.

I bust past Lackey, happy about finally standing up for myself and my girl. No more Mr Nice Guy. No longer the 97-pound puffy white Marshmallow Man getting sand kicked in my face.

I'm finally a star, baby.

In Media, Pennsylvania, at least.

CHAPTER 4

HEADS ROLLING, ASSHOLES RIPPING, GUTS SPILLING

A thousand women are better than six hundred. Especially when they're out of their fucking minds, supercharged with eager-beaver expectation. There's not an empty seat in the Media megaclub. Or a dry one, by the look of things. God I love these Ladies. Their hair's not quite as big as their Manhattan sisters', skirts not quite as short, they're not quite as stylish or fashionable, but still: yowza!

As I enter the main room I catch Johnny's eye and give her a little wink: Hey, baby!

Lights out. Music up. Video starts.

KABLOOIE!!!

The room detonates with deafening Lady ecstasy.

And I like it: this opening night is so much more fun, because I'm not terrified I'm gonna fuck everything up, and the show is such a rush, it just gushes by so fast.

Highlights:

Nick's track record continues true to form: he has chosen as the Media Construction Guy a man every bit as big as Tiny Tim but even more prehistoric. And, if possible, an even worse dancer. Again, the beauty is NO ONE CARES. The Media Ladies love him unconditionally.

During my rehydration break I hang with Johnny, and it's great fun: chitting and chatting, lip-smacking and wisecracking, kissing and laughing.

Drenched and happy, I bring the show home, exhilarated by the triumph of my night: from standing up to the moneymen to whipping the Media Ladies into a frothy foam of wild delight.

A jovial buzz fills the huge man-sweat-scented dressing room. It's like we're a traveling all-star team who just conquered the locals. Congratulations abound, and war stories fly:

'D'joo see that crazy blonde in the corner? She almost ripped my cock off!'

'Look at this, man, that big bitch bit me in the ass. Broke skin, dude!'

'Three rows back, right in the middle, huge bazooms?'

'Yeah, bodacious tatas! She was all over me, man.'

Into this group glee whips Nick de Noia:

PISSED!

Heads will roll, assholes rip, guts spill.

Silence follows. Nasty, dangerous, crazy-making silence.

I glance over at the Media Construction Guy, expecting he'll be the victim of this hit'n'run. Imagine my horror when Nick de Noia turns his flame-throwing eyes on me.

Me?

Oh shit:

ME!

What did I do?

What did I not do?

I gird my loins for the onslaught, as Nick takes one balletic step toward me and launches:

'Who the *hell* do you think you are?'

I, of course, realize this is a question no one should ever answer.

'This is MY show, mister,' Nick continues, 'and no one fucks with MY show.' Nick gets all mocking now. 'Oh, you want your *girlfriend* to sit ringside. So you can play little kissy games with your *girlfriend*.'

Degradation, humiliation, and shame flood through me, and I'm acutely aware of the stares of the men.

'No one puts themselves above MY show. NO ONE. When they told me that you threatened not to go on, I was flabbergasted. How dare you? I made you, and I can break you like that.' Nick snaps his fingers, illustrating how easily he can break me.

Shame turns to anger, and the bile rises in me.

'Don't you EVER threaten MY show!!! Is that clear? Do we understand each other? After all I've done for you, I cannot believe you would treat me like this. This is CHIPPENDALES, mister. This is not the David Sterry Show, and if you don't understand that, I'll find someone who does.' With a malicious point of his finger, Nick punctuates his tirade with a threat, turns dramatically, and storms out.

Anger rattles madly through me, as I mutter:

'I'm gonna kill that asshole!'

If I'd been thinking I most certainly would not have followed. When a snake bites you and pumps you full of venom, you do not follow the snake as it slithers away. But I am *not* thinking. So I follow, all instinct.

I bust through the door into the hall, quickly catch up to the back of Nick, grab his shoulder, and spin him around so he's facing me. My true, pure, unfiltered, uncensored, righteous indignation catches Nick by surprise, as the words pour out of me:

'Don't you EVER yell at me in front of those guys. I have to work with them every night, and if they don't respect me, I'm fucked out there. From now on, if you have anything to say to me, you take me aside, you look me in the eyes, and you tell me like a man.'

Nick looks shocked. Caught off guard. And like the bully on the playground, when confronted, he backs down.

'Well, uh . . .' Nick stops, at a loss for words. 'All right then.'

As I smile in triumph, Nick turns and glides away. He never ever yells at me again. In fact, these are the last words I ever exchange with Nick.

And I become the fifth person I've heard express a desire to kill Nick de Noia.

CHAPTER 5

ROADKILL ON THE HIGHWAY OF LIFE

'Crazy Eddie's dead.'

The Snowman says it like he's telling me it might rain later or that the Yankees lost yesterday, so it doesn't register. It's Wednesday, 7 P.M., I've already done two shows in Media this week, and I've just arrived sleep-deprived in the lobby of Chippendales. I suspect I'm having an audio hallucination, so I say:

'What?'

This time the Snowman says it with a what-are-you, stupid? 'tude:

'Crazy Eddie's dead.'

No matter how long I look into his *Village of the Damned* blue eyes, I still can't understand what he's saying. I'm so tired I can't think straight, and jagged confusion fills my voice:

'What are you talkin' about?'

'Crazy Eddie's dead, motherfucker. He's fucking dead. The dude died.' The Snowman's so light and blithe it still doesn't sound like he's describing death, so I feel like I'm not getting the story right:

'Wait a second. Are you saying that Crazy Eddie the DJ is dead?'

'What are you, a retard?' The Snowman does Nick: 'Helloooooo!' Back to regular voice: 'Crazy Fuckin' Eddie is fuckin' dead, dude!'

'Holy shit,' I mutter as it sinks in.

'Fuckin' A right, man. It's survival of the fittest, take no prisoners, kill or be killed.' The Snowman starts to strut off.

'Wait a minute!' My urgency to buy and imbibe drugs stops him. 'I need to get some . . . I need to buy some—'

'Yeah, I'll catch up with you before the show.' The Snowman freezes me out.

'Yeah, but I need it now and—'

'Dude, take a fuckin' chill pill, the Snowman will catch you on the rebound.' He then parades his mustache past the super-huge Men pics and disappears through the red velvet curtain into the wild wetlands of Chippendales.

Crazy Eddie is dead. That beautiful redheaded freckle-spackled maniac with the Mad Hatter laugh, who could drive a crowd to euphoria with the magic of his music and make you love life every time you laid eyes on him, is dead.

The Swedish prime minister just got assassinated. The Chernobyl power plant in the Soviet Union exploded and nuclear fallout laid waste to the land. President Reagan just vetoed legislation that would crack down on apartheid in South Africa. The US national debt just topped $2 trillion.

And now Crazy Eddie's dead.

Long live Crazy Eddie.

I just wish I'd gotten a chance to tell him I loved him. Then again, I don't tell anybody I love them. I do a sad, slow, trudge into the overstuffed dressing room.

The Barbarian heaves heavy weights. Prince Charming camouflages his tattoos. Tom Cat dick-pulls his pud till it fills with blood and then snaps black Spandex over it. Slick Rick mercilessly rehearses on Slick Rick Island.

Business as usual.

The more I stand there, the more it pisses me off. Finally I shout:

'Hey, you self-absorbed motherfuckers, Crazy Eddie is dead. Dead! Don't you understand? How about a little respect? A little reverence? A little love for somebody besides yourself?'

Sadly those words never make it from inside my head to the dressing room. I just clump back blackly into the costume room, which sucks even harder 'cuz some dye-jobbed blonde's standing where Johnny should be. Shit. I want to grieve the death of the man who was the life and soul of the partyallthetime Chippendales madness with Johnny. But she's gone.

Arnolpho pops his beautiful Brazilian self into the costume room, gets in close to me, and touching my chest he whispers:

'Did you hear about Miss Eddie?'

'Yeah, I can't believe it—' I say. I hear myself, stop, then continue, 'I mean, I *can* believe it, of course, if you were gonna pick a guy to die around here, it would be Crazy Eddie—'

'Nooooooo,' Arnolpho interrupts, 'if I was gonna pick one person, it would have to be Miss Nick de Noia.'

'Yeah, I suppose.' I chuckle wry and dry. 'I just can't get my head wrapped around it . . .'

'Just say no, bay-bee!' Arnolpho wags his head while waggling his index finger.

'How'd it happen?' I ask.

'God love her, the redheaded stepchild.' Arnolpho crosses himself Catholic style. 'What I heard was, they foun' her this mornin' slumped over the turntable up in the DJ booth, a cigarette in one hand, a drink in the other, an' a pound of coke up her nose, stone col' dead.' Arnolpho takes an expertly timed pause and puts on a funny grieving face: 'Died in the saddle, bay-bee, an' I think Eddie woulda wanted it tha' way.'

I can't help but chuckle. I so much prefer his gallows laughter to the narcissistic indifference of the Men of Chippendales.

Arnolpho thinks deeply, and with uncharacteristically serious sincerity, he sighs, saying:

'I'm gonna miss her.'

'Me, too,' I reply.

The show drags and lags like molasses. The new DJ has the music a step ahead or a step behind all night, and it fucks everything up. The Ladies are subdued, and a pall hangs sad over the Land of Chippendales.

For the first time in memory, Big Alice, the greatest Chippendales groupie ever, leaves early.

Every time I look up at the booth and don't see that crazy shock of red hair, I get a lump in the pit of my hump that slides sickly from my heart into my belly. If I wasn't so high I'd cry.

Now that Nick is gone, the show, as predicted, has gone straight to the dogs. Guys are barely going through the motions of dancing, whipping straight into their Kiss & Tip as soon as humanly possible. Again the Ladies don't seem to notice. But

I do. Sadly, even I have a hard time caring anymore.

By the time the show's over, I'm fried and fucked, roadkill on the highway of life. After I've thanked everyone I take off my top hat and get very serious.

'Ladies and gentlemen, could I have your attention.'

Maybe because I say it like David Henry Sterry and not the Master of Ceremonies, I get the club to shut the fuck up. Which is not easy at this point in the evening, because everyone's so full of hooch and either horny or tired or looking to get higher. But I instantly get 'em spooky quiet.

'Chippendales lost a rare soul recently when Crazy Eddie passed away. For those of you who don't know him, Crazy Eddie was our DJ. But he was also our funny bone and our heart and soul, our musical maestro who made our lives more fun every day. I'd like to have a minute of silence for Crazy Eddie, who died way too young.'

Considering what a small thing it is, a minute can last, under certain circumstances, bizarrely long.

This is one of those minutes.

When someone in the back of the room starts talking, three or four people violently *Shhhhhhhh!* them. When the longest minute in the history of Chippendales is over, I point up to the DJ booth in the sky and I say:

'Thanks Eddie, we miss you.'

I readdress the crowd:

'I'd like to leave you with the words of Crazy Eddie . . .' I turn my voice into his rapturous rasp and scream:

'"Paaaaaaaaaaaaaaar-tay!!!"'

When the crowd howls and the new DJ cranks 'Thriller,' I can hear the ghost of Crazy Eddie laughing his ass off.

And so the House of Death claims its first victim.

CHAPTER 6

COWARD! LOSER! LIAR!

'I gotta move,' Johnny says as we lounge in my bed, flushed with love.

'How come?' I ask.

'Carl's closing down the operation.'

Carl is her boss in the loosest sense of the word. He's the dude who's the brains behind the marijuana business and supplies Johnny with product. Since she's no longer working at Chippendales, it's been difficult to keep the product moving.

'So he's getting rid of the apartment?' I ask.

'Yup,' she says.

'Why don't you move in here?'

The words are out of my mouth before I even begin to consider the ramifications of this potentially life-altering question.

'Really?' Johnny doesn't sound surprised.

Now wait a minute. Do I really want Johnny to move in here? I like her. A lot. She's funny and capable and gorgeous. I love being with her, around her, and in her. I love talking to her. I love looking at her, fully clothed, naked, whenever. She cooks, she cleans, she makes crazy love. Sure, why not?

'Yeah . . .' I sound like I'm agreeing to lend someone a quarter.

'Cool . . .' Johnny sounds like she's agreeing to give someone a bite of her pizza.

And thus it is decided.

I'd just moved into a room in a huge, renovated, two-story loft on Fourth Street between Avenues A and B in the East Village. It's on the edge of Alphabet City, where anyone, regardless of race, creed, or color, can satisfy their heroin needs in the time it takes a junkie to nod. Scrawny pasty rockers in tight black pants and Russian grandmothers who moved here in 1911 and still don't speak English. Raving painters and starving poets. Low-level shiny-suited gangsters and slumming yuppies. Jewish cobblers and Arab falafel makers. Actors who will never be more than waiters and playwrights who will never get to quit their dreaded telemarketing jobs. Indian mothers in saris and drag queens in miniskirts with size 17, six-inch-high spiked heels. Reagan's economic boom has not trickled down into Alphabet City. The Gap hasn't got here yet. And the farther you go into Alphabet City, the scarier it gets, until out by Avenue D the sidewalks are strewn with used condoms, needles, and humans – ranting conspiracy theorists, dopers and peddlers, people looking to die and people looking to kill, the hustlers and the haunted and the hunted, the psychopaths and the ripped-up Vietnam vets with their Agent Orange toxic shell shock, the bottom-feeders and their predators. It's only a twenty-minute skate to Chippendales and the Upper East Side, but it seems like a galaxy far far away. Suits me just fine. The grunge and the filth and the juice of the drugs and the buzz of the artists make me feel right at home.

Seven other actor-artist-musician-students live in the huge loft with me. Me and Johnny's favorite is a wisp of a Southern writer-performance artist fellow who puts on a long straight Cher wig and a long flowing dress and sings a Southern gospel ballad in a soulful mournful voice:

'Come home . . . Co-o-o-o-o-me ho-o-o-me. Ye who are weary come ho-o-o-o-me.'

I look over at Johnny lying languid and luscious next to me, and I feel so lucky that she chose me over all the faaaaaaaabulous Men of Chippendales.

But I'm a firm believer in full disclosure, and I feel obligated to reveal my secret before we seal the deal.

'Hey look, I gotta tell you something . . . ,' I start weakly.

'Yeah?' Johnny asks.

'I used to be a . . .'

She waits for me to finish that sentence. When I don't, she asks with no attitude:

'A what?'

'See, when I was younger I was . . .'

Again the words refuse to move out of my mouth.

'You were what?'

'I was . . .'

I desperately want it out, I need to let it go. I owe it to her. She has to understand what she's getting herself in for.

'I used to be . . .'

Pregnant pause.

'A total pain in the ass.'

Johnny looks confused. All this build-up for that?

I kick myself with both feet: Coward! Loser! Liar!

'You're still a total pain in the ass,' Johnny wisecracks. 'You're almost as big of a pain in the ass as I am, and that's sayin' somethin'.'

'I'm afraid I have to agree,' I say with a nod.

The next day Johnny moves in, and we celebrate by making a huge feast of roast beast and homemade french fries, gravy, and biscuits, corn on the cob, fruit cobbler, and ice cream. Then we eat until we collapse and fall asleep in each other's arms.

CHAPTER 7

DOES THAT MAKE ME A SHALLOW PERSON?

The patina of opening-night excitement is solid gone in week two of the Media Experiment. Though the Ladies show up in droves, a powerful boredom sits on my face. Oh, I'm a professional, I give them their money's worth, but my heart is not in Media. Johnny isn't either, and I'm jonesing for her.

After the show I can't get outta that club fast enough. Slouching down the shabby drab hall of the Dirtbag Hotel, where they're storing us, I'm not at all excited at the prospect of staring at the four nasty walls of my dirtbag room. Prince Charming turns a corner as I do, and we practically slam into each other. We have a funny face-to-face moment. Or rather face-to-pecs, since he's 6' 4" and I'm 5' 11" on a good day.

'Hey man, how's it going?' Prince Charming seems happy to see me. Which fills me with way too much well-being.

'Partyin' hardy in Media, baby.' I make a hard-rocker

PARTYYYYY! gesture with my index finger and pinky extended straight out, arm shooting up devilishly.

Prince Charming throws back his coiffed blond locks and laughs. 'You're a funny fucker, man.'

'Yup, that's me, the funny fucker,' I shrug.

He pauses and thinks for a moment. 'You wanna come in for a nightcap?'

'Sure, man.' I try not to sound like an excited homely schoolgirl asked out by the captain of the football team.

As I follow him into his dirtbag room I can't help but wonder why he isn't bringing some crazyhotsexy Media Lady back to fornicate with her. God knows he must have so many gorgeous pick-o'-the-litter babes to choose from. Maybe he's being true to Betsy. Although judging from Johnny's story, fidelity is not one of the ways that Prince Charming is charming.

As always, it's calm on the surface of his pond. But there seems to be some murky shit lurking beneath that shockingly beautiful exterior.

'So what's goin' on, man?' I say, hoping to relieve him of his pent-up-ness.

'Nothin',' he answers, easy and charming. 'What's up with you?'

'Well . . . ,' I say with a sigh, 'I guess the glitz and glamour of Media has kinda worn off for me.'

'Yeah.' Prince Charming chuckles. 'Tell me about it.' He looks at me as we sit. 'You want some blow?'

Ahhhhhh! A man after my own heart.

Chop chop chop, snort snort snort. Ooooooh, that's good. Suddenly I'm loving life again. Loving Prince Charming and his coke. Even loving the Dirtbag Motel.

'Wow, shit, thanks man,' I beam.

But Prince Charming doesn't even hear me. A dense layer of distress surrounds him like Pigpen's funk fog. Where does Prince Charming go when he's troubled? And what does he have to be troubled about, for God's sake? He's beautiful. He works thirty minutes a day at a job where he gets worshipped by hundreds of women while making ten grand untraceable $ a month. He's got a beautiful, nice, albeit disturbingly surgically-altered girlfriend. Here's a man who has a life that a kazillion guys would lose a testicle or two to have. And yet he seems deep in some nasty shit.

I don't quite know what to do. Let him stay in his unhappy place? Try to pull him back? It's like my mind is the autobahn and my thoughts are turbocharged German-engineered speed machines roaring past.

'So, uh . . . what's going on, man?'

Prince Charming beams back into the Dirtbag Hotel, focuses his wild, wired eyes on me, and smiles wryly. Not even a smile really. More a twitch of the lip that admits he's a coke cliché, spacing away in front of someone he barely knows.

It occurs to me suddenly that I've worked with the guy for over a year, partied with him till the sun came up, and I don't know one single thing about him. Where does he come from? Does he have brothers and sisters? Or parents for that matter? For all I know he could be a genetically engineered replicant from the future, sent to save the world by stripping for the Ladies of Earth—

Stop! Focus!

'I don't know, man . . .' Prince Charming shakes his sun-colored rock-star head, 'I mean, what am I doin' here? What's the point? You know what I'm saying?' He leans forward. His hands are so large and perfect.

'Sure, I know what you're talkin' about,' I say, even though I have no idea what he's talking about.

'I don't know . . . ,' Prince Charming sighs. 'All my life, my old man was like, "What the hell's wrong with you?" My old man's a genius with machines. He can fix anything. I swear to God, he can make a motor outta rubber bands and dried bird shit.'

I laugh. Prince Charming is funny. Who knew?

'He'd always be standing behind me rolling his eyes, and then he'd push me outta the way, "Look, ya moron, ya just put the flange on the crankshaft, any idiot could do that with his eyes closed." Yeah, so, I'm like . . . what the hell am I doing with my life, ya know? I make all this money, and I've got four dollars in the bank. By the time my old man was my age, he owned two houses, he had his own business, he had three kids. I mean, what the hell, ya know?' Prince Charming reaches into his bag and doles out more coke.

More coke? Holy moley! We just hoovered down a huge snootful ten minutes ago. I'm not saying no, mind you. *Au contraire, mon frère*, I'm excited to see just how high I can get.

Chop chop chop, snort snort snort. Oh my Lawdy Lawd I can barely swallow there's so much foofoo dust clogging up my facial passages and cavities. My eyes are open wider than they've ever been. I have to consciously force myself to blink 'cuz they're drying out like water evaporating on hot asphalt in the Mojave Desert. All the muscles in my face are clenched too taut. And what is that sound pounding relentlessly? Oh fuck, it's my heart thumping inside my hollow tin

chest. Moisture is forming like dew on the lawn of my forehead. My armpits and crotch are turning into swampy marsh-
land. It's hard work not to hyperventilate. Need liquids! Must
flush water up nose and down throat!

As if reading my mind, Prince Charming pours water from
a big bottle into two plastic dirtbag glasses and hands one to
me. We drain liquid down our throats. The hydration is
magical. He refills his plastic glass, then mine. We gulp until
we drain them again. And there it is, what every coke-headed
mook lives for: that wild-life bliss, and I want to live forever
in this state of grace.

Prince Charming does not seem to be sharing my tran-
scendental intoxication. He seems to be sliding back into his
unhappy place. But this time he catches himself before he
slips away.

'So you and Johnny hooked up?' Pleasantness floats over
his wired-too-tightness.

'Yeah, it's great, she's really . . . amazing,' I say. 'I consider
myself a very lucky guy.'

'Yeah, she's cool.' He nods like he's said something
extremely meaningful.

High as I am, it seems extremely meaningful to me, too.

I have to consciously stop my mouth from saying: Yeah, I
know all about how cool you think Johnny is, seeing's how
you fucked her and all. I really enjoy the fact that I know,
and he doesn't know that I know, that he shagged my now-
girlfriend behind his girlfriend's back. I can't help it; I just
love that Johnny thinks I'm a better fuck than Prince
Charming. Does that make me a shallow person?

'Yup, she's cool,' I agree.

'And Betsy's great,' he adds a little too quickly. 'It's just, uh . . . she's great . . . I don't know . . .' Hard harsh laughter that ends too abruptly. 'You know, you promise yourself you're not gonna . . . but then when they're there, and they're so beautiful, I mean really . . . you know, and nice and sweet . . . I just . . . I can't . . . Sounds kinda stupid, but sometimes it's easier to just do it than to not do it. I know that sounds weird, but . . . so then, after a while you can't remember what lies you told to who, and then it's like you can't even remember what is a lie anymore. And then all of a sudden you run into somebody in the wrong place at the wrong time, and then you're just . . . fucked. I feel so bad, ya know . . . 'cuz Betsy takes it so hard. She gets totally bent out of shape, crying and screaming and throwing shit, I'm afraid she's gonna fucking kill me in my sleep one night.' Again, hard harsh laughter that ends too abruptly. 'Not really. That was a joke. She's not . . . I mean, she's great, she really is . . . See, I try to tell her that it has nothing to do with her, that I love her, but I just can't get her to understand. I mean I love her, I really do, I love her, she's . . . great. I *would* like to have kids with her, get married, have a house, and a dog, all that shit. Yeah, I wanna get a big dog, ya know, like one of those dogs that comes running up to ya when ya get home and jumps all over you . . . But see, the problem is, I just can't . . . I mean, every single night there's . . . it's ridiculous, seriously, you have no idea . . . so what am I gonna do? I should just quit all this shit. It's killin' me. Male exotic dancer. What if I have a kid one day? Is that what my kid's gonna say when they ask him what his daddy does? Am I gonna go to his school on career day and say, "This is a G-string, kids. Lemme show you how to Kiss & Tip." I mean, what kinda life is this? I gotta get the fuck outta here

. . . do something . . . be a man. That's what my dad said to me, he said, "When you gonna grow up and be a man?" I mean, what the fuck, ya know? I don't know . . . it was easy for him. He knows how to do shit. He knows how to get shit done. He can build shit and fix shit. But I mean, come on . . . What else am I gonna do? I don't know how to put a flange on a crankshaft, I'm just, like . . .' Prince Charming looks at me with that desperate need to be understood that only coke can conjure, and asks, 'Do you understand what I'm talking about?'

Thing is, I *do* understand. I, too, feel like I've been denied the instruction manual that would offer the blow-by-blow explanation of how to be a man. I should tell him about me. He'd understand. Him of all people. The urge to purge, once activated, is overwhelming. I have to bite my lip to stop the words from tumbling like dice out of my mouth. But I wanna organize my confession, put it in historical context, explain the inexplicable. My brain finds all this completely confounding. Every time I think of the right way to get into the thing, it seems all wrong. My mind is a land mine in a maze in a combat zone with scud missiles flying all around me. And I can't get out.

'Yeah, man,' I say to the waiting Prince Charming. 'I know exactly what you're talking about.'

He seems much relieved to be understood. With perfect earnestness he asks:

'So you don't think I'm outta my fuckin' mind?'

'Oh no, you probably *are* out of your fuckin' mind, but I understand exactly what you're talking about,' I reply with a deadpanned shrug and nod.

Prince Charming roars a laugh. He laughs and laughs and

laughs. By the end it sounds like the wailing of a miserable guy.

Never in my wildest dreams did I imagine that I, the puffy Marshmallow Man would be feeling sorry for Prince Charming.

I have no idea how long he actually laughs, but it seems like about a month and a half. Finally it dissolves into a chuckle, which turns into a hard sigh, followed by a shake of his great mane. He daubs at his eyes. Prince Charming is in that spot where laughter meets tears. Then he looks off into the universe:

'I mean, what the hell am I gonna do about all this shit?'

The universe does not reply.

Nor do I.

'Just seems like if I don't do something soon, it's gonna be . . . totally fucked . . .'

I glance at the window and see a horrifying sight: The sun is coming up over Media.

Prince Charming and I realize at the same time that we've been talking all night. Or rather, he's been talking and I've been cracking him up with the occasional odd quip.

'Hey man, thanks for the blow,' I say as I rise and stretch my groaning bones.

'Sure, man,' says Prince Charming.

We don't hug. We don't shake hands. And we never mention our night together again.

When I get back to my room it looks so much dirtbaggier than when I left it. I'm beyond exhausted, past dog tired, into shattered. My jaw throbs from all the unconscious clamped clenching, my insides are like miles of barbed wire, and a clammy fog hangs all over me, as I curl fetal into bed and relive every horrible thing that's ever happened to me, while periodically vowing to never ever snort coke again, until sleep mercifully puts me out of my misery.

CHAPTER 8

JAPAN OR FLORIDA OR SOME FUCKING PLACE

Meanwhile back at Sixty-first and First, the pizzeria's still selling most excellent pizza, the bodega's still homely, and at Dangerfield's nobody's still getting no respect. But Nick de Noia's solid gone, and the show's devolved even further into barely controlled every-man-for-himself mayhem. Every time I look up at the DJ booth and don't see the redheaded Crazy Eddie, my heart sinks. Place was never the same once he croaked.

But the big news is: Hallelujah, after watching all these motherfuckers making $ hand over hammy fist, I've finally come up with a scam of my very own. I've never felt more American. Here's how it works. I suss out a bachelorette hen party, identify the instigator (usually a saucy, bawdy, boozing babe), then casually chat her up. I ask if she'd like me to make a special wedding announcement for the bride-to-be during the show. I charge twenty if she looks rich. Ten dollars if not.

Then, at the appropriate moment, I scream into the priceless mic:

'And a big Chippendales congratulations to Gina Maria Bumbansero on her upcoming nuptials. Enjoy your freedom while you still can.'

They always scream ecstatically. As far as scams go it seems harmless, and I can clear $150 cash on a good night. But the show sucks. And the monkey masks are a disgrace.

One Thursday night the Barbarian's Kiss & Tip just goes on and on and on. The fucker will not leave until he's sucked every last cent outta the Ladies. Big Alice yawns. It's so loud, and my head throbs right behind my eyeballs. I'm getting these headaches almost every show now. They make me pukey, woozy, and disorientated. I just plop right down in a seat in the Pit. Nobody gives a shit. I press into my temples hard, trying to shove the pain out of my brain. It hurts as it soothes. I desperately need to focus on something else. Front row just behind the Pit sits a stunner in a clinging forties dress with shiny midnight hair and hell-red lips. My smile eases my head pain a skosh. Lily Tomlin did a bit where she was explaining theater to aliens from another planet. The aliens were much more impressed with the audience than the actors. For the aliens, the audience was the show. That's how I feel here. The Ladies are the show at Chippendales.

Nick has yanked the main stars, and they're in Japan or Florida or Guam or some fucking place. He's booking the show from Cucamonga to Kathmandu to Timbuktu. So Tom Cat is doing Slick Rick's number tonight. I feel a terrible glee when he absolutely SUCKS. He has no moves, he fumbles with his shoes, he trips and falls going up the stairs out of the Pit. Again, the Ladies don't seem to give a shit. They roar when he jacks off his sock, go nuts when he shoots champagne cum all over them, and pant and moan when he strips down to his G-string.

As I take my break during Tiny Tim's pathetic Construction Guy number, I walk past Pretty Peter screaming into the sad face of a bewildered thirty-something Lady with huge poufy sleeves:

'I don't give a fuck where you sit—'

'But you said you would get me and my girlfriends seats in the front row, that's why I gave you all that money—'

'Look, bitch, why don't you go tell somebody who gives a shit!' Pretty Peter doesn't look so pretty anymore.

'Well, then I want my money back,' she insists.

'FUCK YOU!' Pretty Peter screams, then strolls away like he doesn't have a care in the world.

Poufy Sleeves shakes her head and sighs in disgust.

Large Mark is doing the Prince Charming number tonight, and he's even worse than Tom Cat. He's so 'roid-engorged and muscle-chunked that he can only do two or three of the steps required. I automatically look up at the DJ booth to share a mad laugh with Crazy Eddie. But of course, I can't. 'Cuz he's dead. Shit.

A row breaks out after the show in the dressing room. I don't see who, how, or why, but all of a sudden a big silver trash can is flying in slow motion across the room. Pretty Peter, not in the fray, ducks at the last second, and the trash can zooms just past his surprised, horrified face.

CRASH!

The trash can slams into a mirror, smashing the glass.

CHAPTER 9
BIG BLACK BONER III (I AND II MISSING)

Dorothy Dalmatian is a beautiful black-and-white spotted dog owned by Nick de Noia and named after the character his ex-wife, supermodel-actress Jennifer O'Neill, played in the hit movie *Summer of '42*. Nick got custody of Dorothy Dalmatian in the divorce, and she's a gorgeous beast, although extremely jumpy and skittish. Having worked for some time under Nick, I can relate. Johnny and I are dogsitting for him in his stylish yet generic pied-à-terre-ish Manhattan apartment, while he's out conquering the world one G-string at a time.

Dorothy Dalmatian loves Johnny. Her little doggy eyes light up, and her black-and-white tail wags with mad canine happiness when they come face-to-face. Johnny loves her right back with head scratches, belly rubs, and gentle cooing.

Yet another reason to love Johnny. And no bones about it, I am loving Johnny. Living with her has been a boon. She

cooks like Julia Child, my favorite celebrity chef, and sexes me
up like Vanessa del Rio, my favorite celebrity porn star. She
reads great books, she cracks wise, she's got a massive heart
and exudes the earthy yet sophisticated sexuality of a young
Puerto Rican Marilyn Monroe. Plus, and I can't emphasize
this enough, out of all the studs hunks and muffins at Chippendales, she picked me.

So we're having a grand time, hanging out at Nick's, playing
with Dorothy Dalmatian, having sex on as many pieces of his
furniture as we can.

As far as I'm concerned, one of the great pleasures of apartment sitting is getting to rummage through all the skeletons
lurking and skulking in the dark corners of the closets. So
Johnny and I are on a scavenger hunt to discover the dirt
behind the man that is Nick de Noia. Sure enough, at the
back of a closet, buried under a pile of innocuous tax returns,
is a stack of magazines and videos. Get a load of the titles:

Mandongo (a gay *Mandingo* homage)
Top Cock (a gay *Top Gun* homage)
Pee-Wee's Huge Adventure (a gay *Pee-Wee's Big Adventure*
    homage)
Big Black Boner III (I and II missing)

Nick de Noia's closet is awash in cock, much of it big and
black: held in hands, suckled upon, stuffed down throats, slid
up bums, knobbed and veiny, hooded and hanging.

Johnny smirks and tosses off a classic eye roll as she asks:

'Do you think we'd be able to follow the story of *Big Black
Boner Three* if we haven't seen the first two?'

'I think we'd be lost without them,' I laugh.

Dorothy Dalmatian bounds in, sniffs the gay porn, and looks

up at Johnny with big dog eyes, begging to be petted. Johnny scratches Dorothy on her butt, which she wiggles ecstatically while making happy growly doggy sounds.

All of a sudden, Nick de Noia makes a lot more sense.

CHAPTER 10
THE SADDEST GIRL IN THE WORLD

'Ba-by Kil-ler!'

'Ba-by Kil-ler!'

'Ba-by Kil-ler!'

Abortion abolitionists scream at us through pursed pink lips, beaming red anger through small eyes, faces contracted with white-hot hate. And these people call themselves Christians! I'm sorry, what happened to love thy neighbor? Turn the other cheek?

A gaunt bun-haired woman holds up a sign with a picture of a dead bloody fetus in a garbage can, and my stomach flips sickly. I look to Johnny, my pregnant girlfriend, worried how all this horrible shit will affect her. She sneers and flips off the faux-Christian with one of the most defiantly quiet fuck-yous I've ever seen. I'm filled with so much admiration and affection for Johnny that I bust out in a big smile.

A little blue-eyed towheaded angel girl in a flowing flower dress, the very picture of Norman Rockwell Americana, points at Johnny and me, scrunches up her face with childish disgust and screams:

'Ba-by Kil-ler! Ba-by Kil-ler! Ba-by Kil-ler!'

I put my big right hand on the small of Johnny's back, while opening the door of the clinic with my left hand, and usher her in.

Inside the clinic it's too quiet, like everyone's walking barefoot on broken glass sprinkled over very thin ice.

Johnny and I have stepped right into the epicenter of a debate that has rocked America to her core. When does life start? Is abortion murder? Or is it a woman's right to control what happens to her body and her baby? Battle lines have been drawn: pro-choice women liberators and their supporters on one side; conservative, religious pro-lifers on the other. Lately the war's gotten ugly and bloody. Some sick fuck's blowing up abortion clinics, and there's a loony on the loose shooting doctors with a high-powered rifle as they leave clinics. I'm thinking: Is this America or some barbaric fundamentalist state? What happened to life, liberty, and the pursuit of happiness? Am I gonna get blown up in the pursuit of an abortion? I mean, I'm not trying to kill *them* 'cuz they *won't* have an abortion. Don't we both have the right to do what we want? As long as I don't hurt you and you don't hurt me? Wasn't that the whole idea of America?

Johnny and I walk in to a large waiting room where the air is so thick with black, sad misery I can't breathe. All the new life in all these bellies will be dead in a few hours. All the promise of love and future and happy babies will be plucked out and dumped into garbage cans. I feel like crying and collapsing and comforting all these women one by one.

Johnny and I walk up to the intake lady, who's a thick, deep black woman with round brown eyes and pudgy fingers that feature curved, three-inch nails painted in intricate tribal patterns. She's wearing a T-shirt that says: 'WE HAVEN'T COME THAT FAR AND DON'T CALL ME BABY!' Her nails are so long she has to hold the phone several inches from her mouth:

'No, you listen to ME. I want my cable NOW. I took four hours off from work yesterday. Are YOU gonna compensate me for that?!' Pause. 'No, no, I'M talking now. I swear to God, if I don't have my cable when I get home tonight, I am gonna personally make you wish you hadda never been born.' Pause. 'I appreciate it, Julio, you have been very helpful.' Pause. 'Thank *you*.'

I glance at Johnny. She's got faraway eyes. Where is she? What is she thinking? I wanna ask, but I don't wanna upset her.

Fingernails looks at us and with a hint of impatience asks:

'How may I help you?'

Johnny snaps back to reality:

'Uh . . .' She stops, lost, words gone.

'We wanted to . . . ,' I step in, 'we're here about . . . our pregnancy.'

Our pregnancy? Damn. My baby in her belly. My stomach plunges and I have to stop the tears from filling my eyes. My baby in the garbage can. I look at Johnny, who radiates fear, sadness, and uncertainty.

Fingernails hands us a clipboard, gripping it awkwardly between her thumb and forefinger to compensate for the majesty of her nails.

'Fill this out, front and back. Will that be cash or credit card?'

A fancy dinner, a hundred dollars. A bottle of wine, seventeen dollars. A carriage ride, twenty-five dollars. An abortion, priceless.

'Cash,' says Johnny, flat, all the sass and attitude gone. She seems here in body only. She hands Fingernails a large smoothed-down stack of $.

Fingernails hands us a receipt as she recites, like a wax replica of herself delivering her spiel for what seems like the nine millionth time:

'When you have filled out the forms, front and back, return them to the desk. Make sure you fill out the entire form. Do not forget to sign the form on both sides. Failure to correctly fill out your form may result in inconvenient delays in your procedure.' She pauses for less than a moment: 'Do you understand?'

Before we even have time to answer, she says:

'Please have a seat. Thank you.'

There is no please in her *please*, and no thanks in her *thankyou*.

Johnny shuffles to the chair farthest away from the other aborters. I follow. She sits. I sit. The sound of the vicious faux-Christian screams into the room:

'Ba-by Kil-lers! Ba-by Kil-lers! Ba-by Kil-lers!'

Johnny's buried inside her brown curls. The clipboard with the forms sits in her lap. I can't tell whether she's staring at it or lost in the fog of misery hanging in this room. I wanna take her hand and tell her it'll be OK. But how do I know it's gonna be OK? She's about to kill the tiny little life that's living inside her. Murder our unknown child. How do you make that OK? Outside there are rabid, clever, organized hate-mongers who think we are of the devil and will burn in hell with Satan for all eternity. How do you make that OK? There may be a mad bomber planting a homemade explosive device in the basement right now. Or an assassin with a high-powered assault weapon waiting outside to pick off the doctor who performs Johnny's procedure. Who's gonna make that OK?

But I have to do something, 'cuz Johnny looks like she's drowning in a sea of sadness.

'Hey,' I say, 'let's get the forms done, 'cuz we don't want any inconvenient delays in the procedure.'

Johnny doesn't look up, but she snorts a little laugh that makes her curls wiggle.

'Yeah,' she says softly, 'we don't want any inconvenient delays in the procedure.'

I gently take the clipboard.

'Address? 137 East Fourth Street.'

I write it meticulously.

Johnny examines what I've written and says:

'Wow, you have excellent penmanship.'

'Yes,' I say, 'I believe poor penmanship is the sign of a weak mind and a lack of moral fiber.'

'Gotta have moral fiber,' Johnny agrees. 'Where would we be without moral fiber?'

'Morally constipated,' I say.

'Yeah,' Johnny gives a chuckle that fades quickly into misery.

The form is voluminous. Allergic to medications? Small pox? Whooping cough? Scarlet fever? Surgeries? Broken bones? Hospitalized for psychiatric illness? Suffer from depression? Anxiety? Hallucinations?

There are just so many things that can go wrong.

It takes us quite a while, but we wisecrack our way through. Careful not to catch anyone's eye, I survey the group in the waiting room, fifteen of the gloomiest humans I've ever seen.

A Latin-looking lady, late twenties, early thirties, is made up in bright facial colors with a severe pulled-back-tight oil slick of black hair. She's in a tight going-out dress that accentuates her sizable bosom. Next to her is a girl who looks twelve going on thirty-five, with gobs of black mascara around her scary eyes, and a shirt with a yellow happy face that's been shot in the head and bleeds red down her also-sizable bosom. If these two aren't mother and daughter, I'll eat my red high-tops. Angry Daughter is smacking a big gobful of gum, really working it. She blows a big bubble. POP! Many of the abortion seekers and their companions jump in their seats, as if they've been shot at by a crazy antiabortionist. Mamacita lets out an, 'Ayee!' She turns to Angry Daughter and hisses like a Spanish radiator. Angry Daughter turns away in her chair and goes into a tremendous pout, suddenly looking like a twelve-year-old about to have an abortion.

A mid-twenties woman in a buttoned-down blouse over a straight skirt clutches her purse tightly in her lap, like somebody's gonna steal it. She glances at a plain watch on her dark arm and tugs at her skirt. After only a minute or so she glances at her watch again. Looks like if you tapped her gently with a hammer, she'd shatter into a million little pieces. I've never seen a person look more alone.

A tough motherfucker sits across from us. She definitely checks the 'Other' box when it comes to race. She's big and powerful, with maybe fifteen small safety pins in one ear and a tube in the lobe of the other. A tattoo on the upper breast region reads 'ROCKY' in ornate writing. Her eyes are diamonds that could cut you. Safety Pins glares straight ahead like a prize-fighter between rounds. Next to her sits a blonde with a flippy hairdo in a lime green Annette Funicello dress, with a matching lime green handbag and June Cleaver pearls, bare arms covered with wildly colored tattoos full of flames, mermaids, daggers in hearts, and beautiful ladies. There is not one single inch of uninked arm skin. She's slumped in her chair reading a hard-cover book, like she's lounging at a picnic by a lake. If they weren't sitting next to each other you'd never guess they were together. Wonder which one's knocked up.

How did they all get pregnant? And where are the rest of the sperm providers? It's embarrassing to be one of only two men here. How long have we been sitting here? Feels like a hundred years.

Finally . . .

Finally . . .

Finally . . .

A white-coated nurse comes out of a door and says:

'Johnny.'

My pregnant lover rises and we walk toward the door.

'You can't come in here,' Nurse stops me.

Johnny looks back at me, starts to say something, then stops.

'Hey,' I jump in, 'I'll see you when you get out.' I turn to Nurse and ask: 'How long will the, uh . . . when will she be . . . done?'

'It depends, but at least a coupla hours,' Nurse says with professional detachment.

'OK,' I say to Johnny with as much reassurance as I can muster. 'I'll be here when you get out.'

Johnny moves her curls, and I find her eyes. They are wet and sorrow flows out of them. In a choked-up voice she says:

'Thanks.'

'You're welcome,' I reply.

I can't sit in this room of death one more second, so I walk out, carefully noting the time.

I don't wanna think about how my life will have changed by the time I see Johnny again. I don't wanna think about our baby, my baby, in a trash can.

Outside the sun blinds. The faux-Christians are on a food break. Hate and hunger never sleep, but hate clearly gets hungry once in a while. The little blonde poster child for intolerance is eating what looks like a peanut butter and jelly sandwich.

And enjoying it very much.

Head shaking and heart breaking I wander down Third Avenue, mourning my child that will never be. Will I ever get Johnny pregnant again? Will I ever get anyone pregnant again? Do I want this baby? It's her body. She's twenty, she doesn't want a baby, not right now, and really we barely know each other. All of a sudden, I've turned onto Twelfth Street. I know it's a ho' stroll, but I'm never aware of heading to where the ho's stroll.

And yet, here I am, misery unconsciously seeking company.

Immediately I spot a gangly caramel streetwalker in a pair of cut-offs, tank top, and sandals. On the surface she doesn't appear in any way to be someone who's prepared to exchange sex for $. In fact, she looks more like an NYU student who just flunked out or an East Village knockabout considering starting a rock band or out to score a bag of weed.

But my ho'-dar is going off like an air-raid siren. This woman is a prostitute.

Gangly Caramel does no lip licking or eye batting, no tit shaking or ass wiggling. She just nods, and with an empty voice she says:

'Looking for a date?'

'Uh, I don't know,' I say. 'Cuz I really don't.

'You with the cops?'

'God no.' I shake my head like that's the furthest thing from what I am. 'Do I look like a cop?'

'Kinda,' Gangly Caramel says with a little tilt of her head.

Is that what I look like these days? An undercover cop? I gotta seriously think about changing my look.

'Well, I'm not,' I say firmly.

'OK . . . well, do you wanna date?' she asks, sexy as a tax collector.

'You gotta place?' I ask.

'Yeah,' Gangly Caramel says, 'whattya wanna do?'

'Everything,' I say.

'Fifty,' she says.

'Thirty,' I say.

'I gotta get at least forty.'

'All I got's thirty,' I lie.

When Gangly Caramel sighs I can practically hear the wheels grinding in her head.

Risk. Reward.

In the end, $ wins:

'OK.'

Avenue D is a rogue's gallery of strung-out bums and heroin-ravaged freaks seeing demons after five-day binges. A mass of tangled hair and ratty tatters slumbers on the sidewalk. Dead or alive? Hard to say. I step over it. From a bombed-out store-front a disgruntled pitbull rages and roars. For a second, I think it's going to leap right into the street and devour me. But its chain snaps as it reaches the most taut position, yanking

the mighty-muscled beast's vast head back. Reminds me of
Large Mark.

My heart's a racehorse and my blood's a flood as I follow
Gangly Caramel into a building that's in serious need of a stint
in rehab. I'm alive and high at the prospect of getting *everything* from this industrial sex technician for thirty bucks. Or
maybe getting my head bashed in by a psychokiller. Sure beats
thinking about Baby Killers and Johnny and my child in that
crazy place.

An angry voice bombs down a shattered hallway.

'No mothafuckah, I want my SHIT NOW!'

The aggravated hate sounds just like the faux-Christians.

Gangly Caramel shepherds me into a darkened room where
cat urine, burned chemicals, decomposing food, and a slight
whiff of semen perfume the putrid air. It takes several long
moments for my eyes to adjust to the dark. An open pizza box
looks like a toothless empty mouth. Sad soiled panties are
strewn on the floor. Empty plastic vials are strewn everywhere,
the detritus of a narcotics-filled lost weekend.

Someone rustles in another room. A large psychokiller is
gonna bust through the blanket door with a baseball bat and
knock my nose through the back of my head.

'Is somebody in there?' I ask, all tensed up.

'No,' Gangly Caramel says, extremely tweaky, like she's lying.
Or maybe she's just tweaky 'cuz she's a tweaker.

'Somebody's in there,' I say and make a move to leave.

'No, nobody in there. Come on man, don't be like that.'
Gangly Caramel pleads with her eyes. 'Pro'lly the cat. I got a
cat. His name is Freaky 'cuz he gets all Freaky. Come on man,
let's just, you know . . .' Desperation escapes Gangly Caramel
like crack smoke exhaled from junky lungs.

All quiet. I peek a look around a blanket door. Nothing. What the fuck, I shrug, if this is where I die, so be it.

'Come on, I'll take care of you,' Gangly Caramel insists, 'whatever you want.'

It's not sexy, the way she says it. But her utter submission fills me with power, and I like that. I hand her a ten and a twenty. She takes off her clothes. I do not remove my clothes.

Gangly Caramel has a thin long body. I can see her ribs. She does not look at me. I do everything to her. With increasing ferocity I manipulate her so I can go in deep, deeper, deepest, until I make her hurt like I do. She does not pretend to enjoy it. She does not say any sex words. Does not urge me on. Does not complain.

When I'm done she looks wrung out, like a factory worker after a grueling double shift.

It hits me hard how easy it is for Slick Rick and Prince Charming to make five hundred bucks for twenty minutes' worth of kisses and how much Gangly Caramel had to give up for her thirty. So I give her another five dollars and say:

'Thanks.'

'Sure.' Gangly Caramel puts her clothes back on. 'Thanks.'

'Sure.' I say. 'OK.'

'Yeah,' she says. 'OK.'

Then I leave. Halfway down the stairs I realize I forgot to ask her name.

As I walk back out into the filth of Avenue D, I'm filled with emptiness, numb, watching myself trudge through the dregs of the bottom-feeders, dragging my vast sadness with me. I'm sad for Gangly Caramel living in squalor. For Johnny having our fetus scraped out of her uterus. For all those women having abortions while people are screaming about baby killers. For me and my baby.

I've thought countless times over those two decades about what my kid would be doing at any given moment, from diapers to baby teeth to first grade to first crush to prom to college. I see a kid on a bike, in a car, at a restaurant, and I think: My kid mighta looked like that. How different my life would've been if we'd had that baby.

As I slide through Alphabet City I wish I felt guilty about having sex for $ with Gangly Caramel while my girlfriend was aborting our baby. But I just don't. Again I suspect this means there's something terribly wrong with me, that I'm missing something, that I'm irreparably broken. That I'll never be normal.

I hand Johnny a dozen red roses when she reappears in the waiting room, shaky and confused as a newborn fawn. Even through her haze she appears happy that I'm here to meet her. Feels good to have Johnny lean on me. Good to be useful for once.

I sit Johnny down and ask:

'You OK?'

'Uh yeah, I guess . . . ,' she answers all fuzzy.

'What do you want?' I ask.

'I wanna get the fuck outta here,' Johnny says out the side of her mouth.

Gripping my arm and moving gingerly, gamely, Johnny makes her way out of the abortion clinic.

As soon as we hit the street, the haters spring to life, like we're virgin flesh and they're cancer cells hungry to gorge on us. The main hater takes a step forward and launches into the chant:

'Ba-by Kil-ler!

'Ba-by Kil-ler!

'Ba-by Kil-ler!'

I feel an almost uncontrollable urge to shatter her hateful face. Luckily, it's an *almost*-uncontrollable urge. I will turn the other cheek. Treat her as I wish to be treated.

I shield Johnny. She looks completely exhausted and beaten down, like she's aged a thousand years since we last passed the picture of the dead fetus in the garbage can.

I take her back to the loft. All she wants is oatmeal. So I make her some oatmeal. The comfort food comforts her. Without even changing out of her goin'-to-the-abortion-clinic clothes, she slips into bed. I tuck her in and gently stroke her head. Tears appear in her brown eyes, welling and swelling, then weeping wet onto her pillow. She looks like the saddest girl in the world.

'Read to me,' she whispers.

I pick up a copy of *Alice in Wonderland* lying next to the bed.

'"The time has come," the Walrus said, "To talk of many things: Of shoes—and ships—and sealing-wax—Of cabbages—and kings—And why the sea is boiling hot—And whether pigs have wings."'

When I look up, Johnny is asleep.

Suddenly my mind presents me with the image of my baby being born, and this time I don't stop the tears.

CHAPTER 11
TRICKS ARE FOR KIDS

Another Saturday night, and Chippendales is once again crammed-to-capacity with Ladies completely oblivious to the fact that backstage, it's like a pirate ship where the captain's been tossed overboard and mutiny rules.

The stars are back in town, so at least I don't have to suffer through Tom Cat and Large Mark desecrating Chippendales like they're refugees from the *Gong Show*.

I shake my disgusted head and disappear into the costume room, where the replacement costume mistress just depresses me more. My head tightens right up – that by now all-too-familiar behind-the-eyeball ache, back like an unwelcome relative who borrows money, drinks all your beer, makes international phone calls, and leaves floaters in your toilet.

Arnolpho flickers in, all fab in silk and leather:

'Oh bay-bee, wot a week!'

'Hello, gorgeous,' I reply with airkisses on both of his beautiful smooth cheeks. 'How's tricks?'

'Tricks are for kids, sweetie!' He touches me on the chest. I like how his hand feels there. Like I have a real friend.

'Where were you?' I ask.

'Florida, sweetie, and oh Miss Thing, listen to what Miss de Noia did. She booked us into this hhhuge club for two weeks, she gets the money up front, then after the end of the firs' week, she sneaks into the club in the middle of the night, packs up all our stuff, an' takes off. She even steals all the posters, right off the wall. An' where do you thin' all the money from the second week went? Hhmmm . . . lemme think . . . maybe into Miss de Noia's pocket . . .'

'Holy shit!' My eyes bug. 'What did the club owners do?'

'I don' know, dahlin', they di'n't discuss it with me.' Pause for dramatic effect, head tilts as eyebrows arch. 'But I can tell you they looked like some very SERIOUS gentlemen, LOTS of BIG men in tiny T-shirts who looked like they would enjoy terminatin' Miss de Noia with ex-treme prejudice. So it was all very excitin', but bay-by, there's no place like hhhome.'

'Amen, sister,' I nod.

'Well, must go, dahlin', so many to do—'

'So little time,' I reply.

More airkisses, and away Arnolpho swishes.

Tonight's a very special night. Richy Rich, my trust-fund-baby roommate, has decided his best bet to finish his NYU thesis is to do massive quantities of cocaine. And I've come up with a second scam, which I'm very proud of. I discovered I could sell coke to Richy Rich for five times what it cost me to buy it at Chippendales. And Rich is happy to do it, 'cuz my blow is so much better than the stepped-on-by-the-Abominable-

Snowman shit he buys on the street. So Richy Rich has placed a large order with me, and we're all gonna go party in his dad's primo penthouse apartment. I just wanna get through this show, buy my blow, and go partyallthetime with the lovely and talented Johnny till the sun comes up over Central Park.

Luckily I find the Snowman just before I go on.

'Dude, ya gotta pump me up in my intro tonight,' he implores through his famous mustache.

'What's it worth to ya?' I'm sickened by the bastard, but I gots to have it.

'Coke weed speed, whaddya need?' he asks.

'Five grams of blow.' I sound a little too much like a budding junky. But like a budding junky, I don't care that I sound like a budding junky.

'Five fuckin' grams?' The Snowman's fantastically handsome face goes all surprised while his ultra baby blues bulge.

'Yeah, five fucking grams. Is that a problem? 'Cuz I'll be honest, I'm not really feelin' the love tonight,' I spit back.

'No, no problem, I'll have it for you after the show,' he reassures. 'But you really gotta pump me up tonight, man. Seriously.'

Now I see. He's a junky, too.

'I'll do what I can,' I reassure.

Sure enough, I lay it on extrathick intro'ing the Snowman, and he gets the biggest roar of all the nonstars. He gives me the wink, and my sphincter relaxes.

The show drags its sad fat ass. My head hurts too much to even get agitated about it anymore. I've taken to just sitting on the steps away from the speakers during everybody's Kiss & Tip, while making rude remarks into the priceless mic:

'How many male strippers does it take to screw in a lightbulb? I don't know, how many? Male strippers don't screw lightbulbs, 'cuz there's no money in it.'

The Barbarian is out of control. Some designer-dressed over-coiffed skunk-drunk rich bitch grabs him too hard, her nails digging deep into his back. He whips around and screams violently into her face, roaring in pain:

'OWWWWWW! FUCK!!!'

Skunk Drunk pulls back into her pack with terror and screams at her lung tops.

The Barbarian clenches like he's gonna punch her in her rich bitch face and teach her a lesson she'll never forget.

Luckily Sloppy Sam arrives outta nowhere and moves the Barbarian on.

Skunk Drunk and her friends leave in an angry huff.

After the show I track down the Snowman. Drugs and $ are exchanged. My willies melt away, and suddenly I'm skating outta Chippendales, on my way to that de-luxe apartment in the sky.

CHAPTER 12
GAY COKE PAD

A woman screams LOUD. I assume it's one of New York's colorful insane population. Just past the most excellent pizzeria and just before the mom'n'pop newspaper shop. Insanely Screaming pounds on the thick front door of a building that's notorious for containing an apartment known as the Gay Coke Pad. Pretty much self-explanatory. It's a well-known fact at Chippendales that if you're hot and need some coke, you can always get what you want, if you're willing to let a gay man/men suck your wandangdoodlehammer. It's a wonderful blow-for-blowjob exchange program that seems, from what I hear tell, to be a terrific win-win situation – except, apparently, for the crazy lady pounding on the door and screaming:

'I know you're up there getting yer dick sucked, ya miserable piece of shit!'

I'm quite close now, trying to watch this marvelous street

opera as inconspicuously as possible. Upon closer inspection Insanely Screaming is actually a spectacularly exotic and gorgeous creature. Wait a second. Could that be? . . . Betsy, girlfriend of Prince Charming? Holy shit! Up close, with her face contorted in pain and distorted from injections and surgical alterations, eyes too wide and pulled back too far, skin too smooth and too tight, nose too buttony, lips all puffed up, she does look remarkably like a desperate drag queen. I can't believe Prince Charming is in the Gay Coke Pad, getting homosexual head in barter for blow. And yet I can.

Betsy screams from her ovaries, pounding on the door, her nipped and tucked face a twisted mask of misery, her silicone-sacked breasts rock-hard and bouncing unnaturally:

'Get yer ass down here, you faggot cokehead! I know what you're doing up there, ya piece of shit! I'm gonna call your dad and tell him you're a big fag drug addict!'

I want to comfort her, but I'm afraid it would just heap more shame on her if she knew I was witnessing her tragedy.

So I clutch my coke and skate on with a nasty knot in my guts, wondering:

Is this the price you pay for loving Prince Charming?

CHAPTER 13
DROPDEAD BRAINDEAD

Manhattan sparkles and shines, glittering and twinkling through the giant plate-glass windows on the forty-fifth floor of Richy Rich's dad's penthouse apartment. Booming over the state-of-the-art stereo is the loopy thumping bass of 'White Lines (Don't Do It).' I can't help but smile, chopping up white lines on the long chrome and glass table, as I think of Slick Rick popping his pumped-up penis out for the screaming Ladies. You can't put a price tag on memories like that.

As Grandmaster Flash singsongs about how the more he sees the more he does, I'm making an art project with the coke rails, creating a transcontinental railroad that goes coast-to-coast across the length of the six-foot table. It's fun watching Johnny shake her curly mane to the beat, while Grandmaster Flash implores us to get higher and hunger until we never come down.

Richy Rich and his dropdead braindead overpriced-peasant-bloused girly are making out on the couch. If this is his plan for finishing his thesis, I don't see it happening.

When at last I'm done, I shout out in a silly Julia Child soprano voice:

'Coooooooome and . . . get it!'

Richy Rich and Dropdead Braindead break their clinch and come up for air. When he sees my transcontinental cocaine railway tracks he smiles the jaded yet innocent smile of a yuppy puppy and says:

'Cool lines, dude.'

In a shocking disregard for coke etiquette, Dropdead Braindead just dives in nose-first with her rolled-up $20. I really dislike this chick. She's an excellent coke sucker, though; I'll give her that. If they had contests for this kinda thing, she'd be a champion. 'Snorting first for the United States, the defending title holder, Buffy Kennedy Carnegie Rockefeller. Watch her go for the blow gold, folks!'

She snuffs up three feet of coke with the greatest of ease. Impressive. She straightens up, shivers deliciously, and proclaims:

'Holy shit!'

Indeed.

Funny, she is an excellent specimen of gorgeous, fine-featured, selectively bred, blue-blood aristocratic beauty. But she has such an ego-maniacal sense of entitlement, and utter disregard for the Other, that she exudes a kind of antisexi-ness.

Richy Rich snorts and sighs, highly satisfied.

Johnny rolls up a $20 of her own and offers it to me. Her mama clearly raised her right. I wordlessly defer to her. She mutely thanks me and takes a couple of delicate snorts, chasing them with a shot of tequila. She basks in the rush like a cat stretching on a warm rock in the sun. Then she hands me the $20 snorting tube.

Finally it's my turn. Ohhhhhhhh, me oh my, this is exciting. True, it's not as great as that first glorious high. Or the one after that. Or the one after that. Or the one after that. But it's still migh-tee fine.

Johnny puts some James Brown on the wraparound sound system, and here comes 'Sex Machine,' busting, bumping, and grinding all over us. It's as if the hardest working man in show business is right here in the primo penthouse with us, reminding us how great it is to be a coupla young, in-love sex machines. Johnny sways her loose hips to the tune and I put my arm around her waist as we dance on the Manhattan skyline. I can hardly contain my joy. I did it. I came to this god-eat-god city with nothing, and now I'm on the forty-fifth floor, looking down at all the peasants. I got the girl. I'm on top of the world, Ma.

Clearly, there's only one thing to do now:

More coke!

I suck up another foot or so of blow. Suddenly it dawns on me that Richy Rich and Buffy have vanished. He's most likely off writing his thesis, I smirk, and she's probably proofreading it as he goes.

Johnny now brings the mood down, music-wise, with some vintage Janis Joplin moaning about how freedom is just another word for nothing left to lose.

The ghost of Crazy Eddie raises a partyallthetime glass to me, and the coke makes the sadness penetrate all the way to the heart of my bones.

'I still can't believe Crazy Eddie's dead,' I lament to Johnny.

'Crazy Fuckin' Eddie,' Johnny commiserates.

'It's weird . . . I barely knew the guy, in one way . . . but I feel like he was really . . . I don't know, I just miss him.'

'Yeah . . .' She shakes her curls and sighs. 'It's so . . .'

'Yeah, death . . . fuck . . . ,' I sigh.

'Yup.' Johnny nods profoundly.

There's only one thing to do to elevate the mood:

More coke!

I suck up another six inches of snow, and this really gets the engine revved. I shake my head to get my brain to settle. I breathe consciously and carefully, trying to control the overload that's making my needle creep into the red. Ohhhhhhhh, shit! I'm about to blow apart at the seams. It's scary as hell, but I'm just loving the rush. I've never been this alive. Or maybe I've never been this close to death. I can't tell anymore.

'You all right?' Johnny's voice brings me back to the here and now. My ship rights itself and I enjoy the blood carrying all those drugs to my head, heart, and balls.

'Yeah,' I say, trying to smile. But I'm so wired I can't tell whether I'm scary jack-o'-lantern or cool loverstudguy. 'How you doin'?'

'I'm good.' Johnny sounds like she's not entirely convinced.

But worrying about her takes my mind off how my body's all overpumped overheated overcoked—

RELAX YOUR JAW!!!

I open and close my mouth like the Tin Man after Dorothy unrusts him. Cool cool water, that's what I need. I fetch us some from the giant fridge-freezer unit. As I suck it down a great freeze seeps through me, chilling my heat, and crunching ice is nice, tactile, soothing, cooling.

'Hey,' I say with earnest urgency. 'I have something very important to tell you.'

'What?' Johnny's suddenly concerned.

I pause, take her hands, and look deep into her eyes.

'The monkey masks really look like shit these days.'

Johnny tosses back her curly head and erupts. She's much more a smirk-and-chuckle than a howl-with-reckless-abandon kinda girl, so to see her laugh so loud, so long, so hard, and unfettered, really releases that deep-down body-rolling frolicking joy, fills me with bliss. As the laugh fades, Johnny exhales:

'Fuckin' monkey masks . . .'

'Fuckin' monkey masks . . .'

I sigh in reply.

Pause.

I decide to finish the entire rest of my line. I have to work really hard to shove it all into my face, but I feel compelled by a force I cannot control to put every single grain inside me.

When I'm done, it feels like the top of my head's gonna pop off and brain confetti's gonna shoot outta my skull. I can't say it's entirely enjoyable, but it's terribly exciting. Stars shoot in front of my eyes as my throat closes, and my breath races. I can't catch it, it's going too fast. I can hear my own heart amplified to insane volumes, like a mentally ill character in a Poe short story. The ventricles are gonna bust, the valves break, my heart's gonna jump out of my fucking chest, and I'll be able to watch it sputtering, jumping, and flopping around like a fish on the floor.

Sweat rains out of my pores like there's a monsoon inside me. The lights are too bright, and the stars keep shooting. Oh my God, I'm having an aneurysm. I don't know exactly what an aneurysm is, but I'm sure I'm having one.

Blackness seeps in from the edges of my vision. That's it, I'm a dead man. What a stupid fucking way to die. What a moron I am. I killed myself, only I did it before I made a cool record or acted in a great movie or wrote an excellent book. What's the point of OD'ing if you haven't done anything yet? The blackness keeps getting bigger until there's only a pinpoint of light in either eye. David Henry Scary is about to be never-more. My entire existence has been a ridiculous meaningless farce. I am nothing. Less than nothing. Wracked with panic, black envelops me, and I am gone.

CHAPTER 14
ATLAS SHRUGGED

A hand grabs my shoulder and my brain flashes back:

Sharp red hot agony stabs up inside me and travels screaming up through me as a man pins me into a stinking mattress, violent thrusts of raging punishing pain, he's breathing filth into my ear:

BITCH! FAGGOT! PUNK!

I open my eyes and Johnny's face fills the frame of my vision. Am I dead and she's my angel? This doesn't feel like death. But then how would I know what death feels like? Maybe death is being in a primo penthouse apartment looking out over the Manhattan skyline, all coked up with the sexy woman you love.

'Are you OK?' Johnny asks with life and death urgency. Maybe I'm still alive. Have I gotten to the point where I can no longer tell the difference between life and death? I can feel all that coke savagely ravaging my body. Only now it feels like poison.

'David, are you all right?' Johnny demands. I just love how concerned she seems about me. Hearing my name makes me feel real. Wait a minute, I believe I may be alive. I'm aliiiiiiiiiiive! My pulse rate drops, and my heart normalizes. I don't want to have all this coke in me anymore. I don't wanna be a cautionary tale. I don't wanna be poor dead fun-loving Crazy Eddie.

'Yeah, I think so.' My voice sounds strange to me, all thick and froggy, like a bad recording of myself.

'What happened?' Johnny asks tenderly.

'I don't know,' I say slow. 'I couldn't breathe and . . . everything went black and . . . then I was sitting here. How did I get here?'

'It's OK,' Johnny strokes tenderness sweetly into my head. My shirt is drenched wet with sweat, hair clinging hard to my head. I'm shivering with a chill that seems like it's from beyond the grave. Johnny lays my green Cossack coat over me. Now it's her turn to nurse me, and it fills my heart with love.

Before I can stop it, this comes out:

'When I was seventeen, this guy hurt me, really bad, I was in Hollywood and I was all alone, ya know, and he invited me back to his place, he said he was gonna give me a steak, only the steak was drugged, and when I woke up he was . . .'

I can't say the word . . .

'He fucked you up?' Johnny fills in the gap for me.

'Yeah, he fucked me up. It was so . . . painful, ya know . . . it hurt so much, just like my insides were on fire . . . and then I escaped, and then I met this other guy, and he taught me how to be a hustler, ya know, I had sex for money . . . and I never told anybody and . . . then I moved outta Hollywood when I was eighteen, and I stopped, and it was . . . the whole thing scrambled my brains, I keep having these flashbacks, ya know, like nightmares, only you're awake, and I've just never been normal since . . . the whole thing happened . . . I'm just all fucked up . . .'

I realize I'm crying. Not sobbing. Just tears running down my face, and I didn't even know it.

'Well, that sucks,' Johnny says.

No shame. No blame. Love unconditional.

'Yeah, it sucks,' I agree.

I breathe deeper than I have since I was seventeen. I am Atlas and I have shrugged off the world.

She kisses me on the forehead and I sink deep into the relief of her arms.

CHAPTER 15
KILLING HIM DEAD

On April 7, 1987, a man disguised as a messenger walks into Nick de Noia's office on 364 West Fortieth Street and shoots him in the head, killing him dead.

The executioner escapes undetected.

And the House of Death claims victim number two.

CHAPTER 16

ONE LAST SLICE OF MOST EXCELLENT PIZZA

'Fuckin' Nick's dead,' the Snowman reports with great glee, miming a gun shooting me in the left temple. 'Shot in the fucking head, dude. D'joo hear?'

'Yeah,' I say, 'crazy, huh? I mean shit . . . do they know who did it?'

'Probably some buttbanger he fucked over. Hey listen, you gotta pump me up tonight, the place is fuckin' dead.'

He doesn't seem to register the cruel irony of his remark.

'You know what, I got more important things to think about than your intro.'

The Snowman can't quite believe I've rebuffed him. Thinking I'm looking to get my pot sweetened, he says:

'You want a little tootski?'

'No, I don't want a little tootski. Nick just died, man, what the fuck?!'

'Whatever.' The Snowman dismisses me and struts away with his glorious tan, his cut muscles, and his 70s pornstar mustache.

In the dressing room, there's talk of canceling the show, but that doesn't seem right. Nick was all about the show. Plus everyone has their $ to make. I think Nick woulda understood that.

Who killed Nick? Tongues wag as rumors fly. Of course there's not a shred of evidence that anyone was behind the assassination but here's a list I made based on what I heard:

(1) The Edwards Brothers – it's common knowledge that Nick's New York partners hate him with a wild passion and would love nothing more than for him to sleep with the fishes.

(2) The Florida Club Owners – see Arnolpho's story.

(3) The Media Club Owners – apparently Nick left there owing them a big stack of cash.

(4) The Yakuza – ditto several clubs in Japan.

(5) Steve Banerjee – Nick's LA moneyman partner certainly wouldn't shed a tear if Nick ended up cold and lifeless.

(6) 'Some butt banger,' in the Snowman's words.

(7) Any of about a thousand Hosts, Waiters, busboys, technicians, and janitors he ripped off, abused, or tried to grind into dust.

I mean, hell, I myself muttered that I'd like to kill Nick. But what does it take for someone to go from casually contemplating the murder of another human to actually hiring a hitman to blow their brains all over a wall?

It's so sad watching Slick Rick mourn on Slick Rick Island.

You can usually set your watch by where he is in his meticulous preparation for the show. Tonight he's just sitting there in a chair, oozing black pain from every pore, beside himself with a grief so deep and thick you can practically taste it. I ease through the overcrowded room and put my arm on his naked shoulder. He tenses and pulls away, ready to defend himself against an attack. Then he sees it's me and relaxes his guard.

'You all right?' I ask.

'I don't know, Dave.' He looks away, then looks back, brown eyes wet. 'I just can't believe it. It's just unbelievable. I thought they were making it up at first, but . . .' Slick Rick sighs and deflates, being crushed under the weight of his pain. 'Oh man, I just . . . I feel sick to my stomach. I can't believe it. Why would someone do something like this?'

Because Nick was an abusive asshole who loved to use his power to publicly humiliate people? Because he ripped off people all over the world? Because he was a closeted, pent-up, tortured, repressed homosexual pretending so hard to be straight that he raged toxic waste all over people?

I don't wanna say any of this to Slick Rick, so I say:

'I don't know, man. Shit like this doesn't happen in real life.'

'Yeah, I was thinking that, man . . . I feel like my dad just died or somethin' . . . it's just fucking with my head.' Slick Rick shakes his gorgeous distraught head.

'Shit's fucked up.' I shake my head in agreement.

'Yeah,' Slick Rick agrees, 'Shit is fucked up.'

If I'd known this was gonna be my last show, I woulda done it differently. I woulda made my improv scathing. Woulda put every ounce of myself into it. But I don't. And I'm too distracted by the redheaded ghost of Crazy Eddie in the DJ booth and the salt-and-pepper specter of Nick de Noia in the crow's nest.

I do, however, say this at the end of the show:

'I want to dedicate this show to Nick de Noia . . . None of us would be here if it wasn't for Nick. He taught me a lot and . . .'

I can't think of anything else, so I say:

'Thanks, Nick, rest in peace. Good night.'

And that's the last line I say as Master of Ceremonies at Chippendales Male Strip Club.

Later in the crazy-crowded dressing room, as everyone counts their do-re-mi, Slick Rick sits with head in hands, like he's at a nude funeral.

Large Mark, all cuffed, collared, and spandexed, plods through the naked Man bodies. He intentionally slams Slick Rick into a locker, then makes a mock I'm-sorry face, clearly for the amusement of the Snowman and Tom Cat.

'Oh hey, I apologize, I di'n't see ya dere. You OK? I shaw hope so, 'cuz now dat Nick ain't heah to suck yer dick I was worried dat ya might be havin' a hahd time . . . emotionally.'

The Snowman and Tom Cat howl.

Slick Rick springs like a mongoose at a giant 'roided king cobra and drives the unsuspecting Large Mark hard into a locker with a thunderous crunch of muscle meeting metal. Large gasps like a bagful of hot air with a hole poked in it. Bloodlust fills Slick Rick's face as he pulls back his black balled fist, his nearly nude body twitching and bulging, all that pent-up power ready to punish Large Mark.

Tom Cat and the Snowman leap into the fray, grabbing Slick Rick and hoisting him up off his feet. They pin him against a locker and suspend him there in the air, prepared to savage him with the brutal beating they've been dying to give him for the longest time.

I gotta do something. I take a step toward them in the crackling air. I see Slick Rick's nose shatter, blood splattering everywhere, cheekbone smashed, head cracked open.

Just as the Snowman is about to uncock his loaded fist into the face of Slick Rick, a loud large angry voice cuts through the mayhem:

'CUT THAT SHIT OUT! Have a little respect, for God's sake!' It's Prince Charming, and he looks pissed. I've never even seen him peeved, never mind pissed. Because it's Prince Charming, all hostilities cease. Tom Cat and the Snowman drop Slick Rick flat. After an awkward landing, he rights himself and screams at Large Mark:

'FUCK YOU!'

Then he storms into the bathroom, slamming the door behind him.

Large Mark recovers his breath and equilibrium. He and his buddies smirk, scorn, and sneer as they strut out into the club.

The dressing room is after-the-storm quiet, as people go back to their mundane postgame rituals, kinda like a saloon in the Wild West after a gunfight has been averted at the last second by a forceful yet ridiculously handsome sheriff.

While I'm changing, Sloppy Sam comes into the costume room and tells me they're 'letting me go' 'cuz they're 'going in a different direction.' No more Master of Ceremonies in the show. One less mouth to feed. Actually I'm relieved. I just had an audition for an HBO series. These Chippendales headaches are terrible, too, and I'm getting them every night now. Plus I think I have some hearing loss from all the pounding my eardrums have taken here. And frankly, if I never see another bulging G-string I'll be quite happy. I clear out my locker, walk out onto First Avenue, and head across the street for one last slice of most excellent pizza.

CHAPTER 17

FAKE SEX AND TRUE LOVE

Clouds cover Charleston, and a drizzle threatens to dampen us all. Johnny's stunning in a flowing white wedding dress, curls piled high and falling around the soft of her face. As our horse-drawn carriage pulls up to the Southern antebellum mansion, the clouds part and the Southern sunshine smiles on us.

Arnolpho, more dashingly handsome than I will ever be, is Johnny's maid of honor.

When I look at Johnny and wrap my paw around her small hand, I'm so happy. Johnny is marrying me. Today I consider myself the luckiest man alive.

In the pictures taken after the wedding, Arnolpho D'Alencar Araripe Pimenta de Mello and Johnny look like the most hand-some couple ever.

I came to Chippendales to become a star. Instead, somehow, in the middle of all that fake sex, I found true love.

AFTERS

Turns out, as many people suspected, that Steve Banerjee, Nick de Noia's LA $ partner, hired the hitman who blew Nick's brains out. He was caught several years after the murder of Nick, when he contracted to have two ex-Chippendales dancers murdered as they tried to open a male stripper show in London. Banerjee was arrested for both crimes. He killed himself in jail. Turns out his was a dark version of the American Dream: immigrant comes to the USA, makes millions off male stripping, pays an assassin to wipe out his enemies, and hangs himself in prison.

And the House of Death claimed victim number three.

Time gave Slick Rick his revenge on Large Mark and Tom Cat, both of whom ended up fat, divorced, and broke. Slick Rick, on the other hand, went on to become a very successful businessman. Prince Charming and Betsy did not live happily ever after.

I did not see any of the Men of Chippendales again for a very long time. It's strange to spend so much intense time with people and then never see them again. But such is the nature of the topsy-turvy world of male stripperdom. I've poked around and discovered that many of the Men have become personal trainers. Several have done commercials and appeared in TV shows, soap operas, and even *The Sopranos*. Many are married, many divorced. A couple have stayed in the male stripper game.

Many of the beautiful and talented Ensemble Dancers are dead, victims of the AIDS plague that ran rampant in the 90s.

The House of Death claimed them one after another.

Arnolpho d'Alencar Araripe Pimenta de Mello miraculously surfaced about a week before I wrote this sentence. He contacted me out of the blue, and I'm happy to report that he's living large in Brazil and is, according to his e-mail:

'. . . faaaaaaaaabulous, baby!'

Johnny and I were married for eight glorious and torturous years. Today we are the very best of friends. In fact, me and new wife are godparents to her baby.

I quit snorting cocaine the night I almost died. Soon after, I, David Scary, ex-Master of Ceremonies of Chippendales and ex-teenage prostitute, was hired as an actor on an HBO/ Children's Television Network kid's show called *Encyclopedia*. No plastic surgery required.

As for Chippendales herself, it took a long time to recover from the whole assassination suicide thing. She held on at Sixty-first and First until the parent company went bankrupt in the late 80s. In the 90s, the Chippendales name was revived, and the show toured globally. There's still a touring company, and a flagship show is going gangbusters in Las Vegas.

I went back to Sixty-first and First recently to get a look at the old place. Much to my amazement, Chippendales has been replaced by a Bed Bath & Beyond.